MAKING INVISIBLE BUREAUCRACY VISIBLE

A Guide to Assessing and Changing Organizational Culture

MARK BODNARCZUK

Text edited by Cliff Carle
Cover design by Gwyn Kennedy Snider
Text design by Integrative Ink

Published by Breckenridge Press
Boulder, Colorado

The author would like to thank the following for permission to reprint from copyrighted works: Quotation of James C. Collins and Jerry I. Porras from BUILT TO LAST, copyright © 1994, by James C. Collins and Jerry I. Porras, pp. 43-44. Used by permission of Jim Collins.

ISBN: 978-0-9755115-4-1

1. Organizational Culture   2. Organizational Behavior   3. Leadership

Book Category: Business/Management

First Edition September 2009

Breckenridge Press
PO Box 7950
Boulder, Colorado 80306
Tel 1-800-303-2554; Fax 1-888-745-1886
www.breckenridgeinstitute.com

MAKING INVISIBLE BUREAUCRACY VISIBLE

VISIBLE

A Guide to Assessing and Changing Organizational Culture

"We read to know we're not alone."

C.S. Lewis
Shadowlands

TABLE OF CONTENTS

PREFACE

Most managers struggle against the flow of overly complex systems and are often frustrated by an *invisible force* that undermines their attempts to effect positive change. Their instincts tell them that the organization's structures, systems, and culture are preventing them from getting the results they want, but "culture" has remained one of the least understood aspects of organizational life. This book describes how organizational culture often acts like an Invisible Bureaucracy™ that frustrates and undermines the performance of organizations and work-groups.[1] Because over 85% of the root causes of organizational performance problems are in the structures, systems, and culture within which managers and staff members are embedded, putting good people in bad systems can *decrease* their level of performance and *increase* the level of destructive conflict in day-to-day operations. Therefore, focusing on improving the performance of an individual manager or work-group without understanding the context within which they are embedded almost guarantees that change will not be sustainable, because individual managers and staff members are only about 15% of the real problem.[2]

But despite the fact that most individual managers and work-groups have little or no control over the larger organization within which they are embedded, they are still held accountable for their performance and delivering on commitments. The day-to-day reality of Invisible Bureaucracy manifests itself in a number of recurring and troubling questions:

- Why is it so difficult for some organizations to make decisions, and why (once made) do so many decisions go unimplemented?

- Why do most organizations have a gap between the formal rules for how things get done, and the informal rules for how things *really* get done?

- Why does vital business information get filtered, altered, or stopped as it moves up and down through the organizational structure?

- Why do projects that seem to have the full support of top managers and key personnel die a slow death and no one knows what happened to them?

- Why are some organizations able to change in the face of forces and threats from the external environment while others seem to have "Blind Spots" about these issues and fall prey to them over and over again?

- Why do the universal principles of organization development seem to work in some organizations, but not in others?

- Why do change initiatives so often show failed or marginal results?

- Why do so many people find their work to be a substantial part of life's problems, rather than one of the solutions to life's problems?

Interestingly, the process of culture formation has many things in common with the formation of personality. In terms of personality formation, by the time we're old enough to know that we *have* a personality we've had no hand in fashioning it. In much the same way, an organization's culture is like its personality and many managers wake up one day and find themselves with structures, systems, and a culture that they have not consciously chosen; in business relationships that may not be in their best interest; with assumptions about generating revenue and patterns of spending that they have not consciously chosen; with employees who are not matched to the organization's human capital needs; pursuing objectives and goals that don't produce the desired financial and non-financial results.

Ground-breaking studies like Jim Collins' books, *Built to Last* and *Good to Great*, and John Kotter's book, *Corporate Culture and Performance* have shown that while an organization's culture powerfully molds its operating style and can positively (or negatively) affect its performance, "culture" has remained an overly-complex and somewhat mysterious topic for most managers and organizations. One of the keys to simplifying and demystifying the topic of organizational culture is to understand the degree to which an organization's culture is *intended* or *unintended*. An Intended Culture™ is consciously configured to achieve an organization's desired results; e.g., its goals and objectives. An Unintended Culture™ tends to be riddled with ineffective autopilot operations and Invisible Bureaucracy that derail, frustrate, and undermine organizational intentions as embodied in its goals and objectives. Even outstanding organizational performance may be episodic and short-lived because it is an artifact of the specific configuration of internal and external environments within which the organization exists, rather than the result of an Intended Culture. The ability of an organization to change and adapt with conscious intention is the true test of the degree to which its culture is consciously chosen for specific ends.

The approach to creating an Intended Culture described in this book will help you transform your organization's culture into a powerful resource that *effectively* performs day-to-day operations on autopilot; e.g., effectively and seamlessly without thinking about them. When done *effectively*, autopilot operations can be your greatest ally because they increase your ability to compete and achieve your goals. But in most cases the autopilot operations that typify an Unintended Culture are self-defeating because they perpetuate problems with work performance, communication, interpersonal conflict, and decision-making and then derail attempts to create positive change. This unique approach to creating an Intended Culture helps managers take ineffective operations off autopilot, *reconfigure* them, and then *migrate* them back to autopilot operations that produce the desired results. Understanding how these invisible forces actually work begins to transform "culture" into a more reliable resource that can be used to achieve an organization's goals and objectives.

My overall goal in writing this book is to share my experience of helping leaders and managers to assess and change organizational culture in a way that accomplishes six objectives. First, I want readers to "see" organizations differently by first broadening the definition of organizational culture, and then defining it with more precision to eliminate much of the confusion around what organizational culture *is* and why it *matters*. My intention is that readers will learn concrete and tangible reasons why an organization's culture matters (or should matter) to every business owner, top manager, middle manager, supervisor, and staff member in every organization.

Second, I want to address the misconception that an organization's culture can be either "good or bad" *head-on* with a more pragmatic, and operational view that asks – "Does an organization's culture allow it to get the results it wants?" I'd like to underscore the fact that the autopilot operations of organizational culture *are not* Invisible Bureaucracy when they enable an organization to get the results it wants in a self-determined, intentional way. In fact, effective autopilot operations are a competitive advantage. Invisible Bureaucracy as defined in this book is confined to *ineffective* autopilot operations that prevent an organization from achieving its desired results by frustrating and undermining its performance, thus robbing it of its free-will and conscious choice. Invisible Bureaucracy is most problematic because managers and staff members look right at it, and don't see it as indicated by the recurring and troubling questions described earlier. In fact, I've had managers who were A-Level talent tell me, "I wish I'd have known about this material fifteen years ago. Now I know why things have been so difficult in some of the organizations I've been in." Reading and internalizing the principles and practices in this book will enable you to "see" yourself, others, and the world differently and to identify the kind of Invisible Bureaucracy that frustrates and undermines organizational and individual performance. Like a pair of infra-red glasses allows you to see things at night, the material in this book will make Invisible Bureaucracy visible. Once you've learned to see differently, you'll never see organizations (or the people in them) the same way again.

Third, I am convinced that the process of assessing and changing organizational culture must be focused on real business problems – issues that managers care about deeply. It's a mistake to lead with cultural analysis and cultural change. Assessing and changing organizational culture is of little value unless it is linked to (and motivated by) one or more of these six interdependent dimensions of organizational life:

- Generating and retaining revenue

- The effective use and cost of labor as human capital

- The effectiveness and non-labor related cost of operating an organization

- Key performance indicators that measure an organization's performance with high-precision

- The identification and reduction of squandered time and energy

- A focus on sustainability, creating value, and making long-term investments in human, material, and financial resources

If the activities associated with assessing and changing organizational culture cannot be meaningfully linked to one or more of these six dimensions, then they should probably not be done. Diagnosing and changing organizational culture for its own sake is an academic exercise that provides little or no value to organizations and the managers who lead them. But if an organization needs to develop a new strategy or strategic plan; improve its execution and day-to-day operations; implement new IT infrastructure; seamlessly integrate business systems; build bench-strength in leadership and management skills; or improve the decision-making and consensus process for the allocation of human, material, and financial resources, *then* understanding how its culture positively and negatively impacts these issues is not only value-added, it's probably necessary. The key is to lead with a concrete, tangible business issue, *not* the study of organizational culture as an end in itself.

Fourth, I want to offer an assessment model that teaches people how to evaluate an *entire organization*, including the strategic view; execution and day-to-day operations; organizational climate; levels of organizational trust; financial management; corporate life-cycle analysis; and other key areas that shape and define an organization's performance. As such, the book is written for top-managers, middle-managers; human resource professionals; and internal and external consultants who conduct management reviews, performance assessments, change-management activities, improvement projects, organizational interventions, strategic planning activities, culture assessments, and other key initiatives that focus on improving organizational and individual performance.

The fifth objective I want to accomplish is to describe a portfolio of quantitative and qualitative assessment tools that readers could use to empirically test the principles and practices contained in this book in their own organization. Assessment tools like the *Breckenridge Culture Indicator*™ *(BCI*™*)* will provide empirical evidence for the new ways of seeing organizations, and make Invisible Bureaucracy visible in tangible and concrete ways. The book is a comprehensive articulation of the theoretical model that is measured by the BCI and can be used as the basis of a program to train and qualify people to use this powerful on-line assessment tool. This book can also be used as the basis of seminars, workshops, and training programs in the areas of organization development, organizational assessment, cultural assessment, cultural interventions, management development, and leadership development.

Finally, once readers have learned and internalized the principles, practices, methodologies, and tools described in this book, they will be able to intentionally *create*, *manage*, and (if necessary) *destroy* and *reconstruct* an Intended Culture that will produce the desired results within the context of an ever changing business environment. In other words, leaders and managers will learn how to use their organization's culture *as a powerful resource* that facilitates, rather than opposes, achieving organizational goals and objectives. Bottom Line: an Intended Culture is the key to becoming an Island of Excellence® in a sea of mediocrity.

Mark Bodnarczuk

Boulder, Colorado
June, 2009

ACKNOWLEDGEMENTS

This book is the result of many years of research and working with clients through the Breckenridge Institute®. Over the years, there have been many people who have helped to bring this work to its culmination in the form of this book. The most important influence on my thinking in terms of the nature of organizational culture and the conduct of organizational assessments and interventions has come from Edgar Schein[3], Harry Levinson[4], and Chris Argyris.[5] The heuristic power of their respective models and the deep insights they have brought to my work with clients cannot be over estimated.

Jonathan Babicz, Executive Director of the New York Institute of Leadership™ was a sounding-board for my ideas all throughout the writing process and read multiple drafts of the manuscript. Jon has a deep understanding of the principles, practices, and theoretical foundations outlined in this book. He is a coach, mentor, teacher, and practitioner of organizational effectiveness and leadership who has woven these principles and practices into his professional work and the fabric of his life.

I'd also like to thank John Anderson, Anthony Malensek, and Kass Larson for their help, competence, talent, time, professional abilities, and friendship over the course of this endeavor. They've made contributions to my life that are deep and will stay with me forever.

During the final stages of writing this book, I was one of over 125 million people who were inspired by Susan Boyle's performance on the television show *Britain's Got Talent* which was posted on YouTube and many other Internet sites (http://www.youtube.com/watch?v=9lp0IWv8QZY&feature=related). Her initial physical appearance, magnificent performance, and subsequent notoriety show how powerfully who and what we are can be shaped and defined by the "social mirror" of our cultural context.

My seven-year-old son, Thomas Larson Bodnarczuk, constantly amazes me with his insight, perspective, and insightful view of day-to-day life. I've never known another human being who has touched me so profoundly, and been such a powerful catalyst for change and transformation in my life.

Finally, I'd like to thank my wife, Elin Larson who has been a constant source of encouragement, support, and help in the writing of *this* book, and the other two books I've written this year. Her kind and gentle spirit and penetrating insight into the day-to-day realities of our life mean more to me than I can say. As a professional partner, she has been the designer and architect of the IT and computing infrastructure of the Breckenridge Institute® that supports on-line instruments like the BCI™. Without her, this work would not be possible.

FOREWORD

If you have been looking for a book that gives you a comprehensive, understandable, and useful perspective on culture, you are holding it. In the universe of "culture" analysis, this book will give you a complete look at the factors that matter when approaching culture change. Whether for your personal or professional interest, this book provides a penetrating exploration of the deepest unconscious dynamics to the external artifacts and by-products of organizational culture.

A "culture" is created by the collective patterns of group behavior to resolve issues for how people work or live together, manage time and tasks, and relate to an environment that puts demands on the individuals in an organization. This is true whether we are talking about a family or a corporation. I've read as many books as I could find over the years on "culture" in search of a guide to provide a practical model and guidance for understanding the tacit and explicit forces that drive the cultures that human beings create. Now, with this effort, *Making Invisible Bureaucracy Visible: A Guide to Assessing and Changing Organizational Culture,* Mark Bodnarczuk has provided the most complete guide the reader will ever find. Whether or not you use the tool, the Breckenridge Culture Indicator, which is a concrete, hands-on way to access how a culture operates, the concepts in this book are viable and more than merit considerable reflection.

This book brings together the key findings of social scientists and culture researchers in examining how tacit knowledge influences and maintains human systems that affect conflict, financial factors, governance, and the use of time and energy. Importantly, you are given strategies to enhance organizational culture and improve performance. Effectiveness in any endeavor is knowing what to do, and then doing it. With this book as your guide, you have a complete understanding of the "what and how" of organizational culture.

I will resist the temptation to tell you the specifics of why each chapter holds pearls of great value. I do want to highlight some key concepts that help you string those pearls so that the whole of this work is fully grasped.

- Culture is best understood from an organic systems perspective – this means that patterns, contexts, and outcomes of interactions work dynamically to produce an organization's results (planned and otherwise).

- Interdependent beliefs and perspectives about the way people create interaction patterns that reinforce the culture as a whole.

- Interdependent learning loops maintain the interaction patterns which provide considerable "energy" for maintaining a culture (and the hope for changing culture).

- All artifacts of a culture – financial policies, SOPs, information systems, and structures – reflect how the system as a whole works to solve its problems of dealing with people, resources, and the environment.

There are surprises in the chapters to follow as Bodnarczuk shows the link between the levels of trust and the financial potential of an organization. In one of the more remarkable achievements in this field of study and practice, *Making Invisible Bureaucracy Visible*, will make the invisible and heretofore fuzzy concepts about culture very visible, clear, pragmatic, and ultimately useful.

Roger R. Pearman, Ed.D.
President
Qualifying.org, Inc.
Winston-Salem
North Carolina

CHAPTER 1
BUILDING NEW FOUNDATIONS

This chapter uses the broader historical context of the business literature over the last 40 years to help the reader understand the context within which the study of culture in organizations emerged. The goal is to help readers to step outside their tacit beliefs and assumptions about organizations and how they work, and to learn to "see" organizations and organizational culture differently.

The More You Know, the More You See

I was once on a scuba diving trip to the Great Barrier Reef off the coast of Australia, and one of the dive masters who knew a lot about marine life would always say, "The more you know, the more you see." With over 1,500 species of fish, 1,000 species of mollusks and crustaceans, and 600 species of coral, it was easy for divers to get overwhelmed by the sheer number of types of sea life living on the reef. It was also easy to misidentify species because a diver had an inadequate (or incorrect) knowledge of the taxonomies and empirical and theoretical foundations of marine biology. Before each dive, two marine biologists would give workshops on marine life that taught us how to recognize the differences between the myriad fish, coral, and the other sea life that we would likely encounter during our next dive. This new knowledge paid big dividends because divers were able to identify subtle differences in what formerly seemed like an overwhelming visual array of sea life pulsating on the reef.

The process of assessing and changing organizational culture has some important things in common with this diving example. When first entering an organization, it's easy for assessors to get overwhelmed by the sheer number of variables because, like the coral reef, even small organizations of less than 100 people are complex goal-seeking organisms composed of structures, systems, human performers, and culture. It's also easy for assessors to misidentify the underlying causes of organizational and individual behavior if they have an inadequate (or incorrect) knowledge of the empirical and theoretical foundations of how organizations work. In the absence of models that are reliable predictors of organizational and human behavior, it's easy for assessors to misdiagnose what's actually happening in an organization by focusing on symptoms and causal factors, rather than the underlying "root" causes of organizational performance and culture which are often *invisible* and function like an Invisible Bureaucracy that frustrates and undermines organizational and individual performance. Reliable empirical and theoretical models like the ones presented in this book help make Invisible Bureaucracy visible, so the more an assessor *knows* about them, the more they will *see* in terms of being able to help their clients assess and change organizational culture.

For example, Chris Argyris explores the issue of needing reliable models to see the underlying causes of effective and ineffective organizational and individual behavior in his book, *Flawed Advice and the Management Trap*.[6] Argyris evaluates representative examples of over 100 books and myriad articles published by the world's most respected business gurus, and then uses his own theoretical model (theory of action) to evaluate the kind of causal analysis and recommendations for change that these publications give readers. His study includes the likes of Stephen R. Covey, John Kotter, Jon Katzenback, Peter Drucker and other business-literature experts. He concludes that much of the causal analysis and many of the recommendations given by these authors is appealing, and even compelling, but most of it *is not actionable*. In other words, even if a manager could fully implement the recommendations these business luminaries give them, the resulting corrective actions would not lead to the kind of positive change and sustainable improvement that the authors claim it would.

Argyris concludes that, "Since thoughtful and well-intentioned advice givers do not intentionally offer counsel that is full of gaps and inconsistencies, there must be something in the frameworks on which they rely that makes them unaware of these problems – as well as unaware that they are unaware."[7] In other words, the "surface theories" that these writers espouse are based on tacit, unexamined assumptions, beliefs, and models that are not *reliable* in the sense that they do not accurately describe and predict the behavior of organizations and the people in them. So it's important that assessors understand the tacit, unexamined assumptions, beliefs, and models upon which their causal analysis and recommendations are based by evaluating them against criteria like the ones that follow:

- *Reliability*: To what extent are an assessor's causal analysis and recommendations based on an underlying theoretical model of organizations, work-groups, human interaction, and cognitive operations-preferences that is *reliable*; e.g., it describes and predicts the actions, interactions, and overall performance of organizations, work-groups, and the people in them?

- *Validity*: To what extent are the reasoning and assumptions that underlie the causal analysis and recommendations *valid* in the sense that they have been reflected on, made explicit, and subject to public tests and scrutiny to deconstruct organizational defense routines and establish the "organizational truth" of what's really going on in the situation? Validity helps avoid the self-fulfilling and self-sealing cycle that creates and sustains ineffective-invisible cultural norms; organizational defense routines; tacit beliefs and assumptions that are not reliable and are based on stereotypes, and patterns-of-interaction between key personnel that frustrate and undermine high-performance.

- *Being Actionable*: To what extent are an assessor's causal analysis and recommendations *actionable* in the sense that: a) they outline detailed concrete behaviors that will produce the desired results, b) they can be crafted so people can be taught and learn the concepts, behaviors, and skills required to produce the desired results, and c) the implementation of the corrective actions will not be frustrated and/or undermined (overtly-covertly, intentionally-unintentionally) by the organizational context and cultural norms within which they are embedded?

As mentioned previously, it's easy for assessors to misidentify the underlying causes of organizational and individual behavior if they have an inadequate (or incorrect) knowledge of the empirical and theoretical foundations of how organizations work. Field experience with clients has shown that if an assessor cannot clearly articulate the underlying theoretical foundations upon which their causal analysis and recommendations are based, and if their approach to working with organizations (and the people in them) does not satisfy criteria like those listed above, then it's unlikely that their assessment findings and recommendations will lead to long-term, sustainable, positive change in an organization. One of the objectives of this book is to teach assessors to reflect on (and be more aware of) their own tacit, unexamined assumptions, beliefs, and models and the ways in which their knowledge-base and views about how organizations work powerfully shape and define what they "see" when they assess organizational culture.[8]

Different Perspectives on Organizations

Since the industrial revolution in the late 18th and early 19th Centuries, the birth, design and operation of industrial organizations has been characterized by an interdependent balance between two broad "perspectives" for how people explain the underlying causes of an organization's day-to-day operations. The first is a *structures-and-systems perspective* that tends to view organizations as interdependent structures and systems that need to be directed, managed and controlled in order to achieve well-defined goals and objectives. On this view, structures and systems are populated by managers, supervisors, and staff members who must be trained and developed, and can be replaced by other competent people. The *human-performance perspective* tends to view organizations as interdependent work-groups, teams or individual performers who need to be facilitated and inspired, with strategies, objectives and goals that sometimes emerge and morph over time. On this view, *people* are the primary process, rather than structures and systems – in fact, sometimes people are viewed as being irreplaceable. Most people tend to live in the Essential Tension™ between both perspectives, with one or the other being a more dominant way of seeing themselves, others, and the world. In fact, your level of interest in various portions of this book will likely be an indicator of which perspective is your dominant one.

Why is it important to understand this distinction?

The distinction is important because assessors tend to view an organization from their stronger preference; and the causal analysis that they conduct, and the recommendations that they present to clients are shaped and defined by these tacit assumptions and beliefs about the nature and operation of organizations. The fact is that whether a company is in the area of manufacturing, production, transportation, a service industry, R&D, or information technology, they have both the structures-and-systems and human-performance components; e.g., humans working together within structures and systems to accomplish goals and objectives like a cross-functional team. But when unexamined, these biases toward seeing organizations from a specific perspective can cause assessors to misdiagnose why an organization is getting the results they are – good and bad.

Learning to see organizations as interdependent combinations of both perspectives can be difficult because of the tendency in Western Civilization to view the world in a binary way. In their book, *Built to Last*, Jim Collins and Jerry Porras describe this as the Tyranny of the OR, rather than the genius of the AND. I'll quote Collins and Porras at length on this point.

"The 'Tyranny of the OR' pushes people to believe that things must be either A OR B, *but not both*. It makes such proclamations as:

- 'You can have change *OR* stability.'

- 'You can be conservative *OR* bold.'

- 'You can have low cost *OR* high quality.'

- 'You can have creative autonomy *OR* consistency and control.'

- 'You can invest for the future *OR* do well in the short-term.'

- 'You can make progress by methodical planning *OR* by opportunistic groping.'

- 'You can create wealth for your shareholders *OR* do good for the world.'

- 'You can be idealistic (values-driven) *OR* pragmatic (profit-driven).'

Instead of being oppressed by the 'Tyranny of the OR,' highly visionary companies liberate themselves with the 'Genius of the AND' – the ability to embrace both extremes of a number of dimensions at the same time. Instead of choosing between A *OR* B, they figure out a way to have both A *AND* B."[9]

Collins and Porras go on to claim that visionary leaders who practice both-and-thinking do not seek a "balance" between things like low cost and high quality; rather they relentlessly pursue *both* low cost *and* high quality at the same time. They live in the Essential Tension of opposites knowing that these seemingly contradictory ways of seeing actually coordinate and support each other with a synergistic kind of complementarity.[10] When practiced over time, both-and-thinking becomes a new mind-set or way of seeing an organization from both the *structures-and-systems perspective* and the *human-performance perspective* and this is a key element of learning how to assess and change organizational culture. In the next section, I'll discuss some of the established views about the nature and operations of organizations that reflect a primary focus on the *structures-and-systems perspective*.

The Prevailing Wisdom from the
Structures-and-Systems Perspective

Over the last 40 years, the prevailing wisdom in most business schools and boardrooms has been dominated by the *structures-and-systems perspective* of organizations. In fact, an analysis of the top 100 best selling articles from the first 75 years of the Harvard Business Review (1922-1997) shows that 90% of them reflect the *structures-and-systems perspective*, and half of the remaining 10% of articles that cover topics from the *human-performance perspective* were written by a single person –

John Kotter. None of these top 100 best selling articles directly covers the topic of organizational culture.[11]

The driving force of much of organizational theory and the business literature over this 40-year period focused on organizational strategy, structure and processes, with "business" being viewed as a rational enterprise that had two key elements. The *first* focused on *strategic leadership* and *how* things get done in an organization. People who see organizations from this perspective believe that defining a long-term direction, with strategic plans, goals and objectives, and creating and maintaining order and efficiency through structures and systems will result in improved performance. Using a quantitative, data-driven, analytical approach to performance, the organization's strategic goals are deployed and monitored through operations plans, goals, and budgets that direct the week-to-week and month-to-month operations of teams and individuals in organizational units to ensure that those goals and objectives are achieved.

The *second* key element of the structures-and-systems perspective focused on *execution* and *what* gets done in an organization. People who see organizations from this perspective believe that decisive actions, practical solutions to problems, and a short-term focus on clear, tangible goals will result in improved performance. They tend to have a take-charge attitude, are forceful and direct in getting things done, making decisions and get directly involved in day-to-day operations, focusing on *implementing* an organization's goals and objectives through the teams and individuals in work-groups.

The authors and books shown below are representative of the *structures-and-systems perspective* and are some of the thought-leaders that have had the most profound effect on my thinking in writing this book.

- 1970: Alfred Chandler (Strategy and Structure)[12]

- 1977: Alfred Chandler (Visible Hand)[13]

- 1977: Jay Galbraith (Organization Design)[14]

- 1978: Raymond Miles and Charles Snow (Organizational Strategy, Structure, and Process)[15]

- 1980: Michael Porter (Competitive Strategy)[16]

- 1982: W. Edwards Deming (Out of Crisis)[17]

- 1985: Michael Porter (Competitive Advantage)[18]

- 1988: David Hanna (Designing Organizations for High Performance)[19]

- 1990: C.K Prahalad and Gary Hamel (Core Competence of the Corporation)[20]

- 1990: Henry Mintzberg (Manager's Job)[21]

- 1992: Robert Kaplan and David Norton (The Balanced Scorecard)[22]

- 1992: Thomas Davenport (Process Innovation through IT)[23]

- 1993: Michael Hammer and James Champy (Reengineering the Corporation)[24]

Perhaps the best example of viewing an organization from strictly a structures-and-systems perspective and ignoring the human-performance perspective was Business Process Reengineering (BPR). Despite its devastating effects, BPR had a rather uneventful beginning. The creators of BPR believed it showed promise as an organizational tool because it connected three previously existing elements in a new way. The *first* was that the value of technology (information technology) was not simply in doing work more efficiently, but in changing *how* work was organized and performed, so organizations could use information technology to link various processes that cut across functional boundaries. The *second* element was that "business processes" were a useful model for describing how work gets done in organizations. This was a natural extension of the TQM programs that many organizations already had in place where work was characterized as processes. The *third* element was a "clean-sheet-of-paper" approach to organizational change programs. Using this approach, the existing organization was defined as organization "A" and a virtual new organization "B" was created on paper, being built around clearly defined enterprise-wide business processes. As new jobs were developed for organization "B", people in organization "A" reapplied for those jobs and their old jobs in organization "A" were abolished. Bob Filipczak has described the demoralizing effect that reapplying for a job had on employees.[25] Those who were not hired into organization "B" were normally laid-off. The clean-sheet-of-paper approach was welcomed by many senior managers because companies had accumulated myriad policies-procedures (and the jobs associated with them) that were once useful, lost their usefulness, and then threatened to drag organizations into the black hole of Invisible Bureaucracy.

Thomas Davenport, one of the "creators" of BPR (with Hammer and Champy) argued that in the wake of the leveraged buy outs of the 1980s, companies like Ford, Hewlett-Packard, and Mutual Benefit Life developed big financial problems, so they hired "big bucks" consulting firms who promised big savings using BPR. The CEOs, consultants, and information technologists became solidified into what Davenport called the "Reengineering Industrial Complex" – a 51-billion dollar industry by 1995. In the cost-cutting frenzy of the late 1980s and early 1990s, companies began to rewrite their corporate histories by taking activities that were performed under the auspices of *other* programs like TQM and quality improvement, and *repackaging* them as BPR success stories.[26] But most of the BPR interventions failed to produce the promised bottom-line results and consequently, executives were under tremendous pressure to demonstrate the financial benefits of BPR and justify the enormous sums of money paid to consulting firms. When savings failed to materialize as a natural consequence of BPR methodologies, many corporate executives decided to demonstrate bottom-line savings the only *other* way they knew how – by reducing head count.

By 1995, BPR had taken its toll on U.S. workers (especially mid-level managers) with massive layoffs totaling in the millions of people.[27] For example, from 1984 through 1996, AT&T had reduced head count by 212,000 people, with one of the final increments being a reduction in force of 40,000 workers.[28] Also, companies like Capital Holding's Direct Response Group, who were viewed as models of successful BPR interventions, began abandoning their BPR efforts. Other companies who were viewed as BPR role models, like Mutual Benefits Life, almost went out of business. Where did BPR go wrong? Davenport claims that the 1994 CSC Index *State of Reengineering Report* had the answers: 50% of the companies that participated in the study reported that the most difficult part of BPR is dealing with the fear and anxiety of the human performers in their organizations; 73% of the companies said that they were using BPR to eliminate, on average, 21% of the jobs; and of the 99 completed BPR initiatives, 67% were judged as producing mediocre, marginal, or failed results. More specifically, 72% of the companies claimed that survivors believed the restructured organization was not a better place to work.[29] Davenport's view of the fundamental problem with BPR was that it treated people as if they were interchangeable parts in a machine – a view that echoes a myopic focus on the structures-and-systems perspective. To put it another way, whenever you sever the *person* from the *function* (we need the function, but we don't need you doing it), the result is often demoralizing for human performers at all organizational levels.

In a world of increasing stakeholder expectations and decreasing resources, aggressive cost-cutting programs like BPR have taken their toll, and run their course. A number of books published from the structures-and-systems perspective after the BPR era started to recognize the role of the human-performance perspective in building high-performing organizations to a greater degree, especially in the areas of the change management associated with the implementation of new computing systems and IT infrastructure.[30] Perhaps the most important lesson to learn from the BPR experience is that while the *structures-and-systems perspective* of organizations is necessary, it is not sufficient to accurately diagnose what's actually happening in an organization. Focusing on only one of the two perspectives almost ensures that an assessor's causal analysis and recommendations will focus on symptoms and causal factors, rather than the underlying "root" causes of organizational performance and culture. In the next section, I'll discuss some of the established views that reflect a primary focus on the *human-performance perspective*, and the emergence of the study of organizational culture.

Applying the Study of Culture to Organizations

For more than 35 years, the human-performance perspective ran on a separate track from the structures-and-systems perspective largely because the prevailing wisdom in business schools and boardrooms viewed it as "soft" and non-quantitative compared to the "hard" bottom-line orientation of the structures-and-systems perspective. The human-performance perspective has two key elements. The *first* focuses on *teambuilding* and *why* things get done in an organization. People who see organizations from this perspective believe that attunement to the external environment; innovation and radical change, exploring options and new ideas, and engaging with and influencing people to work together and collaborate will result in improved performance. They build alliances and cultivate relationships with people *outside* the organization (the public, interest groups, unions, media, and government agencies) and *inside* the organization where managers and staff members are encouraged to align their efforts with the organizational structures and systems in order to achieve the organization's goals and objectives. The *second* key element focuses on *analysis* and *who* gets things done in the organization. People who see organizations from this perspective believe that building an organization's knowledge-base and capabilities, attracting top talent and supporting and encouraging individual contributors, and analyzing how concepts, ideas, and underlying organizational patterns relate to each other, will result in improved performance. They help achieve the organization's goals and objectives through inner vision, inspiration, and by integrating the knowledge-base and competencies of human performers with the organization's structures and systems to get the desired results.

The authors and books shown below are representative of the *human-performance perspective* as well as some of the most important sources from which the study of organizational culture emerged. While there have been numerous books written subsequently, the ones listed below have shaped and defined the study of organizational culture in deep and profound ways.[31] These are also some of the thought leaders that have had the most profound effect on my thinking in writing this book.

- 1976: Charles Handy (Understanding Organizations)[32]

- 1980: Geert Hofstede (Culture's Consequences)[33]

- 1982: Terrence Deal and Allen Kennedy (Corporate Cultures)[34]

- 1982: Thomas Peters and Robert Waterman (In Search of Excellence)[35]

- 1983: Rosabeth Moss Kanter (The Change Masters)[36]

- 1985: Edgar Schein (Organizational Culture and Leadership)[37]

- 1985: Chris Argyris (Action Science)[38]

- 1985: Ralph Kilmann et al (Gaining Control of Corporate Culture)[39]

- 1987: Howell Baum (The Invisible Bureaucracy)[40]

- 1988: Ichak Adizes (Corporate Life Cycles)[41]

- 1989: Lawrence Miller (Barbarians to Bureaucrats)[42]

- 1989: Allan Wilkins (Developing Corporate Character)[43]

- 1990: Peter Senge (The Fifth Discipline)[44]

- 1992: John Kotter and James Heskett (Corporate Culture and Performance)[45]

- 1994: Jim Collins and Jerry Porras (Built to Last)[46]

The formal study of *any kind of culture* is a relatively recent endeavor in the history of human thought. The word "culture" does not have a corresponding word for its modern meaning in either Greek or Latin and the root of the word in English is the Latin *cultura* – meaning to cultivate in an agricultural sense of tilling and caring for plants, trees, and the soil they grow in; or to breed and tend animals. The word culture was first used figuratively in the sense of the cultivation of the mind or body through education and training in around 1510 in the writings of Sir Thomas More, and had the sense of describing the intellectual or artistic side of civilization by 1805 in William Wordsworth's book, *Prelude*.[47]

Late 18th and early 19th Century writers began to make a distinction between "high" culture; which included the intellectual, philosophical, political, social, architectural, literary, scientific, musical, and artistic works of the Renaissance and Enlightenment; and the "low" culture of the masses (popular culture), including folk music, folk art, sports, legends, stories, and narrative histories of groups of people. Although the notion of "high" culture had a longer history on the continent, it was introduced into the mainstream English world with the publication of Matthew Arnold's book, *Culture and Anarchy* in 1869.[48] During this same time period, the notion of popular culture became identified with a "whole way of life."[49] Allan Bloom identifies Immanuel Kant as the first person to use the term "culture" in the sense of the modern use of the term in his 1795 commentary on Rousseau's proposed unity of high and low culture in the *Social Contract*.[50] T.S. Eliot echoes Rousseau's view that high culture and popular culture were interdependent parts of a more complete model of culture.[51] Johann von Herder was the first person to use the term "cultures" in the sense of making a deliberate distinction between numerous cultural contexts and cultural forms, rather than the notion of a singular, unilateral form of "civilization."[52] From this time on, the newly formed discipline of cultural anthropology came to define "culture" as meaning, "The totality of socially transmitted behavior patterns, art, beliefs, institutions, and all other products of human work and thought."[53]

While the term "corporate culture" was originally coined by Elliot Jaques in his 1951 Ph.D. dissertation at Harvard[54] the mainstream transition point from traditional studies of cultural anthropology to the study of *organizational* culture was the publication of Geert Hofstede's book, *Culture's Consequences* in which he addressed the question about the effect of national culture on organizations.[55] More specifically, he explored the ways in which IBM attempted to establish a "strong" corporate culture and identity that was shared by its employees worldwide. Hofstede's study consisted of 115,000 questionnaires given to IBM employees worldwide. Once analyzed, the data revealed that the work-related values for IBM employees differed significantly from country to country. Hofstede argued that these differences could be explained by the cultural norms in the employee's native country. He used the data collected to identify four "dimensions" that described how national culture influences the work-related values of employees in a single world-wide corporation.[56] He subsequently identified a fifth dimension through studies conducted in China.[57] The five dimensions of work-related values are described below.[58]

- ***Power Distance Index (PDI)***: The first dimension measures the degree of equality, or inequality, between people in a country's society. A high PDI score indicates that inequalities of power and wealth have been allowed to grow within a national culture. These cultures are more likely to follow a "caste system" that does not allow significant upward mobility for its people. A low PDI score indicates that a national culture de-emphasizes the differences between a person's power and wealth. These cultures focus on equality and opportunity for all. The PDI echoes Paul Watzlawick's notion of *Symmetric* versus *Complementary* relationships which is discussed in the section on the *Building Blocks of Organizational Culture* in Chapter 2.[59]

- ***Individualism (IDV)***: The second dimension measures the degree to which a national culture reinforces individual or collective achievement and interpersonal relationships. A high IDV score indicates that individuality and individual rights are the established norm within the culture. Individuals in these cultures may tend to form a larger number of more loosely defined relationships. A low IDV score indicates a more collectivist nature with close relationships between individuals and groups. These cultures reinforce the value of the "group" and extended families, and everyone is expected to take responsibility for other members of groups and society.

- ***Masculinity (MAS)***: The third dimension measures the degree to which a national culture reinforces (or does not reinforce) a traditional masculine work role model of male achievement, control, and power. A high MAS score indicates that a national culture reinforces a high degree of differentiation and discrimination between genders, and that males dominate a significant portion of the society and power structure, with females being controlled by the cultural norm of male domination. A low MAS score indicates that a national culture has a low degree of differentiation and discrimination between genders, and that females are treated equally to males in every sector of society.

- ***Uncertainty Avoidance Index (UAI)***: The fourth dimension measures the degree to which a national culture has a tolerance for ambiguity, uncertainty, and unstructured situations. A high UAI score indicates that a national culture has a low tolerance for ambiguity, uncertainty, and unstructured situations which usually manifests itself as a rule-oriented society that institutes laws, regulations, rules, and controls as a way of minimizing uncertainty. A low UAI score indicates that a national culture has a greater tolerance for ambiguity, uncertainty, and unstructured situations and embraces a wider spectrum of differing views and opinions. This usually manifests itself as a society that is less rule-oriented and more readily able to embrace change and willing to take more (and greater) risks.

- *Long-Term Orientation (LTO):* The fifth dimension measures the degree to which a national culture embraces (or does not embrace) a commitment to either traditional or forward-thinking ideas. A high LTO score indicates that a national culture values and embraces a respect for tradition and a long-term perspective which often supports a strong work ethic where long-term rewards are viewed as the result of working hard in the present. In this cultural context, businesses tend to take longer to emerge and grow, especially for people who are viewed as being from "outside" the culture. A low LTO score indicates a national culture that does not embrace or reinforce traditions and a long-term perspective, and consequently change occurs more rapidly because traditional norms and a long-term perspective do not inhibit rapid change. In this cultural context, business development tends to be typified by innovation and entrepreneurship.

Hofstede's study evaluated the way in which national cultures powerfully shaped and defined the work-related values of IBM employees despite the company's attempts to create a uniform "strong" culture worldwide; e.g., he studied one corporation that was embedded in many different national cultures. But from this time on, researchers and consultants from the human-performance perspective, and the popular business literature, began to attribute the notion of "culture" to *a given organization*, which would be like studying many different organizations, within one national culture.[60] In other words, researchers and large consulting firms like McKinsey began to turn the principles and practices of cultural anthropology *on the organization itself*.

Perhaps the best example of this new approach to studying organizations is found in Terrence Deal and Allan Kennedy's book, *Corporate Cultures: Rites and Rituals of Corporate Life*.[61] They developed a framework for understanding organizational culture that was based on the importance of shared values that manifest themselves as: a) corporate heroes and heroines that serve as concrete role models for how issues should, or should not, be addressed, b) repetitive rituals that connect people to an organization in deeper ways (routine functional meetings etc.), c) ceremonies that punctuate the calendar year and instill a sense of having a common history and mission, and d) stories that teach employees what's really important and function as the social glue that binds people together as having a common identity and purpose.[62]

The notion of organizational culture became common parlance with the 1982 publication of Tom Peters and Robert Waterman's book, *In Search of Excellence*, which was a multi-year study conducted by McKinsey from which Peters and Waterman distilled eight basic findings or "lessons learned" from America's best run companies.[63] Echoing McKinsey's 7-S Framework, their results stressed a central focus on *shared values* that are manifested as organizational culture.[64] More specifically, their research results showed that:

"Without exception, the dominance and coherence of culture proved to be an essential quality of excellent companies. Moreover, the stronger the culture and the more it was directed toward the marketplace, the less need there was for policy manuals, organization charts, or detailed procedures and rules. In these companies, people way down the line know what they are supposed to do in most situations because the handful of guiding values is crystal clear. One of our colleagues is working with a big company recently thrown together out of a series of mergers. He says: 'You know, the problem is that *every* decision is being made for the first time. The top people are inundated with trivia because there are no cultural norms.' By contrast, the shared values in the excellent companies are clear, in large measure, because the mythology is rich." [65]

In the wake of its publication, Hofstede argued that the research findings from *In Search of Excellence* were themselves biased by the kind of national culture phenomenon outlined in his 1980 study. More specifically, he stated that, "Organizations with 'strong' cultures, in the sense of the quote from Peters and Waterman, arouse positive feelings in some people, negative in other. The attitude towards strong organizational cultures is partly affected by national culture elements. The culture of the IBM Corporation, one of Peters and Waterman's most excellent companies, was depicted with horror by Max Pages, a leading French social psychologist, in a 1979 study of IBM France; he called it '*la nouvelle église*': the new church."[66] As shown in Hofstede's 1980 study, French society scored lower on the IDV scale for Individualism than the U.S. companies included in Peters and Waterman's work, consequently the national culture of France encouraged its citizens to be more dependent on hierarchy, rules, and socio-cultural norms. On this view, organizational culture should be viewed as a "sub-culture" within the larger context of the national culture within which an organization is embedded.

By the mid-1980s, Edgar Schein had published his groundbreaking book, *Organizational Culture and Leadership* – one of the seminal works in the development of the study of organizational culture.[67] Schein's was one of the most comprehensive models of organizational culture available. He was committed to moving beyond the more superficial approaches to organizational culture by using the deeper, more heuristic, models of cultural anthropology. Schein's approach would enable managers to understand the hidden and more complex dimensions of organizational life that seemed to defy change. "If we are managers who are trying to change the behavior of subordinates," Schein states, "we often encounter resistance to change at a level that seems beyond reason. We observe departments in our organization that seem to be more interested in fighting with each other than getting the job done. We see communication problems and misunderstandings between group members that should not be occurring between 'reasonable' people."[68] Schein was convinced that the process of assessing and changing organizational culture must be focused on real business problems and argued that, "A culture assessment is of little value unless it is tied to some organizational problem or issue. In other words, diagnosing a culture for its own sake is not only too vast a problem but also may be viewed as boring and useless. On the other hand, if the organization has a purpose, a new strategy, or a problem to be solved, then to determine how the culture impacts the issue is not only useful but in most cases necessary."[69]

John Kotter and James Heskett performed one of the first studies that tried to demonstrate a cause-and-effect relationship between the characteristics of an organization's culture and sustainable financial and non-financial performance, as found in their book, *Corporate Culture and Performance*.[70] Their research showed that high-performing organizations develop an interdependent balance between a focus on vision, purpose, core values, planning, goals, structures, systems, and organizational learning (Theory I, Strong Culture); and a focus on understanding, and being influenced by, market and industry trends, social and cultural values, and the needs and demands of customers in the external environment (Theory II, Strategically Appropriate Culture).[71] These high-performing organizations (characterized as Adaptive Cultures, or Theory III) are able to internally adapt *and* respond to a constantly changing external environment (to be influenced by business realities); and at the same time maintain a deep sense of organizational identity. The data from Kotter's study indicated that achieving this kind of interdependent balance produced long-term, superior financial performance; e.g., net revenue growth, net income growth, return on investment, return on assets, sales growth, and increased market share.

One of the most celebrated research projects to confirm the link between organizational culture and high-performance was James Collins and Jerry Porras' bestselling book, *Built to Last*. This long-range study of corporate history demonstrated that truly great companies develop organizational cultures that are built around: a) timeless principles of leadership and management, many of which have existed for over 100 years, and b) a deep commitment to (and alignment with) a well-defined core ideology.[72] Within the context of *both-and-thinking* which they describe early in the book, they establish an Essential Tension between an organization's commitment to a core ideology (human-performance perspective), *and at the same time* a commitment to driving progress and results through organizational structures and systems that are based on timeless principles (structures-and-systems perspective). Collins and Porras underscore the importance of the principle by stating that, "If you are involved in building and managing an organization, the single most important point to take away from this book is the critical importance of creating tangible mechanisms aligned to preserve the core and stimulate progress."[73]

From the human-performance perspective, the high-performing companies identified in the *Built to Last* study all had a *core ideology* as a primary element of their historical development; where core ideology consists of a combination of *core values* and *organizational purpose*. More specifically, "Like the fundamental ideals of a great nation, church, school, or any other enduring institution, core ideology in a visionary company is a set of basic precepts that plant a fixed stake in the ground: 'This is who we are; this is what we stand for; this is what we're all about.' Like the guiding principles embodied in the American Declaration of Independence... core ideology is so fundamental to the institution that it changes seldom, if ever."[74] In the truly great companies included in the *Built to Last* study, managers and staff at all organizational levels resonated with the core ideology and tended to feel a sense of alignment between the values and purpose of the organization, and the values and purpose of their own lives.

From the structures-and-systems perspective, the *Built to Last* companies all manifested a *drive for progress* using organizational structures and systems that were based on timeless principles of management and that were codified in Big Hairy Audacious Goals (BHAGs). The drive for progress urges continual change in the methods, strategies, practices, processes, policies, resource allocations, and other structures and systems that are used to produce the financial and non-financial results that an organization gets. As Collins and Porras describe it, "The drive for progress is not a sterile, intellectual recognition that 'progress is healthy in a changing world' or that 'healthy organizations should change and improve' or that 'we should have goals': rather, it's a deep, inner, compulsive – almost primal – *drive*."[75] The elements of core ideology and a drive for progress work together to produce what Collins and Porras called "cult-like" cultures which were great places to work for those who buy-into the core ideology. Those who are misaligned with the core ideology and the drive for progress were either ejected like a virus, or self-selected out.

Most of the authors referenced in the last two sections that focused on the *structures-and-systems perspective* and the *human-performance perspective* developed their theoretical models from a specific "perspective" of organizational reality. Which views captured your interest most? Which approaches were least compelling? Which would you use when undertaking the task of assessing and changing organizational culture? It's important to remember that the tendency for assessors to have a preference for the *structures-and-systems perspective* or the *human-performance perspective* reinforces the importance of having a clear understanding of our own philosophical assumptions when assessing an organization's culture, because our assumptions and beliefs about organizations powerfully shape and define the nature of our causal analysis and the recommendations presented to clients. Focusing on only one of the two perspectives almost ensures that an assessor's causal analysis and recommendations will focus on symptoms and causal factors, rather than the underlying "root" causes of organizational performance and culture.

The goal of this chapter has been to use the broader historical context of the business literature over the last 40 years to help readers step outside their tacit beliefs and assumptions and to learn to "see" organizations and organizational culture differently. Readers should note that the distinction between the *structures-and-systems perspective* and the *human-performance perspective* is only the first of many distinctions that will be presented in this book – all of which reflect different ways of seeing organizations, and the people in them. Mastering these multiple perspectives or "lenses" will give assessors powerful insight into the underlying causes and Invisible Bureaucracy that frustrate and undermine organizational performance.

CHAPTER 2
SEEING ORGANIZATIONS DIFFERENTLY

The concepts, models, and tools presented in this chapter will show assessors how to "see" organizations differently by broadening the definition of organizational culture, and making cause-and-effect connections between culture and key performance indicators and measurements that managers care about. Assessors who learn and internalize the material in this chapter will be able to identify the kind of Invisible Bureaucracy that frustrates and undermines organizational and individual performance, and once they've learned to see differently, they'll never view organizations the same way again. These new perspectives will then be used in Chapters 3, 4, and 5 where we present a model for assessing organizations and the key elements of their culture.

An Open Systems Model of Organizations

In this section, assessors will learn to see organizations as open systems that have patterns, structures, and processes. Organizations do not appear in nature.[76] Rather, they are designed, built, and constructed by humans. Organizations are man-made. Once created, organizations take on a life of their own as goal-seeking organisms that manifest the emergent properties of organizational life and energy, and this enables them to act on (and react to) the external environment. They are a product of their history; e.g., their decisions, key events, people, and the financial and socio-cultural forces within which they are embedded. An organization's culture is like its personality with a distinct experience of "what it's like to work here." They have a corporate life-cycle where they're born, they mature, they decline, and then often they die.

In a one-person company, the owner has to perform every function that is performed. They have to obtain materials from suppliers; fabricate products and deliver services; ensure that customers will actually buy their products and services; raise awareness through marketing; sell products and services to customers; and perform financial management functions that control two kinds of dollars: those that come in as revenue and those that go out as operating costs. When a one-person company grows into an organization of 25, 100, or 500 people; the tasks, functions and decisions that the owner handled by themselves must be delegated to groups of people as shown in Figure 1.

EXTERNAL ENVIRONMENT

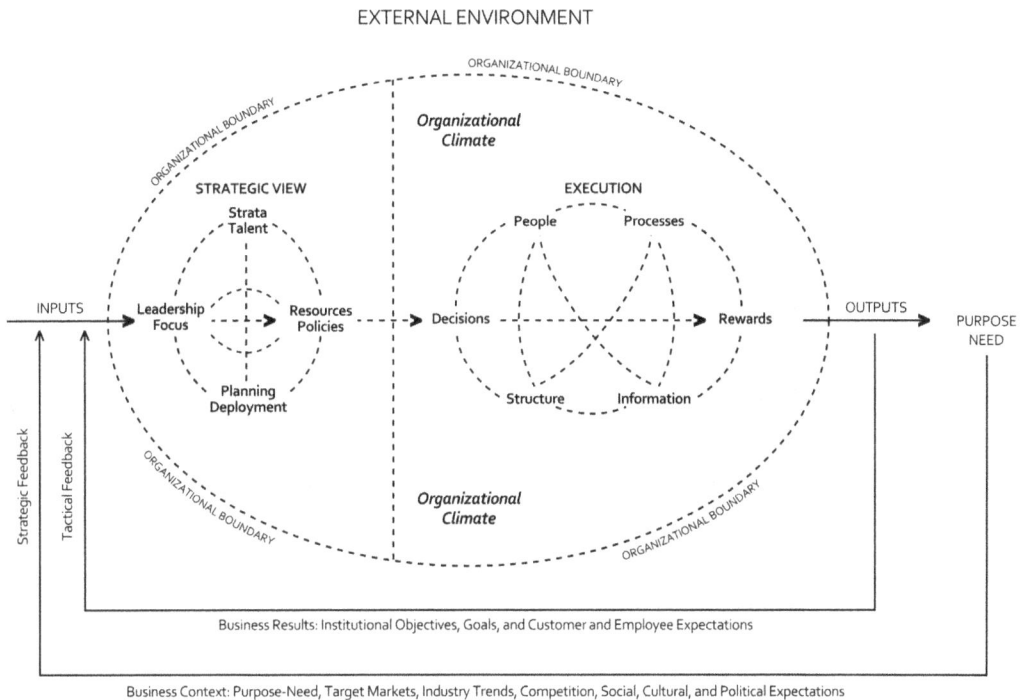

Figure 1

Figure 1 depicts the structures and systems of an organization as an organic, process-oriented system that exists within the context of organizational climate and is open to influences of the external environment, upon which it depends for survival.[77] All living systems are composed of patterns and structures that are linked together by dynamic processes.[78] As mentioned, organizations are like organic, living, goal-seeking organisms where their structures and systems reach a state-of-equilibrium within: a) the context of their organizational climate, and b) the forces and pressures from the external environment outside the organization. Figure 1 has three main elements:

- Strategic View

- Execution

- Organizational Climate

The *Strategic View* defines the overall direction, goals, and objectives of an organization, given its purpose in the external environment. The *Execution* perspective reflects the key elements needed to execute the organization's plans, direction and accomplish its work. The *Organizational Climate* is the day-to-day experience of what it's like to work in an organization and a "window" into the underlying, tacit beliefs, assumptions, and norms of an organization's culture. Perhaps the greatest value in using an open systems model to analyze and characterize an organization's culture is that it provides a framework for focusing cultural assessments on: a) addressing specific challenges or issues that the organization is facing, b) improving business processes and tangible work practices, and c) helping organizations to get the results they want.

Organizations are collective-cultural entities that are led, managed, and changed one person at a time. Studies have shown that a decline in organizational culture is a strong predictor of a decline in overall business performance.[79] Further, a decline in organizational culture is often evidenced by wide-spread destructive conflict and ineffective patterns-of-interaction on the part of managers and staff in response to both the internal organizational challenges; and forces and pressures from the external environment. Given the difficulty of changing destructive and ineffective patterns-of-interaction once they have solidified, they become a strong indicator of an organization's future performance.

Let's review the key elements shown in Figure 1 in more detail. As you review the descriptions below, reflect on ways in which each element manifests itself in organizations that you have worked in, or organizations you have assessed.

- *Organizational Boundary*: All organizations and work-groups (divisions, departments, etc.) have a *boundary* that distinguishes them from other organizational units. Types of boundaries may include: a) *physical* (building, location, geography), b) *time-related* (work shift, time zone), c) *social* (hierarchal, disciplinary, functional), d) *language* (national, industry-based), e) *psychological* (distribution of personality preferences), and f) *beliefs* (shared, unquestioned assumptions, values and stereotypes about how they see the world). An organization's boundaries must be permeable to the external environment in order for the company to survive, but the degree of permeability must be consciously designed and managed. When organizational boundaries are too permeable, the forces, pressures, and demands of the external environment can be overwhelming to managers and staff members. When boundaries have too little permeability, an organization gets cut-off from the resources it needs to survive and grow – too inwardly-focused and introspective.

- ***External Environment***. The external environment is everything that is outside of the organizational boundary. Although organizations must interface with customers and suppliers in order to survive and thrive, there are enormous (but subtle) differences between being *inside* the organizational boundary as an employee, and being outside in the external environment as a customer, supplier, or competitor. Since the vast majority of things in the external environment are not relevant or value-added to an organization's purpose or survival, an organization develops an interaction-style based on its culture and the personality preferences of managers and key personnel. Some organizations try to ignore the external environment and become a closed system. Others attempt to manipulate and control the external environment, which is difficult because they have little or no control over industry trends, market preferences, and competitors. A more effective strategy is to establish an Essential Tension between: a) the strengths and weaknesses of an organization's structures, systems, and climate, and b) the opportunities, threats, forces, and pressures exerted on the organization from the external environment.

- ***Purpose-Need***. All living organisms have a reason for existing – a purpose. Organizations are goal-seeking organisms that can follow the path they choose as long as they meet the needs and expectations of the larger context of the external environment. In other words, an organization must link its vision and purpose to the tangible needs of customers in the external environment. Meeting these needs becomes the organization's purpose – its reason for existing. Dave Hanna argues that elements like the ones shown in the Strategic View in Figure 1 function like an *implicit contract* between the organization and the external environment.[80] Achieving the goals and commitments of this contract ensures an organization's survival. The goals and objectives in an organization's strategic plan should function as internal targets established by managers and key personnel that guide the organization toward fulfilling its purpose in the external environment.

- ***Inputs***. Much like the human body uses food, oxygen, and water from the environment to survive, develop, and flourish; an organization must obtain financial, human, and material resources from the external environment, as well as information on industry trends and the needs of market segments in order to survive and achieve sustainability. When an organization lacks sufficient resources from the external environment, it begins to weaken and will ultimately die.

- *Transformation:* Like any organic system, the inputs into an organization must be transformed by enterprise-wide business processes into tangible goods, products, and services by the elements of the Strategic View and Execution shown in Figure 1. The outputs of the transformation process are exported to distributors and end-use customers in the external environment in the form of goods, products, and services sold by an organization.

- *Outputs:* An organization exports products and services to the external environment to meet the needs of distributors and end-use customers, thus fulfilling its purpose and making good on the commitments that managers and key personnel have made in their implicit contract with the external environment.

- *Organizational Climate:* Probably the most easily understood manifestation of an organization's culture is Organizational Climate; e.g., the day-to-day experience that people have when working in an organization. Like an atmosphere that permeates the workplace, Organizational Climate is characterized by things like level and type of employee morale, confidence in management, openness to change, conflict and pressure, a spirit of creativity and innovation, fair process, and a no-blame philosophy.

- *Business Results (Tactical Feedback):* Tactical feedback is an indicator of the degree to which an organization is on course for achieving the goals it committed to in its implicit contract with distributors and end-use customers in the external environment. Consequently, the data that constitute Tactical Feedback are often called Business Results because they are literally the financial and non-financial results produced by the totality of an organization's activities as an open system.

- *Business Context (Strategic Feedback):* Strategic feedback is an indicator of the degree to which an organization is connected to (and monitoring) the external environment; e.g., industry trends, the needs of market segments, and the activities of competitors and suppliers. While Tactical Feedback tells an organization whether or not it's achieving the goals and objectives that it has set for itself, Strategic Feedback is an indicator of the degree to which an organization is aligned with the realities of its purpose and the tangible needs of distributors and customers in the external environment. Consequently, this is often referred to as the Business Context.

Assessors should evaluate the degree to which the elements shown in Figure 1 are seamlessly integrated with an enterprise-wide IT infrastructure. More specifically, the purpose of seamlessly integrated structures and systems is to allow:

- Data on organization-wide objectives and goals to be transmitted to the correct work-groups so it can be analyzed, digested, and acted on.

- Customer feedback to be transmitted to the correct work-groups so it can be analyzed, digested, and acted on.

- Data on target markets, industry trends, and competition to be transmitted to the correct work-groups so it can be analyzed, digested, and acted on.

- Data on the status of goals and budgets in operating plans to be transmitted to the correct work-groups so it can be analyzed, digested, and acted on.

- The timely retrieval of the business-related documents and records needed to conduct day-to-day work activities in support of enterprise-wide business processes and enabling processes.

Assessors should note that the *more defined* the organization-wide structures and systems shown in Figure 1 are, the *less impact* sub-cultures and the personalities of individuals will have on day-to-day operations because the differing ways of "seeing" and "doing" get eclipsed by these formal ways of operating with end-to-end, enterprise-wide business processes. The *less defined* the structures and systems are, the *more impact* sub-cultures and the personalities of individuals will have on day-to-day operations because the informal power and authority of personality fills the void of formal power and authority that should be defined by structures and systems. In other words, people *are* the processes when structures and systems are not well-defined or operating effectively. Reflect on the day-to-day operations of organizations you have worked in or that you have assessed and ask, "*How much of the job got done by* the formal structures and systems, and how much got done by the informal power and authority of sub-cultures and individual personalities where people *were* the process?"

The Breckenridge Equation

This section will teach assessors how to "see" day-to-day operations and organizational culture through the lens of the Breckenridge Equation™. As mentioned previously, while an organization's culture powerfully molds its operating style and can positively (or negatively) affect the performance of work-groups and entire organizations, "culture" has remained an overly-complex and somewhat mysterious topic for most managers and organizations. The Breckenridge Institute® has identified the constituents of organizational culture and formulated them into an equation that describes what organizational culture *is* in simple, concrete, and precise terms (see below).

POI ↔ COI ↔ ROI = Current Results™

Assessors can apply the Breckenridge Equation to organizations, of any size, in any industry, and in any country; regardless of their governance structure (for-profit, non-profit, government), the products and services provided, number of locations, or corporate life-cycle phase. Assessors can use this simple equation to identify the root causes of organizational performance problems, and to help organizations improve performance at the organizational, work-group, and individual employee levels simultaneously. The key insight is that organizational culture is composed of *all four terms* in the equation, with each term being a distinct (but interdependent) category of business elements that interacts with the others to produce an organization's financial and non-financial results. It's the interaction of all four terms that *creates* and *maintains* organizational culture. The terms of the Breckenridge Equation are defined as follows:

- POI = Patterns-of-Interaction (Do, Informal Rules, Actions, Interactions, Group Learning)

- COI = Context-of-Interaction (Say, Formal Rules, Structures, Systems, Location)

- ROI = Repository-of-Interaction (See, Tacit Assumptions, Belief Structure, Values, Meaning, History)

- Current Results = (Get, Actual Results, Not Planned Results)

Here's how the four terms work together to create and maintain culture in organizations. Day-to-day operations occur as patterns-of-interaction (POI) within the context-of-interaction of an organization's structures and systems (COI). The interaction of POI and COI functions like a group-learning process that creates a repository-of-interaction (ROI) that becomes the shared knowledge-base, tacit beliefs, and unquestioned assumptions that managers and staff members have about the organization and the people in it. Over time, these first three elements settle down on a configuration of organizational patterns-of-interaction (POI) within the larger context-of-interaction of the external environment (COI), and the combination of the first three terms of the equation produces the Current Results; e.g., the financial and non-financial results that an organization actually gets.

If an organization is more or less successful at producing revenue and meeting the challenges of the external environment, the configuration of the terms in the Breckenridge Equation goes on autopilot, slips below the surface of organizational consciousness, and becomes "the way it's done around here." Over time, the specific configuration of the four terms reaches a state-of-equilibrium and solidifies within the context of the forces, pressures, and demands from the external environment. As Hanna puts it, "All organizations are perfectly designed to get the results they get! For better or worse, the system finds a way of balancing its operation to attain certain results."[81] When employees are hired into a new company, they are forced to compare their own ways of seeing the world that they developed while in former jobs with what goes on in the new organization, and to try and make sense of these new ways of working. Seasoned employees have internalized the organization's ways of seeing and working long-ago, so these beliefs about how things are to be done (or not done) are on autopilot and powerfully shape the decisions they make. Employees that don't (or can't) internalize an organization's way of seeing and ways of working don't normally stay in that organization.

Assessors should note that the Breckenridge Equation is a much broader definition of culture than those described in Chapter 1. In fact, most culture theorists focus on one or two of the terms in the equation to define what organizational culture *is*, but few systematically consider all four terms and their interdependency on one another. For example, Edgar Schein focuses primarily on tacit beliefs and assumptions (ROI) and the context (artifacts) in which they happen (COI);[82] David Hanna focuses primarily on observable work habits and practices to explain how an organization's culture really works – the interaction between POI and COI – as producing an organization's Current Results;[83] and John Kotter and James Heskett focus on linking Current Results to the level of flexibility in the POI as found in Theory I (Strong Cultures), Theory II (Strategically Appropriate Cultures), and Theory III (Adaptive Cultures).[84] Each term in the Breckenridge Equation is described in more detail below.

Context-of-Interaction (COI): After decades of research on organizations, it has become *common knowledge* that 85% or more of the root causes of performance problems are in the organizational structures and systems within which people work (COI).[85] In other words, if you put good people in bad systems you'll get poor performance. So focusing on improving performance in a work-group without understanding the context within which it's embedded almost guarantees that change will not be sustainable, because the managers and staff within the work-group are less than 15% of the real problem. The COI is everything that an assessor can see, hear, feel, and experience in an organization including, the business situation; business systems; physical, financial, and human resources; organizational climate; *formal* policies, procedures, power structures, and rules for how things get done; facilities and building layout; geographic location, weather patterns, and physical climate; and what an organization "says" or espouses about itself publicly. The COI functions like a *stage* upon which the day-to-day, week-to-week, and month-to-month activities of the organization are acted out.[86] Most people tend to view the context in which they work as a passive thing, but the context-of-interaction (COI) is far from passive. In fact, it has a powerful shaping influence on what we do (POI), what we believe (ROI), and the outcome of an organization's activities (Current Results). So when attempting to assess and change organizational culture, it's important for assessors to remember that the COI is a vital part of what defines, shapes, and reinforces an organization's culture. The COI is also the most visible part of an organization's culture.

Patterns-of-Interaction (POI): What is *not* common knowledge is that the patterns-of-interaction (POI) that make up most day-to-day operations in companies are performed on autopilot; e.g., they are done out of habit and routine, seamlessly, without consciously thinking about them. It's important to remember that autopilot operations are a doubled-edge sword. When done *effectively*, they can be your greatest ally because they increase your ability to compete and achieve your goals. But in most cases autopilot operations are *self-defeating* because they perpetuate problems with work performance, communication, interpersonal conflict, decision-making, and then derail attempts to create positive change. Here's how most POI are formed. Managers and staff members watch or participate in the work processes that make up day-to-day operations as a joint-group learning process (POI) within the context-of-interaction (COI) – the stage upon which the organization's work is performed. The POI are the *informal* ways of working; budget and resource allocations; policies and procedures; informal power structures; language, acronyms, and "insider" references and descriptions to historical events, stories, and traditions; rituals, ceremonies, and celebrations that recall an organization's history and identity; and the unwritten rules for how things "really" get done in an organization. The combination of POI happening within the context of COI is the most powerful mechanism for embedding culture. While the physical actions and interactions of managers and staff members are *visible* to observers, the ineffective autopilot operations that function as patterns-of-interaction (POI) are largely *invisible* to those acting out these cultural norms because they are tacit, unquestioned, and taken-for-granted assumptions about how the world works. Assessors should note that ineffective patterns-of-interaction are the single biggest component of Invisible Bureaucracy in most organizations.

Repository-of-Interaction (ROI): Culture is most frequently described as the underlying assumptions, tacit beliefs, and attitudes that an organization holds in common (ROI), but as shown by the Breckenridge Equation, this is only one of four terms that defines the constituents of organizational culture. The ROI is a collective repository of group-history and group-learning that functions like a lens through which managers and staff members see (and interpret) day-to-day operations and the realities of organizational life. The ROI constitutes an organization's belief structure and body of knowledge, including the unique capabilities and the intellectual property that allow an organization to create its products and services and its accumulated business experience and knowledge base. It includes an organization's accumulated history; key events, stories, heroes; prohibitions; rituals, ceremonies, traditions; and "folk wisdom" about how things should (or should not) be done. The ROI also includes the collective (group) and individual characteristics of personality; e.g., the distribution of personality type across the organization and in work-groups, as well as the individual personality types of managers and staff members. The ROI functions like an emotional "scoreboard" upon which people *unconsciously* keep track of the emotional messages they receive from each other and from the organization. This includes, what behaviors and attitudes get rewarded, how decisions are made, what employees should focus their time and energy on, and what specific POI and COI "mean" within that unique culture, given the organization's history and accumulated learning about how to succeed in the external environment.

Studies have shown that the repository-of-interaction (ROI) can also function like a kind of "group mind" where individual memory, external memory (knowledge recorded in external media like books and computers), and what Daniel Wegner calls Transactive Memory *combine* to form an intricate and extremely complex memory-system in organizations and work-groups.[87] For example, John is good at analyzing financial data, technical details, and keeping projects and tasks on track. Linda is good at understanding customers' real needs, building relationships, and creating common purpose and synergy with her direct reports. Together, they form a group memory system because his competencies, skills, and areas of expertise are different than (and complement) hers. Developing an effective Transactive Memory system in an organization where managers and staff members have reached group consensus on who knows what, is a key indicator of effective working relationships. In a very real sense, the patterns-of-interaction (POI), repository-of-interaction (ROI), and Transactive Memory developed by managers and staff members *combine* to create a work-group's "culture" that is distinct and unique from the sub-cultures in other work-groups. Over time, it becomes a work-group's organizational reality.[88] This is why losing key personnel and top talent can be so devastating to a work-group – it loses a significant part of its knowledge, competency, skill-base, and group-memory.

Current Results: An organization's current results consist of its *actual* level of financial and non-financial performance and *actual* level of customer satisfaction, as opposed to the goals or key performance indicators (KPIs) that an organization defines for itself. Over time, the four terms in the Breckenridge Equation tend to settle down on a configuration of organization-wide patterns-of-interaction (POI) that emerge within the larger context-of-interaction of the external environment (COI), and this creates the actual results that an organization gets – good or bad. Because all four terms function interdependently, an organization's actual results reinforce the other three cultural elements like a "social mirror" that reflects the way things are – organizational reality.

The Breckenridge Equation allows assessors to analyze organizational culture from two very different, but interdependent perspectives: a) tops-down analysis, and b) bottoms-up analysis. A *tops-down analysis* looks at culture from the perspective of collective-shared patterns of POI, COI, and ROI that powerfully shape the actions and interactions of managers and staff members organization-wide, or in specific work-groups. From this perspective, culture has *emergent* properties that take the form of patterns, structures, and processes that are not directly reducible to the actions, interactions, and personalities of individual managers and staff members, although they function as "culture carriers" who have a powerful effect on creating, reinforcing, and maintaining cultural norms. A *bottoms-up analysis* looks at organizational culture from the perspective of the building blocks of culture in groups of 2s, 3s, and 4s, with the primary issues being the fact that over 85% of the sources of organizational performance problems and conflict in work-groups come from outside the work-group in the organization's structures, systems, and culture. From the bottoms-up perspective, the actions, interactions, and personalities of individual managers and staff members cannot be "added up" to equal collective-cultural norms, although as mentioned, managers and key personnel function as "culture carriers" who have a powerful effect on creating, reinforcing and maintaining the elements of culture.

As described in Chapter 1, writers such as Kotter and Heskett have characterized organizational culture using descriptors such as "strong" culture, "strategically appropriate" culture, "adaptive" culture, and even "weak" culture. But at a deeper level, the key is to understand the degree to which the configuration described by the Breckenridge Equation is *intended* or *unintended* in terms of getting the desired results. An Intended Culture is consciously configured and embedded to achieve an organization's desired results. An Unintended Culture tends to be riddled with ineffective autopilot operations and Invisible Bureaucracy that derail organizational intentions as embodied in an organization's goals and objectives. Even outstanding organizational performance may not be created by an Intended Culture and be short-lived because it's an artifact of the internal and external contexts within which that organizational configuration exists. The ability of an organization to change and adapt with conscious intention is the true test of the degree to which an organization has an Intended Culture. Assessors should note that whether a leader is the founder of a new company, or a top, line or middle manager in a well-established company, one of their most important tasks is to intentionally *create*, *manage*, and (if necessary) to *destroy* organizational culture to get the desired results for an organization or work-group. In other words, they are responsible to create an Intended Culture that is designed to get the desired results, within an ever changing external environment. The precise definition of culture presented with the Breckenridge Equation gives assessors a powerful set of tools for helping clients at all organizational levels accomplish this.

The See-Do-Get Process

Prior to the 20th Century, millions of people died from diseases that could have been easily cured by an antibiotic like penicillin. For years, the world's leading bacteriologists had searched for the missing piece to this medical puzzle. Many times they were looking right at it. But they always "saw" the penicillin mold as a pest that contaminated countless bacterial cultures and slowed their progress toward finding a way to save innocent lives. In the late 1920s, a London doctor named Alexander Fleming suddenly began to see this so-called "pest" as exactly the bacterial killer scientists had been searching for. From that moment on, everyone saw penicillin differently. It was instantly transformed from a problem, to a resource. The new challenge then became how to quickly produce it, not to protect ourselves from it. This is one example of the principle, "what you see is what you get." Something you "see" as a *negative* can be transformed into something *positive* by changing how you "see" it.

The See-Do-Get Process® is a meta-model that describes how organizational culture is created, managed, and deconstructed. More specifically, the purpose of culture (any culture) is to teach people how to see the world, and there are *active*, *tacit*, and *disciplinary* teaching processes by which organizational culture is promulgated in groups of people. Using the See-Do-Get Process will reveal underlying patterns-of-interaction and behaviors that happen all around you, but are not well-understood or seen to be what they are – it will help to make Invisible Bureaucracy visible.

Active Teaching Process

A customer (Curt) walks into a store and a new sales person (Sarah) and her manager (Jeff) are standing at the register checking an order. Jeff comments quietly about Curt, "He always gives us a hard time," so they ignore him, trying to avoid conflict. Curt reads this emotional message in their behavior and actually feels ignored. After a few minutes of just standing around, Curt snaps critically, "Hey, young lady! I need some help over here!" Sarah looks at Jeff and thinks to herself,

See – You said he'd give us a hard time!

The See-Do-Get Process is a way of describing how our knowledge and beliefs are shaped by how we see ourselves, other people, and the world around us (see Figure 2). First, we are taught to see the world a certain way and specific behaviors and emotions naturally flow from that worldview because we believe that it is "reality." When we act these behaviors out in relationships, people read our body language and respond to the message they see in us. Their response reinforces how we see them, how they see us, and over time these responses begin to create patterns-of-interaction in our relationships.[89]

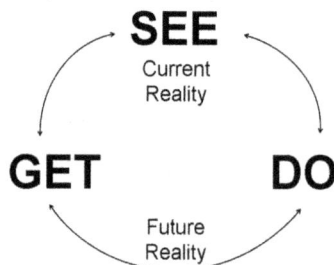

Figure 2

In terms of organizational culture, managers and staff members are actively taught how to see themselves, coworkers, customers, suppliers, competitors, and the external environment in which they are embedded. For example, John starts a new job as an Account Executive in the Sales Department at the SciTech Company and as he begins calling on his new accounts, his manager Sally says, "That's not how we do it around here. Let me show you how we want you to see our customers, and the people in the Production Department." Over coffee and while riding to appointments with clients, Sally teaches John how to see the Production Department as a major roadblock to delivering on commitments; the HR Department's lack of business knowledge as the reason that they can't attract top talent; and top managers as being out of touch with the day-to-day realities of running the business. The Active Teaching Process is one of the primary ways that organization-wide and work-group culture is passed on to both new and existing employees. So work-groups actively teach employees to see the world a certain way, with the goal that specific actions and interactions will naturally flow from that worldview. When an experienced manager or more seasoned employee models (acts out) these cultural norms, new (or less experienced) employees take note of (and absorb) their actions, interactions, and body language. If the manager or seasoned employee is more or less successful in getting the desired results in terms of achieving their performance goals and objectives, this reinforces the cultural norm in the mind of the new employee and creates a shared understanding that, "this is how things ought to be done around here."

Think about it – managers come to see employees as lazy. Employees in that same organization learn to see top managers as distant and uncaring. The R&D Department sees the Sales Department as incompetent. The Marketing Department sees the Sales Department as too short-term focused. The Engineering Department sees the Production Department as doing sloppy work, and the Production Department sees Engineering as arrogant. You see your boss as a moron, and then wonder why she never assigns you to more interesting projects or gives you the compensation increases you think you deserve. The See-Do-Get Process applies to everyone, everywhere.

Tacit Teaching Process

It's impossible *not* to communicate, so many of the most powerful lessons that managers and staff members learn about organization-wide and work-group culture are tacit; e.g., unquestioned, non-verbalized messages that teach powerful lessons about how things should (or should not) be done in a given organization. At an individual level, a person sitting at a table saying nothing is communicating because 55% of communication is non-verbal (body language), 38% is tone of voice, and only 7% is word choice; which is why e-mail is often a problematic form of communication – it leaves out 93% of the message. The overall configuration of an organization communicates; e.g., the entire configuration of non-human structures, systems, facilities, office spaces, public areas, and geographical location. There are specific places that employees feel comfortable going, or not going; ways they are encouraged to dress, or not dress; and greetings that they give top managers, middle managers, supervisors, and staff members that are appropriate, or inappropriate. In fact, the underlying purpose of formal organizational policies is to *encourage* specific behaviors, and *discourage* others – policies are organizational statements of belief about how things should (or should not) be done. So assessors should try to identify what messages an organization is sending. What ways of seeing are the managers teaching to new and existing employees? To what extent are managers and key employees all teaching the same message, or are they espousing different, competing, or even contradictory ways of seeing themselves, others, and the world? The key is for assessors to remember that *everything* in an organization communicates, including inanimate objects and configurations of structures, systems, facilities, office spaces, public areas, and geographical location.

The Tacit Teaching Process is often experienced as a "gap" between the formal (espoused, written) rules for how things get done in organizations, and the informal (behavioral, unwritten) rules for how things are *really* done – with this "gap" being the tacit, unspoken, unquestioned organizational reality which managers and staff members are taught through the See-Do-Get Process. For example,

- Managers and employees observe a "gap" between the formal (espoused) statements that the organization makes about itself, and the informal (behavioral) ways that things are actually done. This forces people into a Pragmatic Paradox™ where employees receive conflicting, contradictory, or duplicitous messages; and the only way to keep the *informal rules* of how things "really" get done is to break the *formal rules* that are stated as public policy. For example, an organization's formal (advertised) rule-policy espoused to customers is that its sales persons do not pressure customers into buying – "Just come in and look at our selection" customers are told publicly. However, the informal rule-policy that is discussed in weekly meetings and seminars on cross-selling and is built into the compensation structure for sales persons is to, "sell, sell, sell…."

- If a manager or staff member attempts to discuss the conflicting, contradictory nature of these messages they will most likely encounter what Chris Argyris calls organizational defense routines; e.g., patterns-of-interaction that protect organizations (and the people in them) from embarrassment or threat.[90] Defense routines also make it highly unlikely that "gaps" like the ones discussed above will ever be detected or corrected. More specifically, the fundamental rules of organizational defense routines identified by Argyris are to: a) bypass such situations and act as if they are not happening, b) give inconsistent answers and "manage the meaning" of the situation by reinterpreting it (we said this, but we really *meant* that), c) make the bypass, inconsistent answers, and reinterpretations undiscussible, and d) make the undiscussibility undiscussible.[91] If a manager or staff member were to continue to press on the discrepancy between the formal and informal policies on selling, they will likely discover overt and covert social sanctions against making such situations matters of public discussion. These social sanctions may even involve real or perceived retribution. This is a form of Organizational Entrapment™ where the organization and the people who work in it use overt and covert strategies to keep others from moving beyond the impasse of the Pragmatic Paradox and finding a solution that actually corrects the problem.

- If circumstances force situations like a duplicitous customer policy into public awareness (customers reveal it to newspapers) and the organization recognizes the problem and makes a commitment to course correction, this sends a *constructive* message that narrows the "gap" between the formal and informal rules of the game. But if the organization maintains its defense routines and survives the confrontation; the gap widens, trust in the organization decreases, and the level of *destructive* conflict created by the Pragmatic Paradox is intensified for managers and staff members. Over time, as an organization's defense routines survive repetitive confrontations, they are strengthened and its climate and culture become increasingly duplicitous; e.g., the opposite of what we describe in Chapter 3 as a Just Culture™.

It is important for assessors to note that organizational defense routines can be acted out by people through patterns-of-interaction and behaviors like the ones described above – what Argyris calls "first-order errors." They can also manifest themselves as "second-order errors" where defense routines are actually designed into the organization's structures and systems; e.g., the context within which managers and employees work.[92] For example, the formal (advertised) statement of the organization about itself is that it welcomes any and all feedback from customers, but the systems by which customers are supposed to give that feedback send them into an organizational black hole, and any feedback that actually "penetrates" these systems is never responded to by the company. To reiterate, it's impossible not to communicate, and many of the most powerful lessons that managers and staff members learn about organizational culture are based upon tacit, unquestioned, undiscussible actions and interactions like those described here.

Disciplinary Teaching Process

One of the most powerful mechanisms for defining and shaping how people see themselves, others, and the world are disciplinary paradigms. A disciplinary paradigm is composed of the education, training, experience, work-related tools, membership in professional organizations and unions, disciplinary indoctrination, and technical standards that *define what it means* to be competent in a particular field or profession.[93] Being accepted as a *competent* member of a disciplinary paradigm requires people to master a body of knowledge; learn problem-solving methodologies; and to adopt the working-level assumptions of that community of practitioners for how to effectively analyze and solve work-related problems. In many organizations, people with different disciplinary paradigms are grouped into functional units like R&D, marketing, sales, production, engineering, and accounting, as well as organizational populations that extend from line-level staff up to top managers. So whether an assessor is trying to gain insight into organizations composed of customer service reps, particle physicists, oil-field workers, Information Technology (IT) professionals, sales managers, engineers, telemarketing workers, medical professionals, or people who provide administrative support to senior managers; assessors should remember that the disciplinary paradigms to which managers and staff members belong, and the sub-cultures that form around these paradigms, can powerfully shape and define an organization's or work-group's culture.

The See-Do-Get Process is a key element of achieving organizational change because it shapes and defines the kind of *commitment* that managers and staff members have (or do not have) to creating sustainable change. In any change initiative, the question is, "To what extent will the change process require *external* versus *internal* commitment to accomplish, and is this message clear and unambiguous to all participants?" External commitment means that participation in the change process is part of a manager's or staff member's roles, responsibilities, and performance goals that they will be evaluated on. In other words, external commitment means that people support organizational change simply because it's part of their job. Internal commitment means that managers and staff members have adopted the knowledge, skills, models, and philosophy associated with the change process as part of their personal value system and paradigm. Consequently, people who have internal commitment tend to share the values embedded in the change process and support them in both their personal and professional lives. Different levels of commitment should be required by different populations in the organization; e.g., top managers, middle managers, and supervisors should have internal commitment to the principles and practices embedded in the organizational change, while staff members may only need external commitment. The See-Do-Get Process is a process for redefining and reshaping how people see themselves, others, and the key issues involved in creating and sustaining organizational change.

Four Ways of Working

In this section, assessors will learn to "see" organizations through the lens of the Four Ways of Working™. Let's begin by exploring how this perspective on organizations has emerged over the last 250 years, and then describe how assessors can use this model to assess and change organizational culture. Michael Hammer argues that, "Most companies today – no matter what business they are in, how technologically sophisticated their products or services, or what their national origin – can trace their work styles and organizational roots back to the prototypical pin factory that Adam Smith described in his book, *The Wealth of Nations*, published in 1776."[94] This new way of working was based on the principle of dividing the enterprise-wide business process of making pins into specialized tasks that workers performed as one-or-more steps in the pin-making process. This division of labor (fragmentation of work) into separate tasks increased the productivity of pin makers by a factor of hundreds. Over time, work was broken into smaller and smaller pieces, with groups of people who performed similar tasks being grouped into organizational functions; e.g., sales, production, administration, financial management, etc. Not surprisingly, workers who were successful at performing tasks were naturally drawn to those organizational functions because they had the skills, preferences, natural talents, and personality needed to perform that kind of work. The See-Do-Get Process powerfully shaped and reinforced the functional approach to accomplishing work in organizations, and the roles of individual workers in accomplishing that work. Functional groupings of specific kinds of capabilities have become collective ways of working that form the organizational design in most modern corporations. In fact, the practice of designing organizations around similar functions has been so engrained into our global culture that most people have never worked in an organization that wasn't structured around functions. Consequently, many managers and staff members mistakenly believe that organizational *structure* and organizational *functions* are synonymous – but they're not.

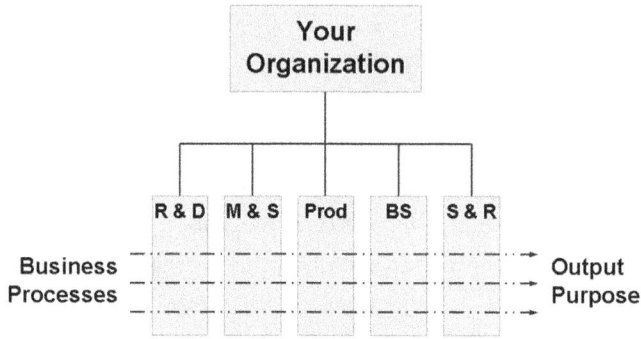

Figure 3

Assessors should note that an organization is a *structure* for grouping people and other resources to achieve a common purpose. A *function* is a field (a disciplinary paradigm or kind of work) that involves similar professional skills, tools, and capabilities. These functions are often concentrated into departments as shown in Figure 3; e.g., the Research and Development department (R&D); Marketing and Sales (M&S); Production (Prod); Business Services (BS); and the Shipping and Receiving departments (S&R). These are often pejoratively called, "functional silos" – vertically oriented structures through which business processes flow horizontally, as shown in Figure 3. Organizational functions have their own vocabulary, acronyms, and sub-cultures, and often work-group members view themselves as members of *that* sub-group, not as a part of the overall organization; e.g., "I'm in the Accounting or Sales department." In some cases, lines of communication between these different functional units break down and people squander enormous amounts of time and energy on toxic interpersonal or inter-departmental conflicts rather than doing productive work. Over time, "we versus they" thinking solidifies as one work-group optimizes its own performance at the expense of other functions, and ultimately at the expense of the overall organization.

Our modern concept of how work is done in 21st Century corporations is the result of: a) grouping similar kinds of work, professional skills, tools and disciplinary paradigms, and b) populating them with people that have similar work styles, interests, talents, cognitive preferences, and personality types. After more than 200 years, organizational functions have solidified into well-defined generic cultural norms that represent four different (contradictory) philosophies for how to accomplish work and to improve organizational performance. We call them the Four Ways of Working, which are defined below.

Type 1: Production (What Things Get Done)

Type 1 (Production) focuses on *execution* and *what* gets done in an organization.[95]

When an organization manifests the Type 1 (Production) way of working, they believe that decisive actions, practical solutions to problems, and a short-term focus on clear, tangible goals will result in improved performance. They have a take-charge attitude and are forceful and direct in getting things done, making decisions, and getting directly involved in day-to-day operations. Type 1 (Production) also focuses on *implementing* the organization's goals and objectives through the teams and individuals who make-up work-groups.[96] They exhibit the following other characteristics:

- Top managers can make tough choices and have the determination and resolve to persevere in achieving the organization's goals and objectives, even in the face of challenges and obstacles.

- The number of approvals needed to make decisions is kept to a minimum to expedite the decision-making process and the number of managerial layers has been purposefully designed to achieve their goals and objectives.

- Decisions have a bias toward action and producing practical solutions (issues don't get "studied to death"); meetings are action-oriented and result in task assignments, due dates, milestones, deliverables, and follow-up. Managers only support decisions that implement or accelerate achieving the goals and objectives as outlined in an organization's strategic plan.

- Work assignments and goals are clearly defined and communicated (milestones and deliverables are understood); lines of authority for reporting and decision-making are clearly defined and focus on achieving results. Roles, responsibilities, and authorities are clearly defined to eliminate confusion about who does what.

- The communication style is open and direct (people go directly to others to discuss problems, rather than involving others and feeding the "grapevine"), and all employees are free to present the unvarnished truth about organizational matters without fear of retribution.

Type 2: Connection (Why Things Get Done)

Type 2 (Connection) focuses on *teambuilding* and *why* things get done in an organization. When an organization manifests the Type 2 (Connection) way of working, they believe that attunement to the external environment; innovation and radical change, exploring options and new ideas, and engaging with and influencing people to work together and collaborate will result in improved performance. They build alliances and cultivate relationships with people *outside* the organization (the public, interest groups, unions, media, and government agencies), and *inside* the organization where managers and staff members are encouraged to align their efforts with the organizational structures and systems in order to achieve the organization's purpose, goals, and objectives.[97] They exhibit the following other characteristics:

- Top managers build a broad consensus and commitment among managers and key personnel around the overall direction and goals defined in the strategic plan, and they can clearly communicate the organization's purpose, goals, objectives, and core values to people inside and outside the organization.

- The focus is on anticipating and acting on changes from the external environment (sometimes even before the details of a situation are fully understood); experimenting with multiple strategies and lines of action to anticipate changes in the external environment, and then letting the results determine the best choices. These data and information are used to identify new products and services that will meet the changing needs and demands of customers in new (or existing) market segments.

- Managers use regular operations meetings and periodic events to build group identity (annual planning, team-building sessions, retreats, holiday gatherings, etc.), but managers and staff members still see themselves as part of the whole organization, not members of a specific department or sub-group. Consequently, they communicate and cooperate with other departments and functional units so that key information is shared; e.g., the left hand knows what the right one is doing.

- People are energized by radical change that results from interacting with customers and the external environment and they believe that innovation and creative approaches to identifying and solving problems will enable the organization to achieve (or exceed) its goals and objectives.

Type 3: Direction (How Things Get Done)

Type 3 (Direction) focuses on *leadership* and *how* (that) things get done in an organization. When an organization manifests the Type 3 (Direction) way of working, they believe that defining a long-term direction, with strategic plans, goals and objectives, and creating and maintaining order and efficiency through structures and systems, will result in improved performance. Using a quantitative, data-driven, analytical approach to performance, the organization's strategic goals are deployed and monitored through operations plans, goals, and budgets that direct the week-to-week and month-to-month operations of teams and individuals in organizational units to ensure that those goals and objectives are achieved.[98] They exhibit the following other characteristics:

- Top managers have set a clear direction for achieving the organization's mission and purpose and this institution-wide planning process is codified into a written strategic plan that defines the organization's goals and objectives. They use a balanced array of "vital few" performance measures (KPIs) to monitor the organization's progress toward achieving its goals and objectives.

- High-level policies are aligned with (and support) achieving the strategic goals and objectives and these policies send a consistent set of signals that reinforce the desired behaviors. They encourage the desired behaviors and discourage actions and interactions that frustrate and undermine the organization's core values and its ability to achieve its goals and objectives.

- Managers use strategic goals, along with organizational unit plans, goals, and budgets to direct their week-to-week and month-to-month operations. They use fact-based decision-making with quantitative data and scientific analytics, not just business experience and intuition. They only budget for, and commit resources to, things that help them achieve the organization's goals and objectives and are consistent with the organization's values.

- Regular operations reviews of goals, objectives and budgets are conducted to keep the outputs of business processes and projects on track. In addition, the performance of business processes is regularly analyzed to eliminate unnecessary steps and tasks that negatively impact achieving the organization's goals and objectives.

- The organizational structure allows the right people to work together on the right tasks to achieve the organization's goals and objectives, and the lateral working relationships and lines of authority between organizational units are defined; e.g., who can say no to whom and under what circumstances.

Type 4: Integration (Who Gets Things Done)

Type 4 (Integration) focuses on *analysis* and *who* gets things done in the organization. When an organization manifests the Type 4 (Integration) way of working, they believe that building the organization's knowledge-base and capabilities, attracting top talent and supporting and encouraging individual contributors, and analyzing how concepts, ideas, and underlying organizational patterns relate to each other will result in improved performance. They help achieve the organization's goals and objectives through inner vision, inspiration, and by integrating the knowledge-base and competencies of human performers with the organization's structures and systems to get the desired results.[99] They exhibit the following other characteristics:

- Top managers are viewed as being competent to lead the organization and have a deep commitment to building the organization's knowledge-base, capabilities, and professional standards as well as understanding how the organization's structures, systems, culture, and human performers relate to (and integrate with) each other as an interdependent, organic whole.

- People analyze the root causes of organizational performance in the structures, systems, and culture and don't blame individual employees for organizational performance problems. They analyze and question the reasoning, assumptions, and attitudes that motivate the organization's decisions (the problem-solving process is a matter of public scrutiny).

- People understand how their individual work assignments and goals contribute to achieving the organization's goals, as well as the way that their day-to-day decisions relate to (and impact) the organization's overall performance. They discourage "we versus they" thinking, so one department or functional unit's performance is not optimized at the expense of others; e.g., they see themselves as working toward common goals and a common purpose.

- People use their history and culture (stories, heroes, traditions) as a rationale that helps employees identify with the organization's purpose and core values, and to teach new and existing employees how problems should (and should not) be handled.

- Managers have a comprehensive method for mapping out the organization's current and future talent needs, identifying and attracting top talent, and for mentoring key personnel using an effective succession management process. They encourage people to look for new cutting-edge knowledge to add value to the organization (to read widely, participate in professional societies, etc.), and they ensure that people are assigned work that they have the knowledge, skills, and problem-solving abilities to perform successfully.

While the exact combination of the Four Ways of Working within a specific organizational function is determined largely by the cultural norms within the overall organization, the list below shows some typical combinations found in companies.

- Sales (**1234**)
- Marketing (**1234**)
- Production (**1234**)
- Engineering (1**23**4)
- R&D (1**2**34)

- Accounting (**1234**)
- Finance (**1234**)
- Legal (**1**234)
- Personnel (1**23**4)
- HRD (1**23**4)

Every organization and its work-groups have all Four Ways of Working, but they often manifest themselves hierarchically as a dominant, auxiliary, tertiary, and fourth preference for how work is performed and how performance is improved. Functional units in organizations almost always have a stronger preference for one (or possibly two) of the Four Ways of Working and rarely does an organization have an equally strong preference for them all. For example, if an organization's culture has a dominant Type 1 (Production) and auxiliary Type 3 (Direction) way of working, leaders, managers, and staff members will tend to use these two ways of working almost exclusively when solving problems. The less developed ways of working almost always exist somewhere in the organization, but they are *eclipsed* from the day-to-day reality of operations and are either undeveloped or not seen as viable ways of working. In some organizational functions, they are marginalized, dismissed, demonized, and consciously repressed – pushed far below the surface of organizational consciousness, so that even the thought of using them as a valid approach to solving problems becomes undiscussible.

For example, if a new employee was hired into a company that was dominated by Type 1 (Production) and Type 3 (Direction) from an organization that was dominated by Type 2 (Connection) and Type 4 (Integration) and suggests that their new organization use these two ways of working to solve a critical problem, it would probably be viewed as a "soft" touchy-feely approach that is out of place in the hard-hitting, quantitative culture of that organization. So through body language (rolling eyes); comments (we've already got that covered); and the See-Do-Get Process; the new employee quickly learns from more culturally "savvy" members of the organization – "that's not how we do things around here." If the new employee continues to press the issue, organizational defense routines will begin to arise to protect the status quo of the Type 1 and Type 3 ways of working, and over time long-term employees will shake their heads and begin to wonder if they've made a hiring mistake.

Ideally, a work-group or functional unit should be adaptable enough to refocus their preferences from one combination of the four ways to another depending on the forces and pressures from the external environment, and internal pressures and demands. But most times this does not happen because in many organizational functions, the Four Ways of Working reach a state-of-equilibrium that tends to be *imbalanced* in one direction, often at the expense of other seemingly contradictory (but much needed) work practices and beliefs. In other words, they come to "see" some ways of working as more reliable or effective than others through the See-Do-Get Process, and then they dismiss other ways of accomplishing goals and improving performance. It is important to note that the tendency to "see" organizations from *either* the structures-and-systems perspective *or* the human-performance perspective described in Chapter 1 emerges from the Four Ways of Working. More specifically, managers and staff members who "see" organizations through the lens of Type 1: Production (What Things Get Done), and Type 3: Direction (How Things Get Done), tend to have a structures-and-systems perspective of organizations. Managers and staff members who "see" organizations through the lens of Type 2: Connection (Why Things Get Done) and Type 4: Integration (Who Gets Things Done), tend to have a human-performance perspective of organizations.

Individual-Collective Paradox

This section will teach assessors to see organizations as collective-cultural entities that are led, managed, and changed one person at a time – what we call the Individual-Collective Paradox™. The issues associated with the Individual-Collective Paradox have been debated since Greek times under the auspices of reductive-atomistic versus emergent phenomena.[100] A more recent example of this debate is John Locke's 17th Century model of society as an aggregation of autonomous, independent, individuals as described in his, *Two Treatises of Government*; rather than Jean-Jacques Rousseau's 18th Century view that society was an emergent, organic, collective entity as found in, *The Social Contract*.[101] In our case, the question is: in what ways is organizational culture a socio-cultural phenomenon that is the property of organizations or work-groups; and in what ways is culture ultimately reducible to the actions, interactions, and beliefs of individuals in an organization – or both?

When assessing and changing organizational culture, assessors should view individual managers and staff members (with their personalities and unique ways of seeing) as being like *magnets* within the *electromagnetic field* of organizational culture. So, asserting that organizations are led, managed, and changed one person at a time means that while the organizational structures and systems associated with the context-of-interaction (COI) and the patterns-of-interaction (POI) between small-groups of 2s, 3s, and 4s can be disrupted and changed at an organization-wide or work-group level; the tacit, unquestioned beliefs and assumptions of people in organizations (ROI) must be changed individually. As William Bridges points out, *change* is immediate, but the psychological adjustment on the part of individual managers and staff members (*transition*) is often a long and protracted process, and some people do better at it than others based on their personality, life experience, and their level of psychological health.[102]

The Individual-Collective Paradox argues that while the collective-cultural actions of organizations can be "mapped" to the actions and interactions of individual performers that are either: a) autopilot responses of cultural norms and personality, or b) conscious decisions to act out (or not act out) the dictates of culture and their personality; that they cannot ultimately be "reduced" to the actions of individuals. So when it comes to socio-cultural phenomena like organizational defense routines, assessors should focus on the individual manager's or staff member's responsibility for perpetuating organizational defense routines because an organizational culture that defends against recognizing its Blind Spots can only maintain its power if individuals consciously (or tacitly) agree to act out and embody the culture's norms and edicts. Alternatively, Chris Argyris emphasizes the organization's role in maintaining defense routines because they occur frequently as Blind Spots that are independent of an individual's conscious choice – they are built into the organizational structures, systems, culture and are unconscious organizational habits that are on automatic pilot.[103] Regardless of whether you focus on the individual or organizational side of the Individual-Collective Paradox, it is a circular, self-reinforcing process that begins with individual actors who create cultural norms that go on autopilot, slip below the surface of organizational consciousness, become reified, and then those norms act like a social mirror that reflects back what's expected of managers and staff members in that cultural setting.[104] So while culture initially forms through founders, managers, and staff members acting and interacting (POI) on the stage of the organizational setting (COI); over time, beliefs and assumptions about the nature of the day-to-day interactions of organizational life (ROI) solidify and the combination of the first three terms of the Breckenridge Equation working together produces the Current Results that an organization gets.

Building Blocks of Organizational Culture

While most people think of organizational culture in broad, sociological terms, in this section assessors will learn how to identify the fundamental building blocks of organizational culture as patterns-of-interaction between small-groups of 2s, 3s, and 4s. Most managers in an organization know that effectively leading a work-group takes an enormous amount of time and energy because they have to maintain a balance between conflicting or competing interests in a complex system of coalitions of small-groups of 2s, 3s, and 4s who *see* themselves, others, and the world very differently. But what many managers don't know is that over time the tapestry of these patterns-of-interaction is woven into the fabric of organizational culture. As such, managers have two choices. They can either allow the culture in their organizations to emerge naturally through autopilot patterns-of-interaction which sentences them to struggle against overly complex systems and Invisible Bureaucracy with an Unintended Culture, or they can consciously create, reinforce, and maintain an effective Intended Culture that will help them achieve their organization's goals and objectives.

As mentioned previously, patterns-of-interaction are habitual (autopilot) behaviors, emotional responses, actions, and interactions that occur between people in the workplace, based on the personalities of the managers and staff members involved, and the tacit assumptions, and the unquestioned beliefs of organizational culture. Perhaps the best way to explain how patterns-of-interaction manifest themselves in organizations is to begin with a body of research that has been conducted on one-on-one relationships.

Over the last 20 years, thousands of people have participated in research conducted by the psychologist, John Gottman.[105] He asks a couple to sit in a room and discuss any topic they choose for 30 minutes while the research team video-tapes the couple's discussion. As mentioned earlier, 55% of communication is visual (body language), 38% is tone of voice, and only 7% is word choice.[106] Gottman and his research associates analyze facial expressions, shifts in tone (frequency) of voice, along with other key indicators like increased heart rate. This extensive set of data confirm that people accurately read and respond to the non-verbal emotional messages that people send to each other, *not* just the words they use. Over time, the actions and interactions between people create POI that powerfully shape and define relationships. Once the patterns-of-interaction in the video have been analyzed, Gottman is able to predict with 94% accuracy whether or not the couple will still be married in 15 years.[107] The same principles hold with one-on-one relationships in the workplace.

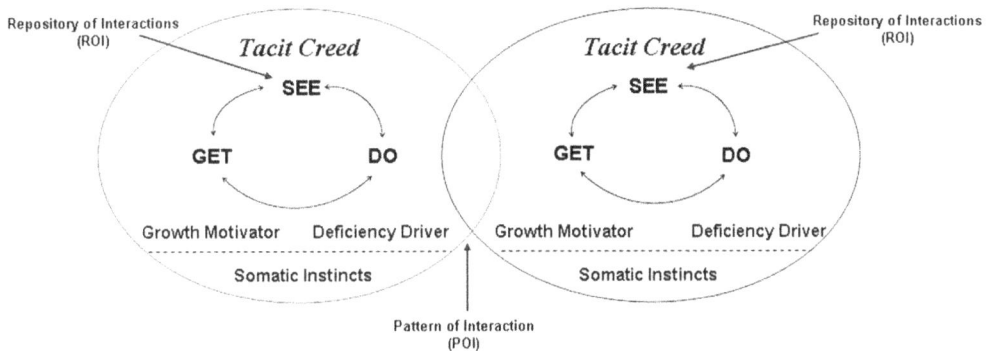

Figure 4

For example, the characteristics of patterns-of-interaction between a manager and a direct report emerge from repetitive problem-solving and discussions about issues that they have in common; e.g., the most effective configuration of organizational structures and systems, how to achieve performance goals, how to motivate employees, how to improve business processes, and how to serve customers. The patterns-of-interaction are powerfully molded by differences and similarities in personality as well as how effectively each person reacts when they are under pressure from the organizational context. Eventually, these POI take on a life of their own and become "objective" in the sense that they can be directly observed in day-to-day interactions and studied in research projects like Gottman's (see Figure 4).[108] In fact, others can often see the destructive nature of patterns-of-interaction much more clearly than the coworkers who are involved because POI tend to be tacit, taken-for-granted, and on autopilot. Reflect on the list of examples below and try to identify actual instances of patterns-of-interaction that occur in your relationships, especially when you're stressed or under pressure. More specifically, patterns-of-interaction can develop from:

- Things you *say* to others and patterns of discussion (debate).

- Things you *do* with others as patterns of action, interaction, or reaction.

- Differences in how each of you "sees" your competencies, skills, talents, and intellectual horsepower.

- Context related pressures concerning business results and achieving key performance indicators.

- Personal traits and habits that manifest themselves in day-to-day operations in the workplace.

- Issues related to your goals and vision for your personal and professional life.

Over time, as patterns-of-interaction solidify, unquestioned beliefs and assumptions emerge and come to reside in the repository-of-interaction (ROI) for each person as shown in Figure 4. In addition to the belief structure, the ROI is a kind of emotional "scoreboard" upon which we *unconsciously* keep track of the balance between the number of destructive and constructive emotional messages we have received from other people. The contents of a person's ROI are often a set of competing, contradictory, and/or paradoxical beliefs that are nonetheless how they see others, and how their relationships actually work. Effective work relationships require an 80-20 ratio of constructive to destructive messages – what we call the 80-20 Rule. When this ratio shifts toward the destructive side, interactions become *spring-loaded* where negative day-to-day interactions build up to the point where people feel that they have to "walk on egg shells" around each other. A destructive balance also makes interactions *toxic* where the chemistry and climate in a relationship becomes unhealthy to one or both of the people involved. Over time, these destructive interactions undermine trust in relationships.

Here are some specific examples of patterns-of-interaction (POI) that assessors can use to identify the causes of destructive conflict in organizations, work-groups, and between managers and key personnel.

Symmetric versus Complementary: Every relationship must be consciously or unconsciously defined (negotiated) by the participants as being either symmetric or complementary.[109] In symmetric interactions, people tend to mirror each other's behavior and emotional responses. Symmetric interactions are based on an assumption of *equality* that has been tacitly agreed to by the participants that tries to *minimize* the differences between the participants. In complementary interactions, one person's behavior and emotional responses complement (are different than) the other's behaviors and emotional responses. Complementary interactions are based on an assumption of *difference* that has been tacitly agreed to by the participants that tries to *maximize* the differences between the participants. Differences can include

46

being assertive-submissive, superior-inferior, primary-secondary, and as being one-up, or one-down. Over time, the actions and interactions of managers and staff members around the Symmetric-Complementary distinction can solidify into autopilot, habitual patterns-of-interaction.

Content versus Relationship: It is important to make the distinction between the *content* element of communication which conveys information and is largely cognitive, and the *relationship* element of communication which is related to the emotions involved.[110] Paul Watzlawick likens the content element to digital (verbal) communication, and the relationship element to analogue (non-verbal) communication; e.g., facial expressions, body language, and tone of voice. Trying to resolve destructive conflict that exists at the relationship-emotional level (non-verbal) by interacting at the content-cognitive level (verbal) tends to *increase* the amount of destructive conflict and the level of cognitive dissonance in the interaction. Over time, the actions and interactions of managers and staff members around the Content-Relationship distinction can solidify into autopilot, habitual patterns-of-interaction.

Event, Pattern, Trust (EPT) Process: Patterns-of-interaction often consist of multiple issues (bundles) that combine to form extremely complex interactions like the Event, Pattern, and Trust (EPT) Process.[111] For example, the first time a manager has to speak to an employee about a negative attitude toward a customer, inconsistent quality in their work, or destructive conflict displayed toward a coworker they are talking about a single event; e.g., the content of the situation in terms of what was done or left undone. The second or third time the manager has to discuss this issue, a pattern-of-interaction begins to form. If the problem continues over time, the employee's actions and interactions begin to undermine the manager's trust in the employee's professional capabilities and eventually it can undermine trust in the overall relationship. The key is to remember that the EPT Process is a bundle of separate interactions that have different consequences, so when one person wants to discuss the current Event rather than the fact that the situation has morphed into a Pattern or a Trust issue, destructive conflict often emerges. Over time, the actions and interactions of managers and staff members around the EPT Process can solidify into autopilot, habitual patterns-of-interaction.

Cross-Road Events: A single event can determine (or change) the entire direction of a relationship between managers, staff members, organizational units, customers, or suppliers. Cross-Road Events have at least four components where the people involved: a) "see" themselves, others, and the situation very differently, b) are under high levels of pressure from external circumstances or circumstances outside their control, c) know the decisions made or direction taken will have important short-term and/or long-term consequences, and d) have a high level of emotional investment in how the process goes, the outcome, and the end-effects. A Cross-Road Event powerfully shapes the initial interaction, and over time subsequent actions and interactions of managers and staff members can solidify into autopilot, habitual patterns-of-interaction.

Organizational Entrapment: Decision-making is often ineffective because people invoke explicit or implicit "rules" that prevent managers, staff members, and work-groups from working through process-related or interpersonal impasses. This is a form of Organizational Entrapment where enormous amounts of time and energy are squandered on destructive conflict.[112] Organizational Entrapment can powerfully shape the decision-making process, business processes, actions and interactions of managers and staff members, and over time it can solidify into autopilot, habitual patterns-of-interaction.

Managers and staff members can become trapped in ineffective and destructive patterns-of-interaction (POI) like the kinds described above because POI are almost always on autopilot. In other words, the POI "have them" rather than the people having control of the situation and doing what would be most effective to address the issues at hand. It's important to note that patterns-of-interaction can (and do) develop around any topic or activity – who talks most in meetings; how decisions are made; whether decisions actually get implemented; the chemistry between a manager and their direct reports; the chemistry in work-group meetings; the chemistry between departments; or how top managers communicate important business issues to their managers and staff. Patterns-of-interaction are constantly forming and morphing in one-on-one relationships between managers and direct reports, in work-groups, between functional units; and in entire organizations. Assessors should remember that there are as many patterns-of-interaction as there are groups of people who interact.

The complexity of these interactions increases exponentially when moving from small-groups of 2s, 3s, and 4s, to groups of 20 or more people because the amount of information processing needed to keep track of the patterns-of-interaction becomes enormous. For example, in a group of 20 people, a manager has to keep track of nineteen relationships between them and others, plus 171 third-party relationships. The dynamics of these third-party relationships change again when they combine into coalitions of 3s and 4s that may have conflicting or competing interests. In a department of 50 people, a manager has to keep track of 49 relationships between them and others, 1,176 third-party relationships, plus myriad coalitions of 3s and 4s that may have conflicting or competing interests. Robin Dunbar has correlated the size of the neocortex with group size and claims that the ideal limit for the number of relationships a person can effectively manage is about 150.[113] The computational power of the human brain begins to overload when the number of interactions gets too large, so as the *quantity* of interactions goes up, the *quality* and *depth* goes down because the human brain only has so much processing power. When we reach cognitive overload, an unconscious cognitive sorting process occurs where we tend to be drawn to people who create the least amount of cognitive dissonance for us because understanding and juggling this many different ways of seeing becomes too complex and time consuming. While we can store data and information about hundreds or even thousands of people outside of our brains using files and computerized systems, actively interacting with more than about 150 people pushes the computational limits of the human brain, and the quality and depth of those interactions and relationships decreases proportionally.[114] The exponentially increasing complexity of patterns-of-interaction between small-groups of 2s, 3s, and 4s is one reason why organizational culture seems so complex and difficult to understand.

A more concrete way for assessors to understand the complex patterns-of-interaction in a work-group of 20 or more people would be to video-tape a series of staff meetings and then analyze them. During a one-hour meeting there are a finite number of interactions that could occur and understanding the patterns-of-interaction over time would reveal important information about the nature of conflict (constructive or destructive), patterns-of-interaction, the formal power structure, and informal-personality power structure within a work-group. Here are five kinds of information that function like five terms in an Interaction Equation™. Analyzing the video-taped recording we would count:

- The number of interactions and who initiated them.

- How many were characterized by constructive, versus destructive conflict.

- How many decisions were made based on these interactions.

- The number of interactions that were actually implemented.

- The degree of impact that implemented decisions had on either maintaining or reconfiguring the performance and day-to-day operational reality of the work-group.

Assessors should note that the number of interactions and how forcefully people advocate for their positions and press for solutions and decisions can be correlated with the personality types of the manager and staff. In addition, assessors can experiment with the Interaction Equation during on-site visits where day-to-day operations are observed as part of an overall cultural assessment.

The Root Causes of Conflict in Work-Groups

As previously mentioned, studies have shown that over 85% of the root causes of organizational performance problems are in the structures, systems, and culture within which work-groups are embedded. Structures and systems are either *consciously* defined with purpose and intent around a strategic direction as an Intended Culture, or they *emerge naturally* from the patterns-of-interaction of the personalities of managers and staff within work-groups, departments, and functional units as an Unintended Culture. Unintentionally designed structures and systems that create contention between managers are the single biggest cause of destructive conflict in work-groups.[115] So focusing on conflict in a "work-group" without understanding the structures, systems, and culture within which it is embedded almost guarantees that change will not be sustainable, because the managers and staff within the work-group are less than 15% of the real problem. Identifying the root causes of conflict in work-groups should always begin by asking four key questions:

- How much of the conflict within the work-group is being created by the organizational structures, systems, and culture that are outside the work-group?

- How much of the conflict within the work-group is in response to dynamic forces and pressures that originate from outside the work-group, or from the external environment; e.g., changing levels of corporate revenue, competitors, customer demands, the efficiency of enterprise-wide business processes or functional units that support the work-group, etc?

- How much of the conflict within the work-group is being created by interacting with other organizational units (or groups outside the organization) that operate from different disciplinary paradigms?

- How much control can the work-group exert over these factors?

The answers to these and other questions will allow assessors to begin evaluating the root causes of performance issues and destructive conflict that come from outside the work-group in a more systematic and rigorous way. They will enable assessors to help their clients better: a) understand how individual group members with specific personalities are likely to respond when subjected to these external forces and pressures, b) anticipate the kinds of conflict-processing strategies that group members are likely to propose in response to organizational forces and pressures, c) utilize *both-and-thinking* to decrease the probability of destructive conflict and create better business solutions in day-to-day operations, and d) manage the levels of destructive and constructive conflict between team members to ensure that the climate within the work-group is positive, motivating and follows the 80-20 Rule, rather than negative and counter-productive.

For example, Stephen was the manager of a work-group in a company where he was held strictly accountable for the milestones, deliverables, and the overall performance of his work-group. But Stephen constantly struggled with destructive conflict between two individuals (Sal and Christy) who had radically different approaches to problem-solving on key projects that had high corporate visibility – the basis of Stephen's compensation. He had tried almost everything to minimize the amount of destructive conflict in the work-group and improve its performance. He has had off-site retreats, done personality testing, and held myriad team building exercises to try to transform the conflict from destructive to constructive. When destructive conflict erupted in meetings in the form of criticism, contempt, defensiveness, or stonewalling, Stephen tried to intervene using the problem-solving tools the group had learned and he tried to discourage this inappropriate behavior by giving Sal and Christy marginal performance ratings and decreased compensation. Stephen had even tried to transfer Sal (the most problematic person) to another department. But each time he tried to take positive steps to correct the situation, Sal and/or Christy went around him to Stephen's boss Jane who intervened and then reversed some or all of Stephen's corrective actions. Subsequently, Jane attended one of Stephen's staff meetings to "set things straight" while Stephen was expected to sit there quietly and say nothing. Jane's boss does the same thing to her. The Board of Directors does the same thing to the company's CEO.

As seen in the case of Stephen and Jane, a frequent cause of conflict in work-groups is a lack of well-defined *accountability* and *authority* for managers. In the absence of such structure, work-groups will establish their own ways of operating based on individual differences in personality, disciplinary paradigm, intellectual horsepower, political connections, etc. When work-groups, departments, and functional units throughout an organization are informally structured around these criteria, destructive conflict often prevails and aligning or changing the organization's direction becomes difficult or impossible. As noted by Elliot Jaques, the manager who leads a work-group should be held accountable for a minimum of four things:[116]

- The outputs of those who report to them

- Creating and sustaining a work-group that is capable of producing the desired results

- Providing leadership for direct reports so they collaborate with the manager and each other to achieve the work-group's goals

- Adding value to the work of their direct reports

The issue of destructive conflict that results from differences in personality is most related to the third element in the above list. But even a complete understanding of the work-group's personality differences *will never* eliminate destructive conflict without the implementation of the other elements of *both* accountability and authority. In Stephen's case, he had *accountability* without some of the *authorities* listed below. Jaques argues that in order for a manager to be successful, they must have at least four basic authorities. This includes the ability to:

- Veto the appointment of new people to the work-group

- Decide on the task assignments of direct reports

- Conduct performance appraisals of direct reports and reward desired performance and discourage poor or inappropriate performance

- Initiate the removal of a direct report from their role in the work-group

Assessors should note that no amount of teambuilding or personality profiling *will ever* transform Stephen's situation into constructive conflict. To the degree that these *accountabilities* and *authorities* are missing, to that same degree work-groups like Stephen's are forced to establish their own ways of operating based on individual differences in personality, disciplinary paradigm, intellectual horsepower, and political connections.[117] One of the main reasons that traditional approaches to using individual personality typologies in the workplace have often produced marginal (or failed) results in terms of long-term sustainable change, is because they have focused on the *local causes* of personality in individuals, without addressing the *common causes* of organizational structures, systems, and culture. In other words, traditional approaches to using personality type in the workplace fail to view Personality in Context®.

Once the root causes of destructive conflict are distinguished and then identified as either common or local causes, it's important for assessors to understand the four ways in which the patterns, structure, and dynamics of conflict actually work in organizations. This includes:

- *Level 1 (Organizational Conflict)*: Two or more work-groups, departments, or functional units experience destructive conflict caused by: a) the structures, systems, or culture, b) differences in disciplinary paradigms and sub-cultures, or c) the personalities of the managers (Border Guards) who lead these organizational units and this negatively impacts the climate and performance of the interacting units *and* the larger organization.[118] Often this kind of destructive conflict optimizes the power position and performance of one organizational unit, and sub-optimizes the overall performance and effectiveness of the entire organization.

- *Level 2 (Work-Group Conflict)*: The work-group experiences destructive conflict with the structures, systems, culture, or with an individual manager or staff member outside the work-group which negatively impacts the group's climate and performance.

- *Level 3 (Interpersonal Conflict)*: People in small-groups of 2s, 3s, and 4s experience destructive conflict with each other which negatively impacts the climate and performance of the work-group.

- *Level 4 (Intrapersonal Conflict)*: An individual experiences destructive conflict within themselves that may, or may not, be created by work-group or organizational activities, but this conflict negatively impacts the climate and performance of the work-group and the organization.

The first two levels of conflict are most often catalyzed by the organizational structures, systems, and culture. The second two levels are most often caused by the personality and level of psychological health of the individuals involved. It's important to remember that in many situations, all four levels of conflict are happening together at the same time, which is what makes dealing with destructive conflict in the workplace so difficult. When destructive conflict at all four levels persists over time, it can go on autopilot and become habitual patterns-of-interaction that frustrate and undermine organizational and individual performance.

So if long-term destructive conflict like the kind in Stephen's work-group is so debilitating, why do managers and staff members tolerate and endure it? There are at least two answers. First, work-groups often lack the ability to change the organizational structures, systems, and culture within which they are embedded, and this accounts for over 85% of the causes of destructive conflict. Second, some work-group members view the cognitive dissonance and psychological pain of staying in destructive conflict as less of a price to pay than the inner turmoil and cognitive dissonance that would be created by disrupting the current way their world is configured. In fact, one of the reasons why deep, sustainable change is so difficult is because it requires physiological changes to the human brain. Studies have shown that the number of synaptic connections in the brains of infants increases to the degree that they interact with their parents, other people, and their environment.[119] During the first years of life, the brain has a high degree of elasticity, but as children mature the See-Do-Get Process interacting in families and the larger culture creates an elaborate system of synaptic, neuropsychological structures that defines how we "see" ourselves, others, and the world. In fact, Clotaire Rapaille argues that the cultural imprinting on the human brain is so powerful that by the time a child is seven years old, she's not just a seven-year-old girl, she's a seven-year-old French, American, or Japanese girl.[120] So when the world outside our heads is "mapped" to (and configured like) our inner cognitive and emotional structures we experience a sense of comfort and psychological safety. When the configuration of the world does not "map" to our inner structures this creates cognitive and emotional dissonance that threatens our sense of "reality" and our identity. As adults, managers and staff members who *see* the world differently and have access to resources and power, begin to *shape* the day-to-day realities of organizational life to conform to the synaptic structures in their heads.

People like Sal and Christy live in two "different worlds" formed by different neuropsychological structures and their destructive conflict is actually a battle to either maintain, or reconfigure, the day-to-day operations of Stephen's work-group to more closely align with the cognitive configuration in their heads. Consequently, Sal and Christy *induce* behaviors and emotional responses in each other with *explicit* and *implicit messages* with the goal of getting the other person to: a) see the world the way they do, b) do what they want, and c) get the results they want.[121] At a more fundamental level, Sal and Christy are fighting to *maintain* or *reconfigure* the world in which Stephen's work-group operates as a way of: a) decreasing their individual levels of cognitive and emotional dissonance, and b) supporting their mutually exclusive ways of seeing which are not aligned with (or in the best interest of) the overall organization. There is little hope of ever stopping this kind of destructive conflict apart from building the kind of effective structures and systems and Intended Culture described in this book.

In the absence of well-defined structures and systems, patterns-of-interaction driven by personality will rule and dominate the day-to-day realities of organizational life. More specifically, when the forces and pressures from outside the work-group bear down on managers and staff members and the autopilot responses of their personalities are activated, a definable pattern-of-interaction (POI) emerges as a cluster of habitual behaviors and emotional messages that coworkers send each other (see Figure 5). The *signature* of an effective work-group is maintaining the 80-20 Rule of constructive to destructive emotional messages in meetings, e-mail exchanges, project activities, one-on-one discussions, customer exchanges, and small-group interactions, even when the forces and pressures from outside (or inside) the organization increase.

Over time, as the patterns-of-interaction shown in Figure 5 solidify, unquestioned beliefs and assumptions emerge from countless cycles through the See-Do-Get Process forming the repository-of-interaction (ROI) that functions like an emotional "scoreboard" upon which work-group members *unconsciously* keep track of the balance between the number of destructive and constructive emotional messages that they've received from others in the group.[122]

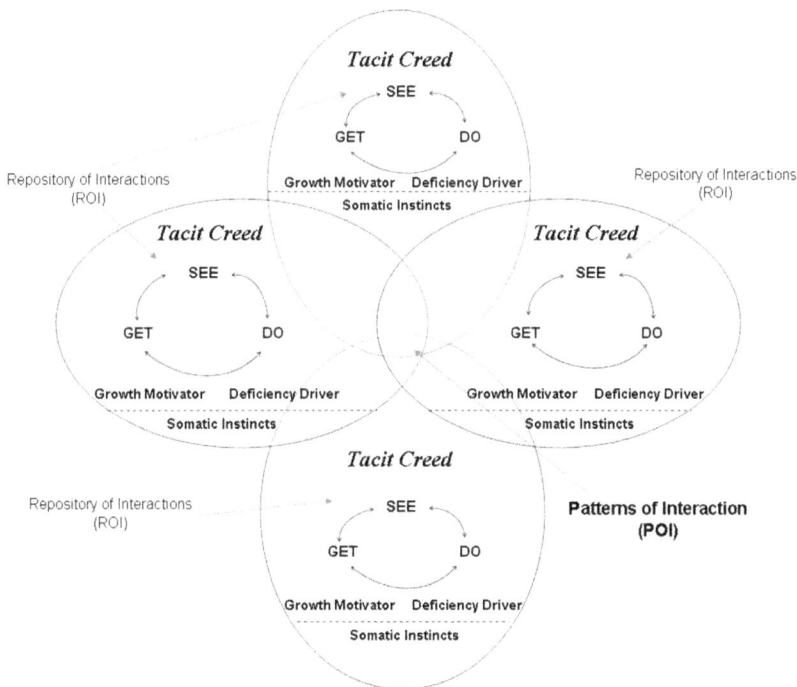

Figure 5

When this ratio shifts toward the destructive side of the 80-20 Rule, the repository-of-interaction for the work-group can become *spring-loaded* where negative day-to-day interactions build up to the point where people feel that they have to "walk on egg shells" around each other. A destructive balance in the repository-of-interaction can also become *toxic* where the chemistry and climate in the work-group becomes unhealthy to all involved. Shifting the ratio from constructive to destructive will undermine *trust* within the group. Shifting the ratio back toward the 80-20 Rule with constructive emotional messages is the most effective way to build *trust* between coworkers.

In terms of the approach to task assignments and day-to-day problem solving, the patterns-of-interaction that develop within a given work-group are governed (in part) by the disciplinary paradigm within which they operate and the body of knowledge possessed by individuals. If the products and services they provide and work-group membership are more or less homogeneous within a disciplinary paradigm (engineering, sales, information technology, accounting, marketing, etc.), then group members will have similar education, training, experience, work-related tools, membership in professional organizations and unions, disciplinary indoctrination, and technical standards. While individual work-group members may have accumulated different bodies of knowledge or embrace different "schools of thought" within a given disciplinary paradigm, the ways in which group members see their professional responsibilities, their interfaces with others, and their role in the larger organization will tend to be shared by virtue of their disciplinary background. The larger the overlap between group members around a disciplinary paradigm, the more identified they will feel with each other and the greater the sense that the group has "shared meaning" and a "shared reality." The less the overlap, the more potential there is for destructive conflict.[123] In addition, the *cognitive conflict* that results from different ways of seeing (even within a disciplinary paradigm) can unintentionally stir up the *emotional conflict* associated with our personality, so cognitive conflict and emotional conflict are inextricably bound.[124] Most people aren't motivated or driven by what they think (cognitive); rather, they are motivated and driven by how strong they *feel* about what they think (emotions). In fact, the level of *rigidity* with which a work-group member holds to their way of seeing is often directly proportional to their tendency to practice either-or-thinking rather than both-and-thinking.

But at a deeper level, the most powerful force in creating the patterns-of-interaction in work-groups is the personality and philosophy of life of the manager who leads the work-group. Traditional approaches to managing conflict in work-groups tend to view all members of a work-group as "equal," but the influence of the work-group manager must be more heavily weighted because they possess formally delegated authority and are accountable for the work-group's performance. This organizational principle about the influence of managers needs to be viewed within the context of neurophysiologic research that has identified a part of the human brain (the amygdala) that produces and senses emotions, and functions like an open-loop system; e.g., our emotional connections to other people (like our boss) help to establish shared moods and emotional responses in entire groups of people. Like an invisible wireless network, work-group members send and receive 93% of their communication through body language and tone of voice. Using another metaphor, the patterns-of-interaction in a work-group are like a stew to which all members contribute, but the manager's influence is the strongest seasoning.[125] Daniel Goleman argues that employees take their emotional cues from the top – everyone watches the boss. Even when a manager is not highly visible their attitudes affect the moods and emotions of direct reports and this ripples down through the organizational levels like a domino effect creating an emotional tone throughout the organization.[126] Over time, a manager's ability to resonate the emotions and moods of their employees *repeatedly* creates either destructive or constructive patterns-of-interaction within a work-group.

Matilda is a sales manager in a medical equipment company. Some days she's your "buddy" and wants to chat over coffee, and other days she's a "high-chair tyrant" who pounds on the table in meetings and demoralizes her direct reports with criticism and contempt.[127] "What mood is she in today?" whispers Jack as he gets to the office. "She's been flip-flopping since I got here," Jill responds, also in a hushed tone; "one minute she's asking me how my weekend was, and the next minute she's hammering me about my sales targets." "Yea," Jack laughs, "you can look at her face when she walks through the door in the morning, and tell what kind of day you're going to have." In any group of humans, the person in the leadership position has enormous power to create either constructive or destructive patterns-of-interaction, so managers like Matilda are like emotional leaders for Jack, Jill, and the other people who report to them.[128] When Matilda transmits destructive emotional messages, Jack and Jill begin to resonate on that frequency. When she sends constructive emotional messages, they resonate on *that* frequency. Over time, patterns-of-interaction emerge that are largely on autopilot, where work-group members are drawn into a destructive cycle of conflict and rehash the same issues over and over again. When managers understand how powerfully they can resonate their staff members and then they use this influence to maintain the 80-20 Rule of constructive and destructive emotional messages, the climate in the work-group will almost always be positive – with much higher levels of work productivity.

In addition to resonating the emotions and moods of group members, the leader's way of "seeing" their direct reports, structures, systems, culture, customers, suppliers, competitors, and the organization's politics powerfully *scripts* work-group members about how they should relate to each other and the larger organization. Howard Gardner claims that the open-loop amygdala of the human brain gives leaders the ability to "manage meaning" for their work-group by promoting ways to interpret situations, and then suggesting ways for work-group members to emotionally react to these situations.[129] As we have stated previously, teaching people how to see themselves, others, and the world is one of the most powerful techniques for building organizational culture. If the structures, systems, and culture in an organization do not allow managers to teach work-group members how top managers *want them* to see the world, other people will teach them according to their own views, interests, and biases of their personality. This almost always results in misalignment with top managers and destructive conflict.

But how can the conflict in work-groups be surfaced and managed as a way of shifting the dynamics and patterns-of-interaction toward the 80-20 Rule? Because 93% of all communication is body language and tone of voice, it's almost impossible not to communicate with everything we say and do. Managers and staff members in work-groups communicate on two levels simultaneously – the *conscious* level of what they say (espouse) about themselves, others, and the world; and at an unconscious (or quasi-conscious) level by the body language and tone of voice that form their actions and interactions in day-to-day life. In addition, people often experience a kind of "inner commentary" about their own actions, interactions, and the actions and interactions of others in their context. Like the italicized mental commentary of the characters in Dan Brown's book, *The Da Vinci Code*, the human mind is like a platform upon which the inner commentary about what we think and feel (but do not say) plays itself out. The model of the Left-Hand Column shown in Figure 6 can be a powerful tool that allows assessors to explore and understand this bifurcated communication and the inner commentary that occurs in organizations, work-groups, and between managers and staff members.

LH COLUMN	RH COLUMN
Cultural Norms and Undiscussible Views (Inner Commentary of ROI)	Socialized Norms and Public Dialogue (Shaped by COI)
What We Think, Feel, Believe, and Assume But Do Not Say and Do (Actual, POI)	What We Say and Do (Socialized)

Figure 6

Based on the work of Chris Argyris and popularized by Peter Senge, the Left-Hand Column can be used as a powerful tool for surfacing and managing conflict in relationships.[130] But it can also be used as a method for exploring the tacit, unquestioned beliefs and assumptions associated with an organization's culture. The Left-Hand Column is the place in our inner-experience where the tacit beliefs and assumptions of an organization's repository-of-interaction (ROI) make their presence known at the fringe of our consciousness. It is the psycho-social place where self-awareness about the strengths, weaknesses, and Blind Spots associated with an organization first emerges into an individual manager or staff member's conscious awareness. It is also the first line of defense for people who choose to censor and block this inner commentary from entering the arena of conscious awareness for themselves and work-groups. It's a gate-keeping function with which managers and staff members "manage" the information that they receive about the organization's structures, systems, culture, and about their own performance within that organizational context. As such, assessors can use the Left-Hand Column as a powerful tool for surfacing and managing conflict that results from the day-to-day operations in an organization.

Follow the Red Flags

The Red Flags that are described in this section are a key to making Invisible Bureaucracy visible in organizations and work-groups, and are the single most important indicator of the degree to which an organization has an Intended Culture or an Unintended Culture. Most organizations have sophisticated algorithms for managing information that they receive that does not "map" onto the way they have learned to see themselves, others, and the world through the See-Do-Get Process. These algorithms are designed to select inputs that agree with the image that the organization has of itself. The rest of the input is ignored or dismissed, but often registers as tacit, unconscious input into the organization's Left-Hand Column and cultural norms. But like the ostrich hiding its head in the sand (if I can't see them, they can't see me), customers, suppliers, and competitors do in-fact see who and what organizations are – how they perform, and the quality, cost, and timeliness of their products and services. Often, an organization is the last to know what customers and others in the external environment have known all along. These beliefs, opinions, assumptions, and views *build* in the Left-Hand Column of our professional and organizational relationships as inner commentary that people think, feel, believe, and assume; but do not say (see Figure 6). People within an organization often have a sense about the issues, beliefs, and assumptions that make-up the content of others' Left-Hand Column because 93% of communication is a combination of non-verbal body language and tone of voice, not what people actually say or espouse. In fact, teasing apart the difference between: a) the non-verbal messages that people inside and outside of the organization send about what they think and feel but do not say, and b) our tendency to impose or project our own unconscious views and the biases of personality on their actions and interactions, is one of the most sophisticated and complex problems in both personal and professional relationships.

At an interpersonal level, things that *others* know about us or "see" in us that *we* don't know about or "see" in ourselves are called Blind Spots. One way to picture this is using the Johari Window which was developed as a tool for raising individual self-awareness and for improving the dynamics and communication in groups of people (see Figure 7).[131] Understanding the nature of Blind Spots *for individuals* is relatively straightforward and intuitively clear. What is often surprising is that an entire organization or a work-group can also have Blind Spots; e.g., Blind Spots can be socio-cultural phenomena. Assessors can use organizational Blind Spots as a window into an organization's culture, ineffective autopilot operations, and Invisible Bureaucracy.

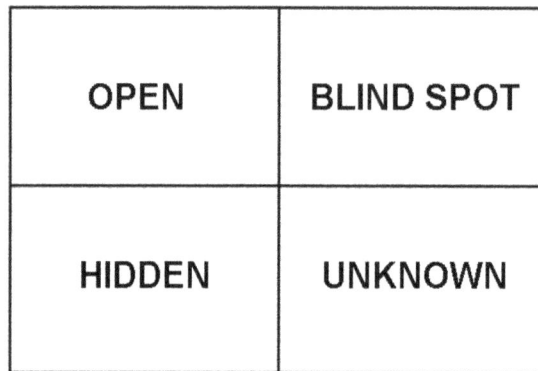

OPEN	**BLIND SPOT**
HIDDEN	**UNKNOWN**

Figure 7

The "open" quadrant indicates things an organization knows about itself, and people in the external environment also know about it; e.g., its brand, level of performance and customer focus, the attitude of its employees, and the quality of its products and services, etc. The "hidden" quadrant represents things that an organization knows about itself that those outside the organization don't – its internal politics, the true competencies of its managers and staff members, internal processes, trade secrets and intellectual property, how employees are treated, and where it pursues excellence or cuts corners. The quadrant marked as "Blind Spot" indicates things that customers, suppliers, and competitors know about an organization; that the organization doesn't "see" about itself; e.g., it says it has customer focus, but then defends itself against customer feedback; it says it's committed to providing quality services, but then doesn't deliver on commitments. The quadrant marked as "unknown" is the repository of things that are unknown to the organization about itself, and unknown to people in the external environment. More specifically, the "unknown" quadrant indicates things that are so paradoxical that those in the external environment would not expect them about the organization, nor would the organization expect them about itself. The combination of beliefs, assumptions, and views that are "hidden" from the external environment, an organization's "Blind Spots," and things that are simply "unknown" are what populate an organization's Left-Hand Column (see Figure 6). They also represent the "gap" between how an organization "sees" itself, how the external environment "sees" it, and the reality of who the organization *really is* – which is a combination of all four perspectives of the Johari Window.

The key to making Invisible Bureaucracy visible is for assessors to help raise an organization's awareness about its Blind Spots. This allows managers and staff members to consciously suspend the gate-keeping function and helps them learn how to purposely *identify* and *eliminate* them. While dealing with Blind Spots can cause conflict and dissonance in an organization, they must be faced *head-on*. Larry Bossidy and Ram Charan call this *confronting reality*.[132] Jim Collins calls it *facing the brutal facts of the situation you're in*.[133] If managers and staff members do not deal with organizational Blind Spots head-on, the knowledge that an organization obtains about itself, others, and the external environment is biased and distorted.

So how *do* managers and staff members become aware of organizational Blind Spots if they are tacit, unconscious, autopilot operations? How can they recognize ways in which organizational Blind Spots express themselves in day-to-day operations if they look right at them and don't "see" them because they are tacit, unquestioned, taken-for-granted, and consequently invisible? The Red Flags are a process that can be used by assessors to help clients identify how organizational Blind Spots manifest themselves in the day-to-day realities of organizational life. The Red Flags make Invisible Bureaucracy *visible* in an organization.

One way to describe how the Red Flags work is by using a metaphor from scuba diving and underwater exploration. The vast majority of the ocean is deep blue sea and the majority of underwater topography even around many tropical islands consists of sandy bottoms and no coral reef. So how do you find the coral reef in such an enormous body of water when the total amount of reef structure in the entire world represents a tiny fraction of the total area of the ocean? Dive operators find coral reef by exploring the underwater terrain and once they locate a good dive site, they tie a mooring ball to a concrete block on the bottom somewhere near the dive site and let it float just below the surface of the water. The mooring ball allows them to find that dive site every time they return.

Finding coral reef in the vast ocean is not unlike finding organizational Blind Spots that lie below the surface of organizational consciousness. If a manager decided to really change an organization or work-group, where would they begin to identify *the most important issues* that needed to be changed given all the issues that occur in day-to-day operations? How would they have any level of confidence that if they put their shoulder to the wheel and hammered through these issues, that this effort would really result in the kind of positive change that we're talking about? The Red Flags are like mooring balls that float near the surface of organizational awareness and indicate that there is an issue below the surface that assessors and their clients need to dive down and explore. Let's discuss three Red Flags.

- Excess Energy

- Unintended Consequences

- Defense Routines

Red Flags exist at both the individual and collective levels as described earlier in the section on the Individual-Collective Paradox. The Red Flags are triggered in response to situations in which an organization or work-group is faced with embarrassment or threat. This is especially true in instances where there's a "gap" between the formally stated (espoused) policies and practices, and the informal ways in which the structures, systems, and culture *actually* work. Whenever an assessor sees one of these Red Flags, they should stop dead in their tracks, take note, and *dive in* to a thorough analysis of the situation using an attitude of empathic inquiry and exploration. Following the Red Flags allows assessors to systematically *link* the underlying forces, actions, and interactions of organizational culture described by the Breckenridge Equation to strategic and tactical decision-making, day-to-day operations, and KPIs, in a cause-and-effect way so that ineffective autopilot operations and Invisible Bureaucracy *become visible*. Let's discuss each of the Red Flags in more detail.

Excess Energy: The first Red Flag is excess, or inappropriate, levels of energy. For example, the emotional response of a work-group to a new marketing plan, organizational change, work procedure, or customer feedback is entirely exaggerated – the emotional response *has you*, rather than you having it. When there's a Red Flag, the level of affect (emotions) displayed by people is entirely out of proportion to what was said or done. Excess levels of psychological energy become stored around an issue like a "hot button" whether it's the installation of new software, getting a new office, selling a new product you don't like, or getting a marginal performance review from a manager you don't respect. Managers and staff members get consumed, taken over, grabbed by the scruff of their emotional necks about issues that to outsiders seem like no big deal. They are gripped by strong emotions, and then an hour later they're wondering why they were so upset about it. When excess energy *has you*, you'll explode because Jane got promoted for playing by the informal rules of the game, and you lost that opportunity because you played by the formal rules. These toxic releases can be overt and aggressive, or covert and passive-aggressive. They can be positive, like being enamored by a new product-line even though it's not selling; or negative, like conflict between the sales department and production about performance targets. When assessors detect excess emotional energy, this is a Red Flag. They should stop dead in their tracks, get curious about what's happening, and then *dive in* and explore the below-the-surface issues with thorough causal analysis.

Unintended Consequences: The effects of Unintended Consequences in an organization are commonly known, but the underlying causes are rarely understood. For example, organizations establish strategies, goals, and objectives, only to have them derailed by ineffective autopilot operations and Invisible Bureaucracy that no one quite understands or can explain (see Figure 8).

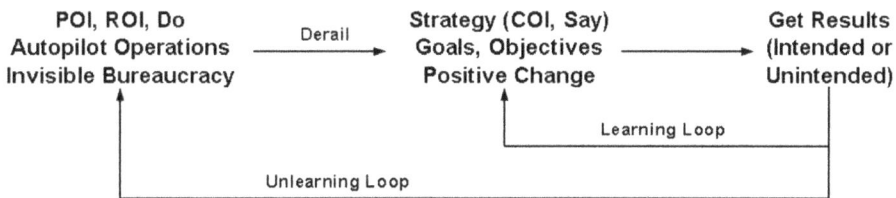

Figure 8

In response, senior managers hire consultants and charter organizational change initiatives to identify and correct the issues that are preventing them from achieving their objectives and goals. These initiatives begin with energy and enthusiasm, but over time they lose momentum and die a slow death and no one seems to know why. Chris Argyris and Peter Senge call this an *unintended* consequence.[134] When a project is off-track and managers know it probably should be stopped, but it isn't, this is also an unintended consequence. Unintended consequences manifest themselves as lost clients, rework, computing downtime, a key hire that goes sour, business objectives and goals that aren't met, and policies and procedures that are not implemented uniformly across an organization. Whenever an organization defines business objectives, sets goals, or develops a plan and they fail to get the desired results because of issues that emerge from within the company, this is an unintended consequence. It's a disruption of organizational intentions (strategy) by ineffective autopilot operations and Invisible Bureaucracy, shown in Figure 8. When assessors encounter an unintended consequence, this is a Red Flag. They should make careful note of the issues and context surrounding the situation, and explore the below-the-surface causes with thorough causal analysis.

Defense Routines: Defense routines occur at both the organizational and individual levels as defined by the Individual-Collective Paradox. At the *organizational level,* Argyris argues that organizational defense routines are designed to protect organizations from embarrassment or threat.[135] They are anti-learning devices that prevent an organization from learning from their mistakes and from making deep, sustainable change. Defense routines can be any policy, procedure, structure, system, or action that prevents an organization from being embarrassed or threatened – and at the same time prevents employees from identifying or eliminating the causes of that embarrassment and threat. Defense routines make the issue invisible like a Blind Spot.[136] For example, let's say managers in an organization say publicly that they want honest staff feedback, but employees who dare to actually give it are punished or fired. In other words, what this organization *says* is not what it actually *does.* This is the Say-Do gap of duplicity. Situations that threaten to expose the Say-Do gap are defended against with enormous amounts of energy. Organizational defense routines might take the form of technical arrogance; the "not-invented-here" syndrome; an attitude that says, "We know what the customer wants," without asking them. Defense routines can also manifest themselves as an unrealistic view of how well the organization is performing without knowing its true operating costs. When an organization is pressed or held accountable for such duplicities, they are normally embarrassed or threatened by the prospect of having the problem exposed. Argyris claims organizations use four strategies to prevent such problems from reaching the light of day.[137]

- Strategy 1: Bypass the real issue

- Strategy 2: Give inconsistent messages about what was actually "meant"

- Strategy 3: When pressed, cover-up the situation (make it undiscussible)

- Strategy 4: When pressed even harder, cover-up the cover-up (make the undiscussibility undiscussible)

Argyris' description of defense routines is revealing and poignant. "Defense routines... *require* people to communicate inconsistent messages, but act as if they are not doing so. In order for these actions to be effective, they must be covered-up while being enacted. In many cases, the cover-ups must also be covered-up. To do this, individuals learn to communicate inconsistent messages, act as if the messages are not inconsistent, make previous actions undiscussible, and make the undiscussibility undiscussible. Individuals on the receiving end of these actions must collude. If they recognize the cover-up, they learn to act as if they do not recognize it. They also expect the deceiver, distorter, or manipulator to not recognize the collusion."[138] Managers and staff members learn how to communicate inconsistent messages and cover-up through countless cycles of the See-Do-Get Process, and they are rewarded for doing so by the unspoken norms and rules of the organization's culture.

For example, accounting firms like Arthur Andersen, who were a symbol of fiscal integrity, couldn't endure the threat or embarrassment of clients knowing that they'd been "cooking the books." Owners and managers who have gone on record saying that they value employees' feedback can't publicly admit that they take retribution on those who give it. Companies that stress hard work and loyalty as the way to get ahead can't publicly own up to the fact that playing the game and managing your way up with "bright" comments in meetings is really the way people get promoted – so these organizations *defend* themselves against people ever seeing them this way. They try to bypass the real issues and give inconsistent messages when the Say-Do gap is probed; they cover-up evidence of organizational duplicity, and when they are really pressed hard, they cover-up the initial cover-up. The current financial crisis is a textbook example of the reality of organizational defense routines.

This kind of psychological and organizational dishonestly is a complex form of self-deception – a refusal to face the organizational truth of the situation. The list below includes a number of actions and interactions identified by Argyris as typical organizational defense routines, plus others learned from field experience of working with clients.[139] It's likely that organizational defense routines are present when managers and staff members:

- Blame coworkers or those outside the organization, but avoid public tests of the validity of the blame.

- Distance themselves from any personal responsibility for problems and issues.

- Argue that they are helpless to effect change in the organization.

- Don't express their ideas until coworkers have made mistakes.

- Do what they want regardless of the organization's decision or formal position on an issue, adopting a "better to ask forgiveness than permission" philosophy.

- Passively "stonewall" decisions or formal positions they don't agree with, hoping the issue will just "die a slow death."

- Frustrate and undermine decisions or formal positions they don't agree with by claiming to be "too busy" with "work-related" activities.

- *Distort* the organizational truth about what's really going on in a work-group to prevent embarrassment or threat; e.g., to "save face."

- Make issues undiscussible in public (LH column) out of fear of retribution, whether real or perceived.

- Criticize their own work-group as a way of cloaking their criticism of others; e.g., "I know we've got problems, but the marketing department is really messed up."

- Express disapproval of using defense routines privately, but refuse to voice their opinions about such matters publicly or in a constructive way.

- Communicate indirectly (they vent frustration about a person or problem to others, but refuse to discuss it with the responsible party).

- Use written communications (e-mails and memos) to build an organizational reality that defends their position while deconstructing the realities built by managers and staff members in other work-groups.

Organizational defense routines are acted out by groups of people through the patterns-of-interaction (POI) described by the Breckenridge Equation. As mentioned earlier, Argyris calls these "first-order errors." They can also be "second-order errors" where defense routines are actually designed into the organization's structures, systems, and culture (COI).[140] Whenever a situation becomes emotionally charged, assessors should ask themselves reflectively, "Is there a defense routine operating here? Is this an *individual* defense routine, or is it an *organizational* defense routine like the ones described above that reflects shared assumptions and tacit understandings of a work-group or the entire organization?"

At the *individual level*, defense routines distort and obfuscate our knowledge about ourselves and other people and prevent us from knowing the psychological "truth" of a situation. We experience the presence of defense routines around two foci of confusion. Managers and staff members can't quite figure out:

- What we are thinking and feeling.

- Whether the source of the problem is in us or in others.

Defense routines are part of the gate-keeping function of the Red Flags that distorts and obfuscates how we see ourselves, others, and the world when we are faced with embarrassment or threat.[141] They prevent us from objectively interpreting: a) our own experiences and emotions, b) the nature of our interactions with others, and c) the nature and characteristics of issues and situations that involve embarrassment or threat. So when we ask questions like those listed below, the gate-keeping function of our defense routines can prevent us from honestly knowing the answers.

- What am I am feeling right now?

- Why am I so bound up emotionally?

- Why do I have so much inner tension about this issue?

- Why am I so upset about this issue?

At the individual level, defense routines are *anti-learning devices* that help people maintain their way of seeing themselves, others, and the world in ways that "map" to the underlying patterns, beliefs, and assumptions of their worldview and personality. Consequently, defense routines are highly skilled actions learned early in life which become habitual, occur on autopilot, and operate below the surface of awareness. Defense routines are hidden, undiscussible actions or patterns-of-interaction (POI) that prevent people from identifying or eliminating what actually caused the embarrassment or threat. Once hidden from awareness as a Blind Spot, defense routines are protected by mechanisms such as hot buttons, inflexibility of mind or position, or a seeming inability to make decisions. Individual defense routines follow the same fundamental sequence as organizational defense routines as described by the Individual-Collective Paradox: a) bypass the real issue, b) give inconsistent messages, c) cover-up the issue and make it undiscussible, and d) cover-up the cover-up by making the undiscussibility undiscussible. For example, an employee knows that his manager is unhappy with his performance and the manager has indicated that she wants to discuss the matter at the employee's convenience, but the employee continually puts off the meeting with the claim that

"I'm so busy" when in reality the employee is the one making his schedule. Defense routines protect us from recognizing or dealing with our Blind Spots – autopilot behaviors that inhibit or undermine personal leadership skills. Accurate self-knowledge is the foundation of self-awareness, and people cannot obtain accurate self-knowledge unless they understand and control for the distortions that result from defense routines, unintended consequences, and Blind Spots.

Argyris contrasts the defensive reasoning that is often present as a part of organizational defense routines, with productive reasoning that typifies managers and staff members who are aware that they may have organizational defense routines and organizational Blind Spots. When organizations use *defensive reasoning*, the premises that managers and staff members use to support their explanations are tacit, unexamined, with hidden inferences, and data that are not easily subjected to objective public debate. When organizations use defensive reasoning, managers and staff members state their conclusion, claim it's valid, and then try to assure others that the only way to test the conclusion is to use *their* logic (trust me, I know what I'm talking about). In organizations that use *productive reasoning*, managers and staff members supply directly observable data to illustrate their arguments, strategies, plans, and to support their performance projections; they make all inferences and assumptions explicit so they're not comparing apples to oranges; and they craft conclusions so that others can publicly debate, test, and improve them. Even when beliefs, assumptions, and conclusions are based on gut-level feeling or intuition, managers and staff members who use productive reasoning articulate these premises *explicitly* so that others can understand the basis upon which their strategies, plans, and recommendations are based.

Assessors should remember that the Red Flags are interdependent and work together to *keep* ineffective autopilot operations and Invisible Bureaucracy invisible to managers and staff members; e.g., to maintain organizational Blind Spots, defense routines, and unintended consequences. Leaders who *can* effect positive change know that their organizations are like a self-regulating system in nature that balances the internal and external demands on its *resources, time, attention*, and *energy* as an open system. Ultimately organizations reach a state-of-equilibrium within a given external environment. This equilibrium may be either: a) the direct result of conscious intent and organizational strategy creating an Intended Culture, or b) the indirect product of ineffective autopilot operations and Invisible Bureaucracy producing an Unintended Culture. Either way, an organization's configuration of structures, systems, and culture will produce predictable results – good or bad – because all organizations are perfectly aligned to get the results they get.[142]

With an Unintended Culture, an organization's ability to make conscious choices and exercise purposeful decision-making to get desired results is impeded because managers and staff members tend to act out of ineffective autopilot operations, the Red Flags, and Invisible Bureaucracy. Its decisions are often reactive, rather than proactive in the sense that managers and staff members lack the ability to insert "choice" between the causes (stimulus) of day-to-day operational performance, and their autopilot responses which are shaped and defined by Invisible Bureaucracy and deeply entrenched cultural norms. This frustrates and undermines an organization's self-determinism and has a number of negative (and very pragmatic) consequences on an organization's overall performance. For example, organizations with an Unintended Culture frequently lack the ability to develop goals and objectives that they can actually achieve because their performance is so often derailed by the Red Flags, especially the Unintended Consequences shown in Figure 8. They also tend to lack the ability to execute and organize day-to-day activities in ways that will enable them to accomplish the goals and objectives that they define for themselves. The Blind Spots, Excess Energy, and Defense Routines that are often manifested in organizations with Unintended Cultures prevent them from accepting feedback from customers and employees because this gate-keeping function tends to screen out data, information, and feedback that are inconsistent with how the organization sees itself, others, and the world. Consequently, an organization's level of performance is probably not sustainable in a changing world because the Red Flags create destructive conflict around the actions and interactions of day-to-day operations, and over time they become patterns-of-interaction that go on autopilot, slip beneath the surface of organizational consciousness, and further reinforce the Unintended Culture.

The Assessment Process

This section gives an overview of the overall cultural assessment process, including both the quantitative and qualitative methodology. The three phases are shown below with a bulleted list of the components of each phase. A more complete description of the items in the three phases is provided in Chapters 3, 4, and 5. This should serve as a general rule of thumb for the process of assessing and changing organizational culture. Sometimes an assessment must be conducted in a different order than the one shown below because of client requirements or peculiarities in an organization's structures, systems, and culture. Other times, a client may only want a sub-set of the items listed below because of practical limitations or for financial reasons.

PHASE 1: The process of assessing organizational culture should begin with an initial research and analysis phase where the assessor tries to establish the overall context of the assessment. This helps to create an initial quantitative and qualitative baseline of performance early-on in the assessment process using the items listed below.

- *Codifying Organizational History*: Identify the key events in an organization's history and how they have helped to shape the organization's identity, culture, and ways of working.

- *Previous Assessments*: Evaluate previous attempts to improve performance and create organizational change, and the degree to which these were successful in creating positive change and getting the desired results. Determine the degree to which the organization is already aware of its performance issues, but has not acted on them.

- *Presenting Issues*: Identify and analyze the initial complaints and reasons why the client first contacted the assessor; e.g., where the "pain" is in the organization.

- *External Drivers*: Evaluate forces and pressures from the business environment within which the organization is embedded, including generating revenue; availability and cost of resources needed to operate the organization; industry and market trends; and competition.

- *Financial and Non-Financial Performance*: Conduct an analysis of revenue, labor, and operating costs; non-financial key performance indicators (KPIs); as well as goals and objectives in the organization's strategic plan and work-group operating plans.

- *BCI Data, Including Verbatim Comments*: Gather and analyze the quantitative and qualitative elements of the BCI Report as an initial baseline and characterization of the nature of the "electromagnetic field" of organizational culture.

- *BTI™ and Majors PT-Elements™ Data for Managers and Supervisors*: Gather and analyze personality type data for managers and supervisors. This is a measurement of the Enneagram and Jungian type preferences of top managers, middle managers, and supervisors as an initial baseline where each manager's personality functions like a "magnet" in the electromagnetic field of organizational culture.

PHASE 2: The data from Phase 1 becomes the foundation of an assessor's *initial working hypothesis* about what's going on in the organization that becomes clarified, refined, and made more precise (or changed) as more data and information are gathered through the assessment process. The key element of this second phase is to allow an Interaction Map to emerge from the interviews, using the quantitative and qualitative data gathered in Phase 1 as a foundation to build on. The overall goal of this phase is to test and validate the working hypothesis using both the quantitative and qualitative data, and to codify the results of this analysis process in a written report and presentation that become deliverables to the assessor's client.

- *One-on-One Interviews and Focus Groups*: Gather qualitative data using structured interviews with individuals and focus groups. The questions used can emerge from the quantitative data gathered in Phase 1.

- *Initial Working Hypothesis*: Allow an initial working hypothesis to emerge from the quantitative and qualitative data that describes what the underlying root causes and effects are that underlie the current results that the organization is getting.

- *Interaction Map*: Build an Interaction Map by allowing the patterns-of-interaction of the organization's informal power structure to emerge from the quantitative and qualitative data. This provides a "window" into the underlying patterns of an organization's culture.

- *Initial Working Hypothesis*: Allow the initial working hypothesis to be shaped, morphed, refined, and changed as the "mapping" between the quantitative and qualitative data gets increasingly refined.

- *Face Validity of Draft Results*: Discuss the data results and conclusions for key elements of the draft BCI Report with the client as a quality and "reality" check, and to ensure the face validity of the assessor's findings and recommendations. Conduct follow-up interviews and observe additional day-to-day operations to further refine the assessment report's findings and recommendations and to increase the precision of its content.

- *Final Written Report*: Make final corrections based on a refined interpretation of the quantitative and qualitative data and produce the final BCI report.

- *Presentation of Results*: Make a presentation of the final results to the client based on their needs and requirements. The final report can be given to the client and followed with a presentation, or the presentation can be made and followed by giving the client the report. This should be based on the client's learning style; e.g., whether they have a preference for reading or hearing information.

PHASE 3: Chapter 5 outlines an overall strategy for improving organizational and individual performance and for shaping and redefining key elements of an organization's culture so that it achieves its desired results. This is actually a process for creating an Intended Culture.

- *Recognizing the Problem*: Use the data from the report and the presentation of the results to establish the degree to which the organization is open to (and capable of) change, and to test the organization's level of "survival anxiety" as defined in Chapter 5.

- *Designing a Path Forward to Desired Results*: Work with the client to develop an improvement plan that will raise ineffective autopilot operations and Invisible Bureaucracy back into awareness; reconfigure the appropriate structures, systems, and patterns-of-interaction to get the desired results; and then migrate them back to autopilot operations getting the desired results through consistent implementation and repetition over time.

- *Measuring Improvement against the Baseline*: Measure the progress toward getting the desired results and improving financial and non-financial performance against the baseline that was established in Phase 2 of the assessment process. This should include conducting a follow-up BCI assessment within 18 months to two years of conducting the initial assessment.

The three-phase process described above utilizes both a quantitative and qualitative methodology. Assessors should build the actual process around the client's needs and what is needed to identify the underlying root causes of performance problems in the client organization.

Using a Qualitative and Quantitative Methodology

In this final section of the chapter, assessors will learn how to analyze and characterize organizational culture using both qualitative and quantitative methodologies. From the qualitative perspective, the See-Do-Get Process describes how "perception is reality" in the sense that the actions, interactions, and the performance of managers and staff members flow naturally from the way they see themselves, others, and the world around them. As described in Chapter 1, qualitative methodologies have their roots in cultural anthropology and the application of the study of national and ethnic culture to organizations beginning in the 1980s. Data gathered about attitudes, beliefs, assumptions, and organizational performance using qualitative methods such as interviews, focus groups, observation of work activities, and historical analysis allows assessors to see beneath the surface of day-to-day operations and to identify ineffective autopilot operations, Red Flags, and Invisible Bureaucracy.

From the quantitative perspective, the Individual-Collective Paradox describes organizations as collective-cultural entities that are led, managed, and changed one person at a time, so data gathered from individuals, work-groups, and the overall organization must be analyzed and interpreted systematically to yield results that have a high level of precision. A quantitative methodology also includes an analysis of financial management, key performance indicators, and data from competitors and industry benchmarks in the external environment. Quantitative analysis of the attitudes, beliefs, assumptions, and performance of groups of people has its roots in statistical methods as defined by the reliability and validity of the overall assessment design, as well as the measurement properties and scoring parameters of the instrument/s being used. This section establishes quantitative criteria against which assessors can evaluate the statistical properties of instruments that are used to assess organizational culture, using the BCI as an example of a tool that gathers quantitative data with high levels of precision.

Assessors will tend to have a dominant preference for either a quantitative or qualitative methodology based on the degree to which they prefer the structures-and-systems perspective or the human-performance perspective described in Chapter 1. Combining the qualitative and quantitative perspectives gives assessors a deeper understanding of the day-to-day realities of an organization's culture than that provided by either methodology when used alone. Using both a qualitative and quantitative methodology increases the precision with which assessors can determine the degree to which an organization has consensus between top managers, other populations, and individual work-groups about key issues affecting organizational and individual performance, including the causes and solutions to the internal and external problems facing the organization.

Structured Interviews and Focus Groups

Structured interviews and focus groups are designed to gather qualitative data on organizational performance and culture in a systematic way. They provide a different perspective than that produced by quantitative data, so the key is for assessors to learn to see organizations from both perspectives. Assessors should gather information about three areas: a) how the organizational structures and systems work, or do not work, b) the behaviors of people they work *for*, work *with*, or who *report to them*, and c) the organizational environment (atmosphere and culture). It is important to establish criteria for the kind of information gathered in interviews and focus groups. More specifically, assessment participants should give their most accurate and honest responses to the questions asked based only on *personal knowledge*, not second hand knowledge, or hearsay. If an individual does not have personal knowledge about the issue under discussion, then this input should not be counted toward the data results.

Assessors can use the qualitative and quantitative data gathered in Phase 1 of the assessment process to formulate questions along specific lines of inquiry. These questions can be used in interviews and focus groups as a way of correlating the quantitative and qualitative data; developing an initial working hypothesis about the organization's performance and culture; and validating the overall assessment results. Assessors should utilize open ended questions like the ones shown below as the basis of interviews and focus groups.

- What results is the organization getting (good and bad)?

- What does the organization need to *start* doing to be more successful?

- What does the organization need to *stop* doing to be more successful?

- What metaphor would you use to describe this organization: "This organization is like…?"

- "Some of the data gathered thus far seem to indicate that the organization is experiencing X. Do you have any personal knowledge about this…?"

The assessors should take detailed notes about the key points mentioned in interviews, and have someone act as a "scribe" to record the information and interactions in focus groups, with the notes being transcribed into summary documents. Depending on the organizational culture, setting, and client needs, assessors may also record interviews and focus group activities using audio or videotape technology if formal permission is obtained from management and the participants. However, in some cultures people may be guarded about the information they provide while being recorded out of fear of retribution.

It is important to conduct interviews with a broad cross-section of the organization that includes every organizational level and a sample from key organizational units. This avoids the issues associated with capturing the views and perspectives of a small (but vocal) minority and misinterpreting them to be the perspective of the overall organization. It also helps to minimize the effect of "lobbying" on the part of specific managers and staff members who want to steer an assessment to conclusions that support their way of seeing themselves, others, and the world of day-to-day operations. This will be described in more detail below under the heading of reliability (sampling error) and validity (coverage error).

For a given sample of structured interviews, it is important to frame the information gathered in terms of how wide-spread specific views or observations are. As a rough rule of thumb, when 80-100% of the people interviewed espouse a given view or perspective, assessors can describe this using the descriptor, "Most people said…." When 50-80% of those interviewed hold a specific view or perspective, this can be described as, "Many people said…" with 20-50% being described as "Some people said…" and 5-20% being characterized as "Few people said…." If no one interviewed espoused a perspective, this should be characterized as "No one said…."

Assessors should try to link the examples, situations, stories, and patterns-of-interaction gathered during interviews and focus groups to elements in the organization's structures, systems, and culture; and to the quantitative data shown in the BCI Report charts and radar graphs. An informal way of doing this is by repetitively asking the question "why" in the face of organizational issues. For example, "Why do the managers consistently fail to work collaboratively, so the left hand does not know what the right hand is doing, even though they know that it negatively affects the organization's overall performance?" The answer might be that managers are territorial because they don't trust each other. The next question might be, "But why don't managers trust each other even though they *know* that this would be in the best interest of the organization? Is it because the budgeting process pits them against each other in a win-lose battle for resources? Does the compensation and performance evaluation system reward the wrong behaviors? Are managers given the authority needed to carry out their scope of responsibility, and are they held accountable for the performance of their work-groups and delivering on commitments?" And so on. In some cases, assessors should use a more formal kind of causal analysis and advanced analytics based on the complexity and importance of the issues identified and client requirements and needs.[143] Assessors should use the power of qualitative and quantitative methodologies to determine the degree to which an organization has consensus between top managers, other populations, and individual work-groups about key issues affecting organizational and individual performance, including the *causes* and *solutions* to the internal and external problems that the organization is facing.

Reliability, Validity, and Interpreting Reported Results

When mapping out the overall design of an organizational assessment, assessors should have a clear understanding of the statistical methods associated with reliability, validity, and interpreting reported results. This section outlines these principles in a practical and straightforward way and describes the parameters that come into play to affect *reliability* (response consistency) and *validity* (truth measurement). We discuss each of these three areas below.

Reliability: There are two measures of reliability: a) sampling error, and b) measurement error. *Sampling error* is based on statistics as part of the overall sampling plan or survey design where data from only a subset (sample) of the total population is gathered, not from everyone in the population of interest. When a sample is drawn (by definition) only that portion of the population is actually measured, so error is introduced into the measurement when data from the sample are used to represent the entire population of interest. Consequently, sampling error can be reduced by collecting larger and larger samples of a population, and when an assessment gathers data from the entire population, rather than a subset, the sampling error is zero. The percentage values associated with sampling error are normally referred to as the "confidence level" of the survey design. Figure 9 shows the confidence levels for a variety of survey sample sizes.

Confidence Level

Population Size	Reliability						
	75%	80%	85%	90%	95%	99%	100%
50	5	9	16	29	44	50	50
100	6	10	19	41	80	100	100
250	6	10	22	54	152	247	250
500	6	10	23	60	218	486	500
100	6	11	23	64	278	944	1,000
2,500	6	11	23	66	334	2,173	2,500
5,000	6	11	23	67	357	3,843	5,000

Figure 9

It is important for assessors to understand the nature of sampling error when planning the scope of an assessment, because the desired confidence level can have a significant impact on the quality of the data gathered and the cost and time commitment required by the client organization to gather both a quantitative and qualitative data sample. For example, the number of samples needed to obtain a 95% confidence level rather than a 99% confidence level in an organization of 50 people, is significantly different than the sample size needed in an organization of 5,000 people (see Figure 9). In other words, in an organization of 5,000 people an assessor can obtain a confidence level of 95% by sampling only 357 people, while the sample number rises to 3,843 people in order to achieve a 99% confidence level. Assessors and their clients should weigh the cost-benefit of achieving this higher level of precision. From the qualitative perspective, the number of people interviewed or included in focus groups is also defined by the confidence levels shown in Figure 9, not just the positions that people have within the organizational structure. In other words, interviewing only a small sample of people introduces sampling error into the data results, while interviewing only managers or select groups of "key" personnel introduces coverage error into the data results as described in the section on validity.

Measurement error occurs as a result of people misunderstanding the specific wording or sequencing of a question, or bias in the survey instrument, and is referred to as "test reliability." Test reliability refers to the extent to which an instrument like the BCI can be expected to reliably perform each time the measure is used. The key measure of reliability with instruments like the BCI is *internal consistency* which is an estimate of how closely the responses to items on a given scale relate to each other. This is a statistically derived value known as Chronbach's Alpha Coefficient. It is generally agreed that an alpha coefficient of .70 or higher indicates adequate internal consistency. To get a sense of what the common range of internal consistency is on other instruments that are very well constructed measures we can examine the reported alphas from other instruments such as the MBTI® Form Q, M, the Breckenridge Type Indicator (BTI), and the Denison Organizational Culture Survey.

- The scales on the MBTI® Form Q range from 5 to 9 items on each scale. The average Chronbach's Alpha reliability for these scales is .74 with a range of .57 to .85. The scales on MBTI® form M range from 21 to 28 items. The average Chronbach's Alpha reliability for these scales is .91 with a range of .91 to .92.

- The scales on the BTI range from 4 to 17 items on each scale. The average Chronbach's Alpha reliability for these scales is .93.

- The scales on the Denison Organizational Culture Survey are composed of five items on each scale, with a range of Chronbach's Alpha reliability of between .62 and .84.[144]

- The scales on the BCI range from 3 to 8 items on each scale. The average Chronbach's Alpha reliability for these scales is .88 with a range of .77 to .96.

The Chronbach's Alpha reliability measurements indicate a very strong connection statistically within the items on each of the BCI scales compared to other instruments. The results of the internal consistency analysis for the BCI show that the measure has been constructed with items that are of similar meaning and utility. Regardless of which assessment tools an assessor chooses to use in the process of assessing organizational culture, it is important that the statistical properties of the instrument provide high levels of internal consistency.

Validity: There are four measures of validity associated with instruments like the BCI: a) coverage error, b) non-response error, c) face validity, and d) criterion validity (best fit). *Coverage error* occurs when the sample does not equally include all elements from the population of interest (the company may have a diverse array of sub-groups). For example, the sample did not include people from entire departments and populations, or only managers, supervisors, and key personnel were surveyed, but staff members were not included in the data sample. Consequently, coverage error can be reduced by ensuring that all elements of the population of interest have been sampled, with coverage error becoming zero when everyone in the population is surveyed. *Non-response error* occurs when all responses are not received from the sample; e.g., 450 people out of a 500 person organization were included in the survey, but only 350 of those invited actually completed the survey questions.[145] Non-response error can be reduced by contacting people a second time and having them complete the survey, and by making statistical adjustments to the data during the analysis phase. The third measure of validity is *face validity*. An instrument is said to have face validity when it "looks like" it measures what it is supposed to measure. In other words, when participants evaluate the results reported on charts and graphs, they recognize that the results map to (and describe) the day-to-day operations of their organization. The fourth measure of validity is *criterion validity* which is also known as "best-fit" validity. Best-fit validity is the degree to which the reported results agree with concrete behavioral criteria that occur in day-to-day operations as judged by trained and experienced organizational and cultural diagnosticians, in combination with a clients own self-evaluation (Face Validity).

Assessors should note that reliability and validity are interdependent. From the perspective of validity, it is better to survey a smaller number of individuals and achieve a higher response rate than to survey a large cross-section of a population and obtain a low response rate. From the reliability perspective, assessors should strive to keep the sampling error as small as possible which requires larger samples, but this may increase the probability of non-response error for the assessment.

What Scores on Radar Graphs and Charts Measure and Mean

This section describes how to interpret the data and reported results from the case-study of the SciTech Company described in Chapter 3. An understanding of how to interpret the quantitative results of the SciTech case-study data will give readers deeper insights into the process of assessing and changing organizational culture. The scores on the radar graph in Figure 10 were generated from BCI data with the SciTech Company. They show the averaged responses by population at SciTech for the Strategic View. The data compare the scores of SciTech's top managers to the scores of all other participants by population level. A score of 100 represents excellence based on the benchmark criteria described in Chapter 3. They are an indication of the degree to which SciTech has consensus between top managers and other populations on the six perspectives of the Strategic View – the degree to which the organization speaks with one voice. The scores are also a "window" into underlying elements of SciTech's culture as characterized by differing perspectives about the causes of (and solutions to) the internal and external issues facing the organization.

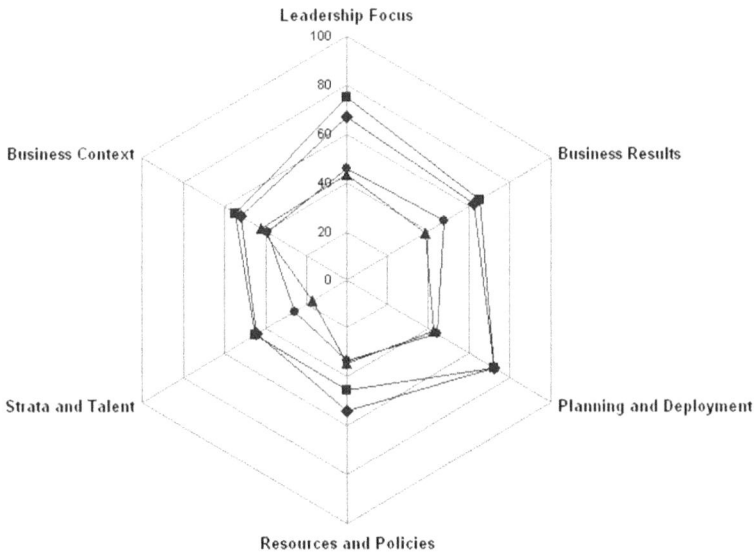

	LF	BR	PD	RP	ST	BC
Top Manager ♦	66.7	62.0	72.0	53.8	44.0	52.0
Line Manager ■	75.1	64.8	72.0	45.0	44.8	54.4
Supervisor ▲	43.2	38.3	42.3	33.9	17.1	41.7
Staff ●	45.6	47.6	44.4	33.2	25.6	38.7

Figure 10

79

The key to interpreting the data on the radar graph is to look for: a) high scores, and b) the degree of overlap between the scores of populations. Similarities and differences between scores are an indication of the degree to which an organization has consensus between top managers and other populations in the six key areas shown on the radar graph and chart.[146] When the scores of top managers and another population differ by less than 15 percent, they appear in black indicating that top managers and other populations see these issues in much the same way (see Figure 10). When the difference between the scores of top managers and other populations is between 15 and 30 percent, the score appears in grey signifying that there is a moderate misalignment between that population and top managers in terms of how they see these issues. When the difference between the scores of top managers and other populations differs by more than 30 percent, the score appears in italics indicating that there is a significant misalignment between that population and top managers in terms of how they see these issues. Misalignments and a lack of consensus are also indicators of squandered time and energy – resources that become unavailable to achieve the organization's objectives and goals.

It is important for assessors to present BCI data and an interpretation of the data as objectively and clearly as possible by *linking* them to day-to-day operational issues and the organization's overall performance. If the client requests a debrief meeting, it's important to maintain the meeting's focus; stay on track; navigate sensitive political or personality issues; question deeply-held assumptions about the organization's processes or way of doing business; and surface and manage conflict with the goal of more effectively utilizing the organization's time and energy. The goal is to provide objective feedback that leads to innovative and creative solutions to the problems the organization is facing. As such, there are five points that must be considered when determining what the numeric values of the scores on BCI scales do (and do not) measure and what they do (and do not) indicate about the organization that is being assessed:

- ***How High is the Score?*** The numeric value of the score on a 0-100 scale is an indicator of the level of organizational excellence based on a set of benchmarks of timeless principles defined for each set of data on a radar graph and its associated charts. Begin with the "critical path" items on the top and bottom of the radar shown in Figure 10 (Leadership Focus; Resources and Policies). As a general rule, the elements on a radar graph that are most important to creating organizational alignment (critical path) appear in the top and bottom positions. After evaluating these two elements in terms of what's actually happening in an organization, it is important to prioritize the remaining elements shown on the radar graph, remembering that in the absence of well-defined structures and systems – personality rules.

- *How Wide is the Spread?* The numeric "spread" of the scores on a specific scale is an indicator of the degree of alignment and cultural consensus between the organization's populations and work-groups around key issues that affect organizational performance. Cultural consensus is measured by the way participants answer the questions, and subsequently by the overall alignment of the scores of populations and work-groups on the radar graphs included in the BCI Report. Managers have the biggest effect on employees because of the emotional resonance they create, and the degree to which they exemplify internal or external commitment for (or against) the configuration of an organization's structures, systems, and culture. In addition, work-groups can be headed by Border Guards who: a) create sub-cultures that are misaligned with (or in opposition to) the configuration of an organization's structures, systems, and culture, and then b) seal-off their organizational unit from effective interaction with the overall organization. The goal should be for an organization and its work-groups *to speak with one voice*, meaning that when a question is asked about the organization that managers and staff members give more or less the same answer, regardless of which organization level or work-group they work in.

- *How Wide is the Gap?* The numeric values of the scores measure what an organization "says" about itself with high precision. But these scores must be validated in terms of the degree to which the principles and practices shown on a radar graph are actually present and effectively operating in the day-to-day life of the organization. The numeric values of the scores *do not* measure this gap. We described this earlier as the criterion or "face validity" of an organizational assessment. For example, the BCI scores may indicate that the organization has a strategic plan that is being executed, but when asked by an assessor to produce a current copy of that plan and concrete evidence that it's being implemented, managers and staff members may not be able to do so.

- *How Intended is the Culture?* The numeric values of the scores *do not* measure the degree to which an organization has an Intended Culture or Unintended Culture. This must be established using the qualitative data from historical analysis, previous assessments, the Interaction Map, and verbatim comments about organizational trust, and the corporate life cycle analysis that are described in Chapter 3. When combined, the quantitative scores and the qualitative data provide powerful insights into how consciously an organization's culture was created, and the degree to which it can exercise self-determinism and freedom of choice in changing directions and morphing its day-to-day activities to respond to changes in the internal and external environment.

- ***How Internal or External is the Commitment?*** The numeric values of the scores *do not* measure the degree to which top managers, middle managers, supervisors, and staff members have internal or external commitment to the current configuration of the organization's structures, systems, and culture; and the degree to which they are committed to its goals and objectives. This must be established through one-on-one interviews, focus groups, verbatim comments about organizational trust, and the observation of day-to-day operations and work processes. When combined, the quantitative scores and the qualitative data provide powerful insights into the current configuration of structures, systems, and culture; the underlying patterns-of-interaction shown on the Interaction Map, and the likelihood that change initiatives will be able to produce the desired results.

Here are some general rules for interpreting the quantitative scores on the BCI radar graphs and their associated charts.[147] An easy way to summarize the data in a BCI Report for a client would be to identify all areas that were Strengths (High-High) and areas that Need Development (Low-Low), prioritizing them by the critical path elements that create (or undermine) alignment that are located on the top and bottom positions of the radar graphs. These can be listed and described in the Executive Summary Report given to clients.

Strength (High-High): An organizational strength is when the averaged scores of population clusters are around 80% or higher. Alignment of populations around that strength is when the scores of top managers and another population differ by less than 15 percent, which appears in black on the chart below a radar graph, indicating that top managers and other populations see these issues in much the same way (they are aligned and speak with one voice). Either the practices and competencies described by this perspective come naturally to the organization because of its culture, core competencies, and the personalities of its managers and staff members; or the organization has worked very hard to develop them through its structures, systems, and organizational alignment. Strengths should be used as leverage points to create change in less effective areas, and to maximize an organization's chances for success.

Misalignment (High-Low): This type of misalignment is where top managers score higher than the averaged score of another population. When the difference between the scores of top managers and other populations is between 15 and 30 percent, the score appears in grey on the chart below a radar graph signifying that there is a *moderate misalignment* between that population and top managers in terms of how they see these issues. When the difference between the scores of top managers and other populations differs by more than 30 percent, the score appears in italics signifying that there is a *significant misalignment* between that population and top managers in terms of how they see these issues. This is a potential "Blind Spot" for top managers and indicates an area in which organizational performance could be derailed and organizational and psychological energy is being squandered. For example, day-to-day operations may be much less effective than top managers realize, or the organization may have ineffective operations and work practices that are known only to populations other than top managers. In order to address this issue, assessors and their client should determine: a) whether this misalignment actually exists, b) how it manifests itself in day-to-day operations and organizational performance, and c) the root causes and underlying patterns of the misalignment.

Misalignment (Low-High): This type of misalignment is where top managers score lower than the averaged score of another population. When the difference between the scores of top managers and other populations is between 15 and 30 percent, the score appears in grey on the chart below a radar graph signifying that there is a *moderate misalignment* between that population and top managers in terms of how they see these issues. When the difference between the scores of top managers and other populations differs by more than 30 percent, the score appears in italics signifying that there is a *significant misalignment* between that population and top managers in terms of how they see these issues. This is a different type of potential "Blind Spot" for top managers and indicates an area in which organizational performance could be derailed and organizational and psychological energy is being squandered. For example, things may be operating more smoothly than top managers realize, or the organization may have hidden capability and skills that are known only to populations other than top managers. In order to address this issue, assessors and their client should determine: a) whether this misalignment actually exists, b) how it manifests itself in day-to-day operations and organizational performance, and c) the root causes and underlying patterns of the misalignment.

Needs Development (Low-Low): Averaged scores of populations that cluster around 60% or lower indicate that participants have agreement that this perspective needs development, and is an area in which organizational performance is being derailed and organizational and psychological energy is being squandered (they speak with one voice). In this case, the practices and competencies associated with this perspective may not come naturally to the organization because of its culture, core competencies, and the personalities of its managers and staff members; or the organization may not have worked to develop it through structures, systems, and organizational alignment. In some cases an organization may have consciously chosen not to adopt this business practice and instead they chose to adopt a different business strategy. Regardless, this could hinder an organization's overall business performance and may be linked to low scores in other portions of that radar graph, or in other interdependent radar graphs in the BCI. In this case, assessors and their client should determine, a) how this problem manifests itself in day-to-day operations and organizational performance, b) the root causes and underlying patterns of the misalignment, and c) how to develop concrete action to improve in this area within the interdependent context of the reported results of the overall BCI Report. Assessors should remember that it's important not to optimize one perspective of an organization's performance, and sub-optimize other perspectives, or the overall organization's performance.

Figure 11 shows the data from the BCI displayed *by organizational unit.*[148] Similarities and differences between scores are an indication of the degree to which an organization has consensus between top managers and work-groups in these six key areas. When the scores of top managers and a work-group differ by less than 15 percent, they appear in black indicating that there is little or no difference in how top managers and this work-group see this issue.

	LF	BR	PD	RP	ST	BC
Top Manager	66.7	62.0	72.0	53.8	44.0	52.0
Business Administration	57.8	42.2	51.6	34.8	29.1	46.2
Business Development	40.6	45.7	49.7	25.0	20.0	35.4
Field Operations	46.7	49.6	48.8	36.4	22.4	40.9
Technical Assurance	78.4	60.6	70.0	47.0	47.1	50.9
Technical Services	49.0	49.0	42.6	33.6	32.3	43.8

Figure 11

When the difference between the scores of top managers and a work-group is between 15 and 30 percent, the score appears in grey, signifying that there is a *moderate misalignment* in how top managers and this work-group see this issue. When the difference between the scores of top managers and a work-group differs by more than 30 percent, the score appears in italics signifying that there is a significant misalignment between how top managers and this work-group see this issue.

Assessors and their clients should remember that misalignments and a lack of consensus are also indicators of squandered time and energy – resources that become unavailable to achieve an organization's objectives and goals.

When interpreting data and scores from the BCI Report it is important to remember that all organizations are perfectly aligned to get the results they get. If some employees in an organization are heading in one direction, and others are going the opposite way and we add up those opposing forces, we would get an overall direction for that organization. But these misalignments are like running a boat full throttle with the anchor dragging along the bottom, or driving a car with one foot on the gas and the other on the brake. In fact, Peter Drucker claims that serious misalignment about an organization's values, beliefs, purpose and direction condemns managers and employees to frustration and non-performance.[149] Deep organizational change requires a sustained effort that realigns the balance of how an organization spends its *time*, *attention*, *resources*, and *energy*. It also means shaping and transforming how employees see themselves, others, and the world around them. Finally, it's important that any corrective action that is taken does not negatively affect organizational performance, work practices, relationships, beliefs, and assumptions that *are* currently working effectively.

The *Ten Cultural Questions* listed below are a mechanism for learning how to see organizations differently. The assessor can use them with clients to gain a "window" into the characteristics of an organization's culture, and to provide a guide for reflecting on (and linking) the scores shown in the radar graphs and charts with the day-to-day activities of organizational life. The questions are also a way for assessors to establish the "face validity" of the data with client organizations. As assessors review the scores and definitions for each perspective on the radar graphs and charts, they should encourage clients to reflect on the following questions and answer them as openly and honestly as possible.

- First, to what extent do the scores *reflect* your common sense experience and perceptions of day-to-day operations in an organization?

- Second, to what extent is one or more of the six perspectives *derailing* effective performance and preventing you from getting the results you want in terms of revenue, labor, and operating expenses?

- Third, if a score is low and there is solid agreement that this set of practices *is not* happening in your organization, is this the result of a *conscious* and *deliberate* strategy because an alternative set of practices was viewed as being more fitting to an organization?

- Fourth, if the omission of the set of practices *was not* the result of a *conscious* and *deliberate* strategy, would implementing a "tailored" version of these practices improve organizational, work-group, and individual performance and help you get the results you want?

- Fifth, if the omission *was not* a conscious, deliberate decision and if implementing these practices would improve performance, what are the *underlying tacit beliefs, assumptions, attitudes, values* (ROI) and ways of "seeing" these practices that prevent them from being implemented?

- Sixth, if the omission *was not* a conscious, deliberate decision and if implementing these practices would improve performance, what structures, systems and *formal* rewards (COI) help to keep the current configuration in place?

- Seventh, if the omission *was not* a conscious, deliberate decision and if implementing these practices would improve performance, what underlying patterns-of-interaction and *informal* rewards (POI) help to keep the current configuration in place?

- Eighth, what messages does the current configuration of POI, COI, and ROI send to employees and customers about an organization and what are these messages encouraging and discouraging?

- Ninth, how much destructive or constructive conflict is the configuration of POI, COI, and ROI creating in the organization and how much organizational and psychological energy is this squandering in terms of revenue, labor, and operating expenses?

- Tenth, how wide is the gap between the *formal* and *informal* rules of the game, how undiscussible is the gap, and how strong are the overt and covert forces that will rise up to derail a change initiative to narrow the gap if they "see" it as not being in their best-interest?

The current configuration of POI ↔ COI ↔ ROI = Current Results™ often creates decision-making bias and predictable errors in judgment at the organizational, work-group, and individual levels. This expresses itself in day-to-day operations and in the way participants answer the questions qualitatively during on-site interviews and quantitatively on the BCI survey questions. Consequently, when the data from qualitative interviews and the quantitative data shown on the BCI radar graphs and charts are combined with the dialogue that results from the *Ten Cultural Questions*, a *window* into organizational culture is created by identifying ineffective autopilot operations, the Red Flags, and Invisible Bureaucracy. An organization's culture is an interlocking set of beliefs, tacit assumptions, "folk wisdom," unspoken rules, and prohibitions (ROI) that manifest themselves in the day-to-day realities of organizational life (POI and COI). The repository-of-interaction (ROI) is an interdependent, complementary, competing, and conflicting ways of seeing coworkers, business processes, strategy, work-practices, customers, and the external environment within which the organization is situated. Using these quantitative and qualitative data, assessors can make these invisible cultural elements *visible* by repetitively asking the question "why" in the face of organizational issues until the underlying causes are identified.

CHAPTER 3
ANALYZING HISTORY, STRUCTURES, SYSTEMS, AND CLIMATE

One of the objectives of this book is to present a model that allows people to assess an *entire organization* with the goal of improving organizational and individual performance. While our main focus is on assessing and changing organizational culture, the principles and practices described below can also be used as a basis for management reviews, performance assessments, change-management activities associated with IT system implementation, improvement projects, organizational interventions, reorganizations, mergers and acquisitions, strategic planning activities, and other diagnostic and improvement processes.

The full scope of the assessment model and a guide to what aspects of organizations should be assessed are presented in the next three chapters – Chapters 3, 4, and 5. This includes a portfolio of quantitative and qualitative tools that assessors can use to empirically test the principles and practices contained in this book with client organizations. These chapters also contain a case-study of the SciTech Company along with other examples of actual cultural assessments and change initiatives that have been woven into the fabric of the text to reinforce the material. While assessors can use the material in Chapters 3, 4, and 5 as a stand-alone template for assessing and changing organizational culture, using an instrument like the *Breckenridge Culture Indicator*™ *(BCI™)* will provide empirical data for the new ways of seeing organizations described in Chapter 2, and help to make ineffective autopilot operations, the Red Flags, and Invisible Bureaucracy *visible* in tangible and concrete ways.

Codifying Organizational History

This section will teach assessors important ways in which an organization and its culture are powerfully shaped and defined by key events in its history. There are two words in Greek for time. The word *chronos* is the etymological origin of the English word chronological, meaning the day-to-day passing of time and events. The word *kairos* indicates an event or series of events that are crucial in an organization's history. A *kairos* event is often a crossroads where significant, and sometimes mutually exclusive, choices must be made – with each path leading to very different outcomes. Consequently, the process of assessing organizational culture should begin by researching and analyzing an organization's history.[150] Assessors should develop a timeline that includes an inventory of *kairos* events, as well as the origin and development of the other items listed below:

- *Kairos (Key) Events*: These are milestones, successes, failures, and internal or external challenges faced over the course of the organization's history that have shaped and defined its identity, strategy, day-to-day work practices, relationships, stereotypes, tacit assumptions, and climate. A description of a *kairos* event should include stories about the people involved who function as role models and exemplars (heroes, outlaws, villains, etc.) that support the underlying beliefs and assumptions of an organization's core ideology.

- *Core Competencies*: This involves exploring the origin and development of specific areas of expertise, technologies, R&D, production capabilities, and human competencies and skills that define what the organization does, and give it a competitive advantage in the external environment. It might also include an analysis of the industry-specific body-of-knowledge and disciplinary paradigms, professional conferences, and publications that have helped to shape or define the organization's culture.

- *Organizational Rituals*: Rituals are repetitive daily, weekly or monthly activities like the Monday morning status meeting, weekly or monthly reports, regular memos and e-mails, daily social activities around the coffee pot, at the water cooler, and informal group meetings in the lunchroom. Over time, these repetitive functional activities go on autopilot and eventually connect people to the organization in deep and symbolic ways that become organizational reality – what it's like to "work" there.

- *Organizational Ceremonies*: Ceremonies are company sponsored special events that employees participate in – celebrations like the annual Christmas party, staff retreats, staff awards, or the company picnic. They become public expressions and ceremonial reminders of the history, beliefs, heroes, relationships, and core values of the organization. Hard-core business related activities like the annual strategic planning meeting; quarterly strategy, budget, operational reviews; and the annual performance appraisal process also become ceremonies and traditions that embody and transmit organizational culture.

- *Symbols*: These are things that represent (or stand for) other things. Unlike visible objects, the ideas, feelings, attitudes, beliefs, and assumptions associated with an organization are difficult to convey or propagate to others because they are invisible and without physical substance. Consequently, they must be exchanged from person to person using symbols that "pair" ideas, feelings, attitudes, beliefs, and assumptions with visible objects (physical artifacts) so these invisible attributes become embodied in a physical artifact.[151] More specifically, symbols are often represented graphically in the form of brands; logos; advertisements; pictures and graphics hung on walls; and publications or websites that symbolize an organization's history, identity, and culture. Physical artifacts can also be objects such as buildings, facilities, a specific location, geography, topography, and other visible components of the organization. Symbols help to guide the actions and interaction of managers and staff members at a very deep level because they embody the core essence of meaning about an organization's culture, and have the capacity to represent and reveal organizational truth and reality either instantaneously or gradually over time.

The historical analysis of areas like those listed above should characterize the original meaning; what these elements have come to mean today; and how these elements reinforce the organization's identity, values, and work practices through the See-Do-Get Process. The goal of this historical analysis is for assessors to determine how the items listed on the timeline have shaped and defined the organization's repository-of-interaction (ROI) as described by the Breckenridge Equation. These deep, historically-based assumptions become decision-making bias and predictable errors in judgment that shape and influence an organization's strategic and tactical decisions, as well as observable day-to-day operations and performance at the organization-wide, work-group, small-group, and individual levels.

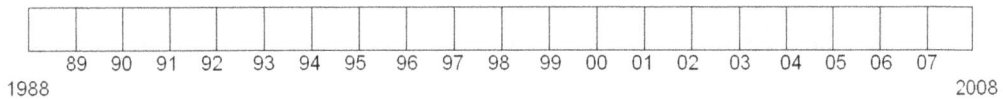

	89	90	91	92	93	94	95	96	97	98	99	00	01	02	03	04	05	06	07	

1988   2008

Figure 12

The results of the historical analysis should be listed in chronological order, and then placed on a timeline like the one shown in Figure 12. Each item should be annotated with its meaning and contribution being explained in terms of the effect that it is currently having on the organization's strategic and tactical decisions and day-to-day operations and performance. When two or more organizations are merged, or when one or more organization is acquired by another, assessors can use the items for each organization and integrate them into a single timeline to create a sense of common identity – a third something from which a new corporate entity and Intended Culture can be consciously created using the four terms in the Breckenridge Equation.

Previous Assessments

A key source of information during an assessment's initial research and analysis phase that will help assessors to identify underlying patterns-of-interaction, autopilot operations, and Invisible Bureaucracy is the analysis of the results of previous assessments. This includes evaluations that have been conducted by the organization (self-assessments), and independent assessments conducted by stakeholders, external entities, regulatory agencies, customers, suppliers, and third-party organizations. The assessor should look for written reports, presentations, and other documentation that is contained in sources like those listed below:

Customer Surveys   Financial Reviews and Audits
Employee Surveys   Reviews of Products and Services
User Satisfaction Surveys   SWOT Analysis
Reviews of Business and Work   Engineering Studies
Processes   Consultant Reports
Employee Improvement Activities

It is also important to identify and analyze "programs" that the organization has conducted in response to previous assessments. For example: a) change initiatives, corrective actions, and improvement plans that were conducted in response to

91

previous assessments, and b) actual changes and improvements that resulted at the organization-wide, work-group, small-group, and individual levels. It is important for assessors to determine the degree to which the managers and staff members in the organization already have an understanding and knowledge of the nature and causes of its performance problems, but have not acted on this knowledge. In other words, the organization has not moved from *awareness* of the issues, to the concrete *action* needed to improve organizational and individual performance.

Presenting Issues

During the initial research and analysis phase, it is important for assessors to formally establish the context of the assessment and the circumstances that led the client to make initial contact and request an evaluation. This helps to create an initial baseline of performance prior to the assessment beginning. It also becomes the foundation of an assessor's *initial working hypothesis* about what's going on in the organization that becomes clarified, refined, made more precise (or changed) as more data and information are gathered through the assessment process. Once the initial working hypothesis has been tested and validated with the quantitative and qualitative data and information collected as part of the assessment, it can be summarized in an initial presentation to the client to test its face validity. This might include the following areas:

- Main "complaint" or "pain" as described by the client and key personnel.

- Key performance indicators (KPIs), goals and objectives that are not being met.

- Issues related to governance or the organization's legal form (for-profit, non-profit, government).

- Issues related to geographical patterns or cross-cultural patterns.

- Special boundary conditions or political sensitivities that may affect the validity of the assessment.

- How the assessment relates to other ongoing evaluations and assessments; e.g., quarterly and annual reviews, individual performance appraisals, etc.

- Initial impressions about the POI, COI, ROI or Current Results that the organization is getting.

Initial impressions that emerge prior to understanding what such things "mean" in an organization's culture are important because assessors have not yet been influenced and shaped by how the organization teaches people to see themselves, others, and the world. This enables the assessor to identify ineffective autopilot operations, Red Flags, Invisible Bureaucracy, and ways of working that people *outside* the organization see, but those *inside* do not because they are based on the unquestioned beliefs and tacit assumptions of culture and are Blind Spots.

External Drivers

Perhaps the single most important part of evaluating an organization's culture is for the assessor to gain a clear understanding of the nature, viability, and sustainability of the organization's revenue streams, and the expectations and pressures that are being exerted on the organization by customers, competitors and other forces in the external environment. More specifically, it's important to determine and document how strong of an impact these external drivers are having on the organization as indicated by the amount of organizational "pain" they are causing. As part of the initial research, analysis, and data gathering phase, and during face-to-face interviews and on-site visits, it is important for assessors to evaluate and document the appropriate items listed under the four categories below and to determine which (if any) are putting pressure on the organization and creating organizational "pain" for managers and staff members.

Category 1: Generating Revenue

The items listed below are part of the Business Results loop of the Open Systems diagram shown in Figure 1. These elements form the basis of a preliminary analysis of an organization's ability to generate revenue, and should be conducted early in the assessment process. A more complete description of issues related to financial management will be presented in Chapter 4: *Governance Issues and Financial Analysis*.

- Growth in revenue levels

- A plateau of revenue levels

- Decline in revenue levels

- Expectations of owners relative to revenue levels

- Growth in funding levels

- A plateau of funding levels

- Decline in funding levels

Changes in an organization's level of revenue almost always create organizational "pain." When revenues are increasing, this often means that an organization is under pressure to recruit, screen, select, and train new employees, and to obtain the equipment and physical space required to make those employees productive. While this is the kind of "pain" most organizations want, this external pressure can reveal latent weaknesses in an organization's structures, systems, and culture. When revenues are decreasing, the opposite kind of organizational "pain" often occurs – deciding which employees, equipment and facilities are needed to stabilize and reverse this trend. Organizations with plateaued revenues who have tried to grow and haven't, face yet a different set of problems and the looming threat that if the external environment changes they may be unable to adapt. The assessor should carefully analyze these data and identify and document key issues and trends that the organization needs to address.

Category 2: Availability and Cost of Resources Needed to Operate the Organization

The items listed below are part of the Business Context loop of the Open Systems diagram shown in Figure 1. A key element of being a high-performing, sustainable organization is the ability to obtain the human, material, and financial resources needed to operate an organization, and to achieve its goals and objectives. This includes the cost of:

- Knowledge and skill-base

- Products and services

- Technology

- Facilities

- Equipment

- Capital and lines of credit

Business environments that have strong competition can make this difficult and can put pressure on an organization. The assessor should carefully analyze the data on the availability and cost of resources and document key issues and trends that the organization needs to address.

Category 3: Industry and Market Trends

The items listed below are part of the Business Context loop of the Open Systems diagram shown in Figure 1. They represent a sample of the kind of issues that an organization may face – forces that can powerfully shape an organization's culture.

- Increase in the growth of the industry

- Plateau of the growth of the industry

- Decline in the growth of the industry

- Changing expectations of customers or market segments

- Changing technological forces or trends

- Federal, state, and local laws' requirements (OSHA, NEPA, FDA, etc.)

- Customer mandated requirements (ISO 9000, ISO 14000, NQA-1, etc.)

- Changes in social, cultural, or legal pressures

- Visibility and scrutiny from the public and media

- Changes from natural/environmental pressures (hurricanes, drought, global warming, etc.)

The pace of change in the business environment, combined with the ability (or inability) of the organization's structures and systems to adapt to that change, should be carefully analyzed and documented by the assessor, including key issues and trends that the organization needs to address.

Category 4: Competition

The list below describes one of the most crucial drivers from the external environment – pressure from competitors. Michael Porter claims that there are seven key areas that need to be addressed in order to create a competitive strategy and competitive advantage (see list below).[152] The assessor should analyze the organization's operations and track-record relative to:

- Competitors who are the known low-cost producers in the industry (cost leadership).

- Competitors who have better differentiation (uniqueness) in the industry for attributes that are widely valued by customers (quality, level of service, timeliness, reliability, customization, etc.).

- Competitors who have more clearly defined and sharply focused target-market segments, which identify who will buy and who will promote the organization's products and services.

- Competitors who achieve superior performance through well-defined business processes, IT infrastructure, and/or tighter cost controls.

- Competitors who have a more externally focused and customer-oriented culture and way of doing business.

- Competitors with a resource and performance record that is more credible with customers.

- Competitors who do not play by the generally established rules of the industry or the disciplinary paradigm.

One of the key factors to understanding competitive forces and pressures from the external environment is the "self fulfilling prophecy" that emerges from the See-Do-Get Process. Here are some questions that assessors can help client organizations ask in order to identify areas for improvement.

- How do people in the external environment "see" us? How do we "see" them?

- What do they expect from us? What do we expect from them?

- How do they interact with us? How do we interact with them?

- How do they affect our results? How do we affect theirs?

- How could we cause people in the external environment to "see" us differently? How can we learn to "see" them differently?

- How could we influence them to modify their expectations of us? Which of our expectations do we need to modify?

- How can we cause them to interact with us differently? How should we be interacting with them?

- Are there important competitive drivers from the external environment that we are not monitoring?

Asking these and other questions is a strategy for raising tacit assumptions and beliefs back into organizational consciousness, reconfiguring them, and then migrating more effective actions, interactions, and patterns-of-interaction back to autopilot operations.

Understanding the changing needs of customers and the ability of competitors to meet those needs is a key element to establishing sustainable growth in organizations. As a general rule, customers want increasingly high product and service quality, customization to their needs, and increasingly competitive prices. In other words, they want better customer value. If an organization can't provide customers with the value that they want and their competitors can, more than likely those customers will migrate to a competitor.

Case Study of the SciTech Company

The SciTech Company is located in the northwest corner of North Dakota near the Canadian border. Founded in the early 1900s as a mining company, the company was later purchased by the federal government as a part of mobilizing America's natural resources to support the country's national defense. SciTech's main office is in Minot, North Dakota with its field operations located about 45 miles north where the mining actually takes place. The Director is a federal employee who reports to the Assistant Secretary for Land and Minerals Management, in the U.S. Department of Interior (DOI), and has a staff of federal employees who head SciTech's five departments. Most of the actual work done by the organization in the field and in the town office is contracted to PSI Engineering which supplies the administrative, technical, and operations personnel needed to accomplish the vast majority of SciTech's day-to-day work. In other words, SciTech has a matrix configuration where the federal employees had approval authority for financial, human, and physical resources, and PSI supplied the people to accomplish the organization's day-to-day activities. The PSI contract was headed by a Program Manager who was the senior manager for PSI staff in town and in the field, and who functioned as the counter-part of SciTech's Director for contractor personnel.

Through historical analysis in the initial phase of the assessment, we learned that in the mid 1990s, DOI Headquarters in Washington, DC decided to shut SciTech down, and as a result the organization had begun to dismantle its structures and systems as part of the decommissioning process. As a way of saving the facility and their jobs, the SciTech Director and his staff developed a vision for transforming the SciTech facility into a state-of-the-art R&D and testing facility that would provide developers of new mining technologies a place to test their innovations in an operating mining environment. SciTech's level of appropriations-based funding prior to the decision to decommission the facility was about $20 million per year. Because they would charge customers for these services, they would need much less appropriations revenue to operate the organization, and would eventually be able to run strictly on revenue generated from customers. The SciTech Director and key line managers developed a strategic plan that projected that they could reach $20 million dollars per year in revenue within three years (thus freeing themselves from the need of appropriated funds), and $50 million per year in revenue within seven years. With the strategic plan in hand, the SciTech Director approached the DOI Assistant Secretary with a proposal that would shift SciTech's revenue mix from being almost 100% appropriations based, to being generated by clients (users) who would pay to use the facility. This would transform SciTech into a "hybrid" organization for the first three years with its revenues coming from appropriations, the sale of mining products to customers, and conducting R&D and testing in their field operation.

After receiving the approval of DOI Headquarters to implement the strategic plan, SciTech was reorganized to carry out its new mission, goals, and objectives. The Technical Services Department was populated largely by engineers, geologists, and project managers who were responsible to plan and oversee the R&D and testing activities in the field for SciTech clients. The organization-wide IT function also reported to the Head of the Technical Services Department. They were physically located in the town office, but routinely travelled out to the field when clients were on-site conducting R&D and testing activities. The IT work-group routinely visited the field to conduct maintenance and support on the IT infrastructure. The Field Operations Department personnel carried out the day-to-day activities of mining, and were the support staff used to actually conduct R&D and testing activities. They were physically located in the field, and occasionally visited the town office to attend training sessions and planning meetings. The Business Administration Department was responsible for the traditional financial management services (finance, accounting, procurement) as well as the life-cycle asset management of SciTech's facilities, equipment, and property. The Technical Assurance Department had responsibility for compliance with environment, safety, health regulations as well as mandated quality assurance requirements. While the day-to-day activities of environment, safety, health, and quality were a line management responsibility, Technical Assurance was responsible to provide training, auditing, and compliance support to SciTech's line managers and their staff. The Business Development Department was located in the town office and was responsible for SciTech's public relations, marketing, and sales functions which included maintaining the website, attending trade conferences, and conducting on-site (in the field) exit interviews with clients when their projects were complete. The new direction outlined in the strategic plan created and reinforced some interesting dynamics between SciTech's managers and staff, the most important of which are shown and described on the organization's Interaction Map in Figure 13.

The Interaction Map

From the very beginning, the assessor should begin to build an Interaction Map of the client organization. An Interaction Map emerges from interviews, on-site observations of work-processes, and other quantitative and qualitative data that are designed to identify the key underlying issues, patterns-of-interaction (POI), cultural norms, and the informal power structure around which day-to-day operations revolve. Assessors will often find that the underlying structure, dynamics, and patterns-of-interaction of an Interaction Map will emerge around the Four Ways of Working as tacit, taken-for-granted attitudes toward accomplishing work that are shaped by the distribution of personality type in an organization.

When built correctly, an Interaction Map provides a "window" into these invisible dynamics that can be empirically identified using the Red Flags. Because managers and staff members tend to "see" the world so differently, most organizations are typified by a combination of both constructive and destructive conflict. An Interaction Map characterizes the nature of constructive (synergistic) dynamics as well as ineffective autopilot operations, Red Flags, and Invisible Bureaucracy by showing how managers and staff members interact with each other within the context of an organization's structures, systems, and culture. It's important to note that the interaction of dynamic forces shown on an Interaction Map are ultimately reducible to small-groups of 2s, 3s, and 4s – the building blocks of organizational culture described in Chapter 2. Figure 13 is an Interaction Map that shows the key patterns-of-interaction (POI) that emerged during the BCI assessment of the SciTech Company.

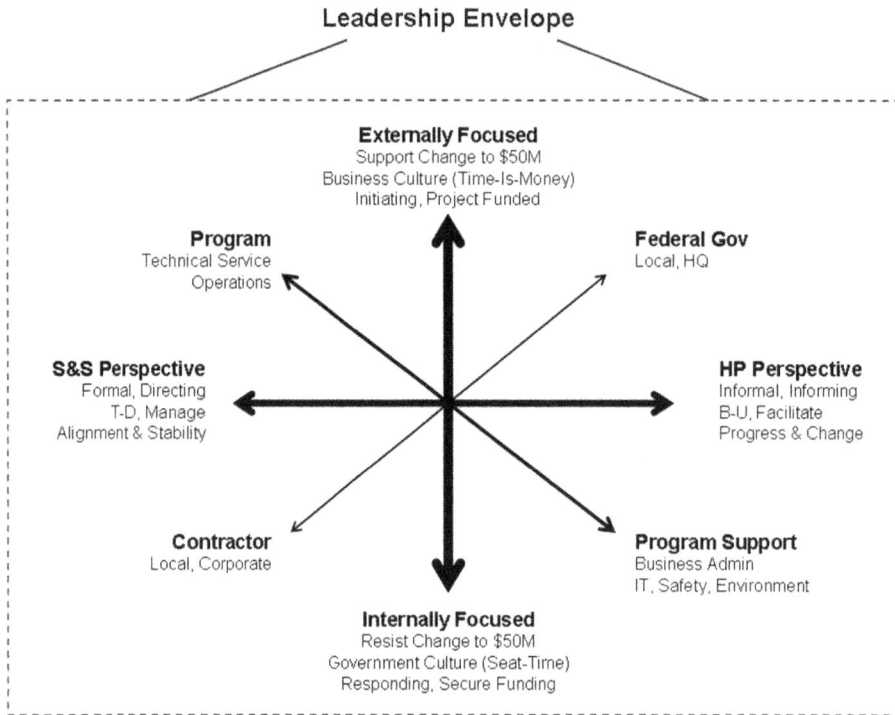

Leadership Envelope

Externally Focused
Support Change to $50M
Business Culture (Time-Is-Money)
Initiating, Project Funded

Program
Technical Service
Operations

Federal Gov
Local, HQ

S&S Perspective
Formal, Directing
T-D, Manage
Alignment & Stability

HP Perspective
Informal, Informing
B-U, Facilitate
Progress & Change

Contractor
Local, Corporate

Program Support
Business Admin
IT, Safety, Environment

Internally Focused
Resist Change to $50M
Government Culture (Seat-Time)
Responding, Secure Funding

Figure 13

The conflict associated with the patterns-of-interaction (POI) depicted on an Interaction Map are often intensified or mitigated by the personalities of managers and key personnel, combined with an individual's or work-group's capacity and desire to learn, see value in other perspectives, and embrace change. More specifically, conflict is either intensified or mitigated by the degree to which an individual or group is dominated by *either-or-thinking* rather than *both-and thinking*; e.g., where the best elements of both sides of the axis can be embraced for the overall good of the organization. All of the axes shown on the Interaction Map in Figure 13 are interdependent, but the thickness of the line indicates the degree of destructive conflict along that axis that affects all of the other axes. The thicker the line, the more destructive and intense the conflict is. The primary axis of destructive conflict shown on the Interaction Map in Figure 13 is the Externally-Internally Focused axis. The secondary axis of destructive conflict is the Structures and Systems-Human Performers Paradigm axis, with the tertiary axis being the Support-Program axis. There were no significant issues and destructive conflict occurring across the SciTech-HQ-Federal- Contractor axis.

The elements shown on an Interaction Map function as sub-cultures or "stereotypes" where stereotypes are defined as oversimplified ways of grouping, binning, or "branding" people based on external factors. For example, what organization a person works in, their organizational level, how long they've worked for the organization, where they are located geographically, and their role relative to the organization; e.g., contractor, customer, supplier, etc. SciTech's Interaction Map reveals an interdependent tension between the main stereotypes and sub-cultures in the organization, with the highest probability for destructive (not constructive) conflict occurring between the elements that are directly opposite each other on the Interaction Map, and those that have thickened lines.

Every organization has an Interaction Map, although the stereotypes and sub-cultures that populate it and the tensions between them vary widely from organization to organization. Stereotypes function as tacit, unexamined "short cuts" that allow people to quickly make sense of the day-to-day interactions in their personal and professional life. For better or for worse, the constructive or destructive tone of this conflict powerfully shapes the Organizational Climate, and over time it becomes woven into the fabric of organizational culture through patterns-of-interaction (POI). The fact that stereotypes are incomplete (or incorrect) does not stop them from powerfully shaping the day-to-day reality of organizational life through the See-Do-Get Process. A more detailed description of each axis shown on the SciTech Interaction Map in Figure 13 is given below.

Externally-Internally Focused Axis: This axis in Figure 13 represents ways of "seeing" and perspectives on how the organization should be operated that extend outside of the SciTech organization to the external environment. Most people at SciTech manifest some aspects of both perspectives, but have a preference for one end of the axis over the other based on their personality type, and their tendency toward *either-or-thinking* rather than *both-and-thinking*. This is the most problematic axis on the SciTech Interaction Map and is an underlying cause of destructive conflict and informal power struggles in almost all of the other axes.

Externally Focused Perspective

This perspective has a *primary* focus on generating revenue, serving clients, and client satisfaction as the reason for SciTech's existence; and a *secondary* focus on the organization's internal operations as the way to achieve the primary focus. The net result of holding the Externally Focused perspective is to provide *support* for the changes to organizational structures, systems, and culture needed for SciTech to achieve its $50 million goal. People who hold this perspective *initiate* interactions with the external environment, and are focused on increasing project revenue as a way of controlling SciTech's destiny, rather than reactively depending on fluctuating levels of appropriated funds which are not directly tied to the organization's performance. They tend to view time-as-money, so the amount of work-time that they spend in "social-discourse" is minimized and the amount of time spent on tasks that directly contribute to achieving SciTech's goal of $50 million is maximized, thus increasing the overall *pace* of work performed. This perspective has a number of similarities to a for-profit, industry-style business culture where managers and staff tend to *initiate* contact with clients and prospects in order to identify and secure the projects and revenue needed to meet their project-funded revenue goals. Their ways of working and decision-making are influenced *primarily* by client requirements, feedback and other forces from the external environment, and *secondarily* by their own technical capabilities, professional interests, core competencies, and work preferences. Consequently, managers and staff who hold this perspective tend to bring "fresh blood" and A-Level talent into the SciTech organization to stimulate change, innovation, and improvement. They are less concerned about maintaining what might be perceived as their "territory" and the status-quo than those who hold more strongly to the Internally Focused axis.

Internally Focused Perspective

This perspective has a *primary* focus on internal operations, and a *secondary* focus on generating revenue, serving clients, and client satisfaction as the reason for SciTech's existence. The net result of holding this perspective is to create *resistance* to the changes to organizational structures, systems, and culture needed for SciTech to achieve its $50 million goal. People who hold this perspective tend to *respond* to external forces, like fluctuating levels of appropriated funds which are not directly tied to the organization's performance, rather than proactively increasing project revenue as a way of controlling SciTech's destiny. They tend to view work-time as "seat time" (put in your eight hours), so the amount of work-time that they spend in "social-discourse" reflects a more leisurely pace of work, and the amount of work-time spent on tasks that they deem important (but may not directly contribute to achieving SciTech's goal of $50 million) is greater than those who hold strongly to the Externally Focused end of the axis. The Internally Focused perspective has a number of similarities to a non-profit, government-style culture where managers, supervisors, and staff members tend to *respond* to contact that is initiated by clients when they are approached about projects needed to meet their project-funded goals, but they tend not to initiate contact. Their ways of working and decision-making are shaped *primarily* by their own technical capabilities, professional interests, core competencies, and work preferences; and *secondarily* by client requirements, client feedback, and other forces from the external environment. Consequently, managers, supervisors, and staff members who hold this perspective tend to value a "seasoned" perspective from long-time SciTech employees, rather than the "fresh" perspectives that newer employees tend to bring. In addition, they are much more concerned about maintaining what they perceive to be their "territory" and the status-quo at SciTech than those who hold strongly to the Externally Focused end of the axis.

S&S-HP Paradigm Axis: The Structures and Systems and Human Performance axis in Figure 13 represents ways of "seeing" and perspectives for how work should be performed within the SciTech organization. This axis mirrors the distinction between the *structures-and-systems perspective* and the *human-performance perspective* outlined in Chapter 1. In other words, should SciTech be viewed as an interdependent configuration of structures and systems, an interdependent configuration of human performers, or a combination? Most people at SciTech manifest some aspects of both perspectives, but have a preference for one end of the axis over the other based on their personality type, and their tendency toward *either-or-thinking* rather than *both-and-thinking*. This is the second most problematic axis on the SciTech Interaction Map shown in Figure 13, and is an underlying cause of destructive conflict and informal power struggles in almost all of the other axes.

Structures and Systems Perspective

This perspective is typified by a tops-down (T-D), formality of operations, with a task-time project orientation that tends to see the work accomplished by SciTech as an interdependent set of structures and systems that need to be directed, tightly managed and controlled (rather than people being facilitated and inspired) in order to achieve well-defined goals and objectives. On this view, structures and systems are populated by managers, supervisors, and staff members who must be trained and developed, but who can be replaced by other competent people; e.g., the structures and systems are the primary process, not the people that populate them. This perspective tends to tightly control the financial and non-financial data used to run SciTech and to discourage shadow-systems; e.g., they operate with only one set of data and information. SciTech managers that hold to this perspective tend to use *directive* language in their communications rather than *informing* language. They tend to make T-D, action-oriented, deliberate decisions that implement and execute the organization's strategic and tactical goals and objectives. In addition, SciTech managers who hold this perspective create alignment and stability by monitoring and evaluating their progress toward achieving the organization's objectives and goals, and keeping the organizational units they are responsible for on-track with key performance indicators (KPIs). This T-D structures-and-systems perspective tends to focus the organization's day-to-day decision-making and activities on achieving quantitatively defined goals, objectives, and KPIs, and to discourage "lobbying" on the part of managers, supervisors, or staff members.

Human Performance Perspective

This perspective is typified by a bottoms-up (B-U), informality of operations, with a human performance orientation that tends to see the work accomplished by SciTech as an interdependent set of teams or individual performers that need to be facilitated and inspired (rather than tightly managed and controlled), with strategies, objectives, and goals being allowed to emerge and morph over time. On this view, *people* are the primary process, rather than well-defined structures and systems (people are sometimes viewed as being irreplaceable). This perspective tends to loosely control the financial and non-financial data used to run SciTech which encourages shadow-systems; e.g., they operate with multiple sets of data and information. SciTech managers that hold to this perspective tend to use *informing* language in their communications rather than *directive* language. Their decision-making tends to be B-U where they consult with (and gather input from) many sources and people with differing perspectives, thus allowing solutions to problems to emerge bottoms-up and contextually – *even after* strategic and tactical goals and objectives have been defined and agreed upon. SciTech managers who hold to the human-performance perspective encourage digressions and the morphing of goals and objectives as a way of refocusing the organization on new outcomes and new KPIs, rather than seeking alignment and stability around previously agreed-upon goals, objectives, and KPIs. This B-U human-performance perspective tends to encourage "lobbying" on the part of managers, supervisors, or staff members.

Program-Program Support Axis: This axis in Figure 13 represents ways of "seeing" and perspectives that extend outside of the SciTech organization to requirements from the external environment; e.g., SciTech-HQ and other government agencies and entities. Rooted in SciTech's relationship with the mining industry is the perspective that increasing production, and maintaining cost and schedule are *mutually exclusive* (incommensurate) goals with: a) preserving the environment, and the safety and health (ES&H) of employees, b) ensuring quality (QA), and c) being financially accountable. At SciTech, this axis is powerfully shaped by the context of these cultural norms. Most people at SciTech manifest some aspects of both perspectives, but have a preference for one end of the axis over the other, tending toward *either-or-thinking* rather than *both-and-thinking*. This is the third most problematic axis on the SciTech Interaction Map and is an underlying cause of destructive conflict and informal power struggles in almost all of the other axes.

Program Perspective

This perspective tends to believe that increasing revenue, satisfying SciTech's customers, and achieving the organization's strategic goals and objectives *are not* mutually exclusive (incommensurate) with protecting the environment and the safety and health of SciTech employees (and contractors) and ensuring financial accountability. Responsibility for ES&H, QA, and financial accountability is a line-management responsibility and line managers can be *trusted* to know the requirements, interpret them properly, and implement them as a day-to-day part of doing their job. On this view, people in the support functions act as advisors and consultants who facilitate and enable SciTech's enterprise-wide business processes and periodically act as an independent check on implementation. This is the model used by for-profit companies and is closely aligned with the Externally Focused perspective on the Interaction map. This perspective is also typified by "thinking" compliance where the application of requirements from SciTech-HQ and other government agencies is based on responsibly managing the risks associated with ES&H issues, and ensuring financial accountability as a way of *achieving* SciTech's strategic goals and objectives. In other words, program support elements like ES&H, QA, finance, and accounting are a *means* to the end of SciTech achieving its purpose – they are not an end in themselves.

Program Support Perspective

This perspective tends to believe that protecting the ES&H of SciTech employees, ensuring quality (QA), and financial accountability are mutually exclusive (incommensurate) with increasing revenue, satisfying SciTech's customers, and achieving the organization's strategic goals and objectives. On this view, responsibility for ES&H, QA, and financial accountability is a line-management responsibility, but line managers cannot be *trusted* to know the requirements, interpret them properly, and implement them as a day-to-day part of doing their job. On this view, people in the support functions view their job as ensuring that line managers comply with the support staffs' knowledge, interpretation and implementation of the requirements independent of the impact that this has on SciTech's end-to-end business process or strategic goals and objectives. They also view their job as requiring them to monitor and audit line management's implementation of the requirements against the support staff's interpretations of the requirements. This is the model used by non-profit and government organizations and is closely aligned with the Internally Focused perspective on the Interaction map. This perspective is also typified by a "compliance" mentality where the application of requirements from SciTech-HQ and other government agencies and entities is based on a "one-size-fits-all" approach to implementation rather than responsibly managing the risks associated with ES&H, QA, and ensuring financial accountability as a way of achieving SciTech's strategic goals and objectives. On this view, the purpose, goals, and objectives of program support organizations like ES&H, QA, and finance become ends in themselves, sometimes at the expense of achieving SciTech's strategic purpose, goals, and objectives; e.g., the tail of support services wags the dog of the organization's purpose, goals, and objectives.

Federal Gov-Contractor Axis: This axis in Figure 13 represents the contractual and management relationship between SciTech and its contractor. While there are episodic issues that arise along this axis because of ambiguities in the way the contract between SciTech and its contractor PSI Engineering is written, interpreted, and executed in day-to-day practice; this axis is relatively unproblematic to day-to-day operations. On occasions when this axis becomes problematic, it is often attributable to the personalities and communication skills of the people involved and the way they interpret the requirements of the contract.

SciTech Leadership Envelope: The role of the SciTech Director and the PSI's Program Manager is to understand, orchestrate, and integrate the different (and often opposing) forces shown on the Interaction Map within the leadership envelope shown in Figure 13. The actions and interaction of the SciTech Director tend to be externally focused and on the human-performance perspective side of the Interaction Map (top, right side), while the contractor's Program Manager's actions and interactions tend to be Internally Focused and on the human-performance perspective side of the Interaction Map (bottom, right side). At this point in SciTech's corporate life-cycle and in order to maintain a course toward a $50 million SciTech, the assessment team recommended that both senior managers should more strongly embrace the externally focused and structures-and-system perspectives as criteria for decision-making, and in the actions and interactions that they have with their managers and staff.

As described in Chapter 2, the Left-Hand Column can be used as a powerful tool for surfacing and managing conflict in relationships.[153] But it can also be used as a method for exploring the tacit, unquestioned beliefs and assumptions associated with an organization's culture and the underlying dynamics of the Interaction Map shown in Figure 13. The minds of managers and staff members become a platform upon which the inner commentary about what they think and feel (but do not say) plays out. The model of the Left-Hand Column shown in Figure 14 can be a powerful tool for exploring and understanding this bifurcated communication and the inner commentary that occurs organization-wide, in work-groups, and in small-groups of 2s, 3s, and 4s – the building blocks of organizational culture.

LH COLUMN	RH COLUMN
Cultural Norms and Undiscussible Views (Inner Commentary of ROI)	Socialized Norms and Public Dialogue (Shaped by COI)
What We Think, Feel, Believe, and Assume But Do Not Say and Do (Actual, POI)	What We Say and Do (Socialized)

Figure 14

The Left-Hand Column is the place in our inner-experience where the tacit beliefs, assumptions, ineffective autopilot operations, Red Flags, and Invisible Bureaucracy that underlay the Interaction Map make their presence known to managers and staff members. It is the psycho-social place where self-awareness about the strengths, weaknesses, and Blind Spots associated with an Interaction Map first emerge into conscious awareness. It is also the first line of defense for people who choose to censor and block this inner commentary from entering the arena of awareness for themselves and work-groups – the gate-keeping function with which people "manage" the information that they receive about the organization's structures, systems, culture, and about their own performance within that context.

Focus on Key Stakeholders

Having established a performance baseline with the organization's history, previous assessments, presenting issues, and external drivers; and having built an Interaction Map of the client organization, assessors should evaluate the organization's operations against a number of *benchmarks* that are indicators of high-performance and organizational excellence. The first set of benchmarks evaluates the degree to which an organization is focused on all of its key stakeholders. John Kotter and James Heskett argue that a long-term vision for sustainability requires a focus on six key stakeholders:[154]

- Customers

- Owners, Shareholders (Taxpayers)

- Employees

- Leadership

- Community

- Society

It is especially important to focus on customers; owners and shareholders (in the case of the government, taxpayers); employees; and leadership because these constituencies have powerful interdependent links between them. In other words, when managers and staff members are focused on the interests of owners and shareholders, their goal is to ensure that an organization performs well economically over time. But the only way to accomplish this in a competitive marketplace is to focus on satisfying customers, and the only way to satisfy customers in a competitive labor market is to focus on the people who create the products and deliver services to customers – the employees. In much the same way, the only way to make the organization's operations effective and create improvement is to value, teach, and use the established principles of leadership and management which is an indicator of a company's ability to learn, adapt, and serve all stakeholders more effectively. A focus on the community and the larger social structures of society echoes Collins' view that truly great companies are concerned with more than just profitability; e.g., "Profitability is a necessary condition for existence and a means to more important ends, but it is not the end in itself for many of the visionary companies. Profit is like oxygen, food, water, and blood; they are not the point of life, but without them, there is no life."[155]

The need to focus on all six key stakeholders raises philosophical issues associated with the question: What is the purpose of a business? There are two broadly debated theoretical answers to this question: a) the Business as Property Theory, and b) the Stakeholder Theory. Assessors and the people they work with should understand their tacit assumptions and beliefs with regard to this issue. Business as Property Theory argues that a business is "property" that belongs to the owners, and as such the owners have the right to operate it as they see fit within the confines of the law and morality. Workers voluntarily exchange their labor for wages from the owner. From this perspective, workers have no more right to tell owners how to operate their organization than owners have the right to tell people how to spend their wages. Milton Friedman argues that the main purpose of a business is to maximize profits for its owners, and in the case of publicly traded companies this is the stockholders.[156] Stakeholder Theory argues that people who have a legitimate interest in a business should have a voice in determining how it is operated, where stakeholders might include employees, customers, and even society as a whole (given environmental impacts and an organization's ability to create jobs which affect the economy).

The scores on the radar graph in Figure 15 show the averaged responses of all populations at SciTech for the six Key Stakeholders using the BCI and compare the scores of top managers to the scores of all other participants by population. When the scores of top managers and others differ by less than 15 percent, they appear in black indicating that the scores are *aligned* and there is little or no difference in how the populations see this issue. When the difference between the scores of top managers and other populations is between 15 and 30 percent, the score appears in grey signifying that there is a *moderate misalignment* in how the populations see this issue. When the difference between the scores of top managers and other populations differs by more than 30 percent, the score appears in italics signifying that there is a *significant misalignment* between how top managers and the populations see this issue.

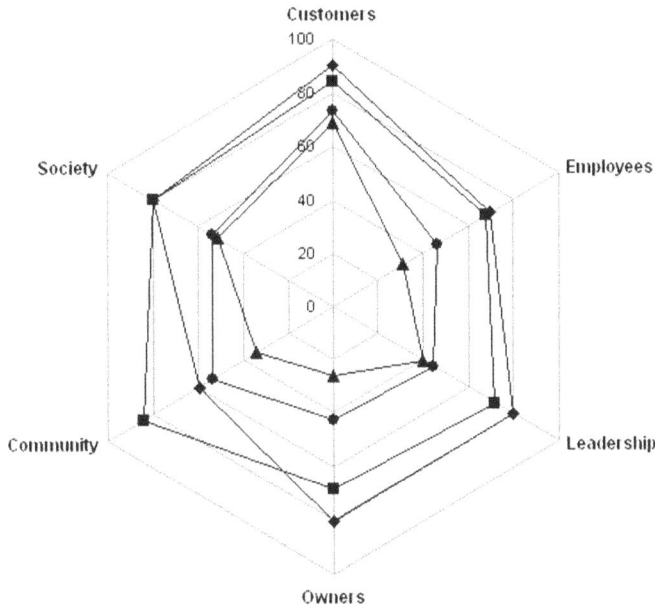

	CUST	EMP	LDR	OWN	COMM	SOC
Top Manager ◆	90.0	70.0	80.0	80.0	60.0	80.0
Line Manager ■	84.0	68.0	72.0	68.0	84.0	80.0
Supervisor ▲	68.6	*31.4*	*40.0*	*25.7*	34.3	51.4
Staff ●	73.3	46.0	*44.6*	*42.1*	53.7	54.0

Figure 15

The data in Figure 15 indicate that customer focus is probably a Strength (High-High) for the SciTech organization because the scores tend to cluster around 80%, although all scores should be validated using objective evidence from day-to-day operations; e.g., customer satisfaction surveys, exit interviews, repeat business, etc. SciTech's consensus that customer focus is a key aspect of the organization's operations can be used as common ground to discuss the importance of improving their focus on the other five Key Stakeholders.

The data in Figure 15 also indicate that there are significant misalignments between top managers and line managers; and the supervisors and staff in a number of areas, including the Leadership area and the Owner (Taxpayer) area. The scores indicate that while top managers and line managers believe that the road to effective operations and improvement is to value, teach, and use the established principles of leadership and management, the supervisors and staff members are either not getting this message from top managers and line managers, or they do not see evidence of this belief put into practice in day-to-day operations.

Notice that the scores of supervisors are even lower than the scores of staff members, which probably indicates that supervisors may be negatively shaping and defining the ways in which staff members see themselves, others, and the overall organization. As a general rule, whenever there are scores that indicate a significant misalignment (italics), assessors should explore these areas with clients to determine the reasons for these scores. More importantly, in the case of SciTech there is an overall pattern of moderate to significant misalignment through the entire data sample as revealed on almost all radar graphs. This indicates a deep lack of consensus about almost every aspect of how the organization is led, managed, and operated. This lack of consensus is reflected in SciTech's organizational climate, culture, and the organization's overall level of effectiveness and productivity. This interpretation of the data is also supported by the amount of time and energy that SciTech squanders on: a) rework, poor or inconsistent quality and service, work-arounds, timeliness, downtime (organizational energy), and b) poor or ineffective communication, exchanges of negative energy, people frustrating or undermining positive change, fear of retribution, power struggles between managers and coworkers (psychological energy) as described in Chapter 4. Time and energy are an organization's most valuable resources, and when squandered they become unavailable to achieve an organization's goals and objectives.

Figure 16 shows the same data binned by work-group which allows assessors and their clients to identify specific organizational units that have higher (or lower) levels of consensus with top managers about the nature of day-to-day operations within the SciTech organization – in this case, the degree of focus on the six Key Stakeholders. Viewing the data by work-group can reveal "pockets" of alignment (or misalignment) that are often related to the specific manager who heads an organizational unit. Work-group managers often function as "Border Guards" who fight to protect a work-group's human, material, and financial resources; who navigate and manage the organizational and cultural politics that exist in organizations; and who powerfully shape and define the sub-cultures within their organizational units by the emotional tone and resonances that they create. The sub-culture within a specific work-group is also shaped and defined by the leadership and management style of the work-group manager; the characteristics of their personality and level of psychological health; and the degree to which they are either aligned (or misaligned) with top managers (and other work-group managers) about how to approach the day-to-day realities of organizational life. As described in Chapter 2, the building blocks of organizational culture consist of small-groups of 2s, 3s, and 4s who are work-group managers and supervisors – Border Guards who define the nature of the underlying patterns-of-interaction on an organization's Interaction Map.

The Field Operations and Technical Services work-groups at SciTech have the lowest scores on the chart shown in Figure 16. In fact, three out of the six elements shown on the Key Stakeholders radar for these two work-groups show scores that indicate significant misalignment with top managers. This is a pattern that repeats itself throughout the data gathered for the SciTech case-study described in the remainder of this book.

	CUST	EMP	LDR	OWN	COMM	SOC
Top Manager	90.0	70.0	80.0	80.0	60.0	80.0
Business Administration	81.8	43.6	*41.8*	60.0	74.5	78.2
Business Development	77.1	57.1	54.3	60.0	77.1	77.1
Field Operations	74.6	44.6	*48.8*	*34.2*	40.8	*49.6*
Technical Assurance	75.7	74.3	72.9	74.3	72.9	74.3
Technical Services	71.3	*40.0*	*42.6*	*38.3*	67.0	58.3

Figure 16

This type of scoring pattern often indicates the existence of warring factions of Border Guards and their functional silos that try to optimize their own work-group's performance, while sub-optimizing the performance of other work-groups and ultimately the overall organization. Consequently, focusing improvement efforts on these two work-groups and their associated managers and supervisors can be high-leverage for assessors and their clients because the scores focus the attention of follow-up interventions on the work-groups within which ineffective autopilot operations, the Red Flags, and Invisible Bureaucracy are most likely to be found.

Strategic View

The set of benchmarks described in this section enables assessors to evaluate the degree to which a client organization takes a strategic (100,000 foot elevation) view of the external environment and its internal operations. The benchmark criteria are based upon the principles taught by business experts such as Jim Collins, Peter Drucker, Jay Galbraith, Robert Kaplan and David Norton, Harry Beckwith, Al Ries and Jack Trout, Larry Bossidy and Ram Charan, Michael Porter, Edwards Deming, numerous articles in the *Harvard Business Review*, and the Global Organization Design model developed by Elliot Jaques.[157] The left side of Figure 17 shows the six perspectives of the Strategic View, which consists of:

- Leadership Focus

- Resources and Policies

- Planning and Deployment

- Strata and Talent

- Business Results

- Business Context

An assessor can "see" an organization from any one of these six perspectives, and while all six are important to building a high-performing organization and understanding an organization's culture, the two key elements of the Strategic View are Leadership Focus and Resources and Policies because they are the critical path to creating organizational alignment and stability. The six perspectives of the Strategic View map to the context-of-interaction (COI) term of the Breckenridge Equation described in Chapter 2, and are a way of viewing organizations like SciTech from the structures-and-systems perspective described in Chapter 1.

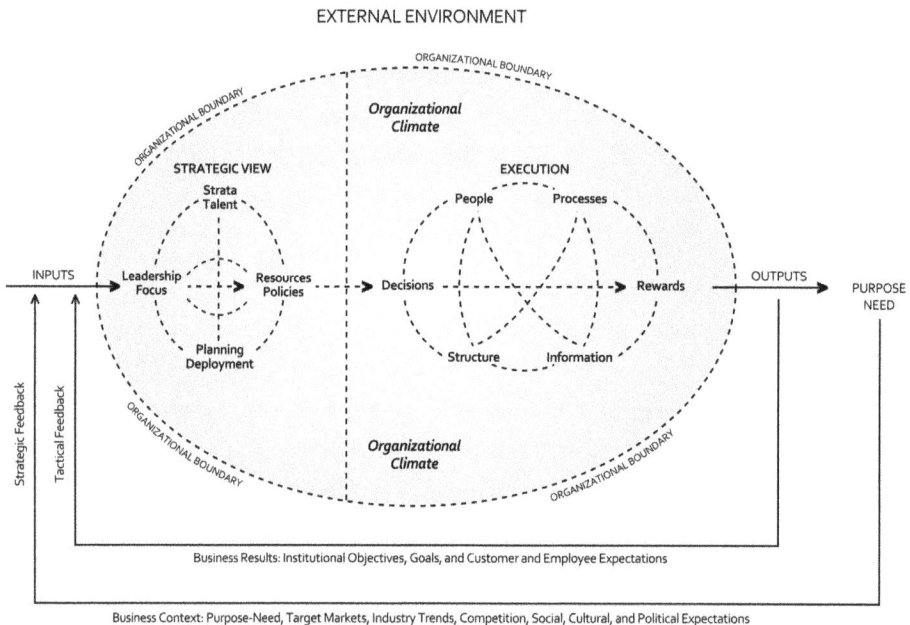

Figure 17

Let's define each of the six perspectives of the Strategic View in more detail, beginning with the two critical path elements: Leadership Focus and Resources and Policies.

Leadership Focus: This perspective helps assessors to evaluate the degree to which top managers in an organization have set a clear direction for achieving an organization's mission and goals and can clearly communicate the organization's purpose, goals, and core values to people inside and outside the organization. It also indicates whether top managers have identified the most important sources of revenue that drive financial performance and whether they use a balanced array of "vital few" performance measures to focus the time and energy of the entire organization on a common purpose and direction. The Leadership Focus perspective is an indicator of the degree to which top managers do what's in the best interest of the organization, rather than being motivated by self-interest. It indicates the degree to which top managers are viewed as being competent to lead the organization (they know what they're doing), can make tough choices, and have the determination and resolve to persevere in the face of obstacles.

Resources and Policies: This perspective focuses on the degree to which management only budgets for, and commits resources to things that help the organization achieve its goals and objectives and are consistent with the organization's values. It also indicates whether the level of human, financial, and physical resources is adequate to achieve the goals and objectives defined in the organization's strategic plan, and whether the allocation of financial and human resources, equipment, and space send a consistent set of signals that reinforce the desired behaviors. The Resources and Policies perspective also evaluates the degree to which high level policies are aligned with (and support) achieving the strategic goals and objectives, and the extent to which the compensation system motivates people to achieve their goals.

Business Results: This perspective focuses on the degree to which the organization monitors and measures its overall performance to determine whether it's achieving its goals and objectives, and the extent to which the organization focuses its time and energy on revenue growth, increasing profits, and cost cutting (see Tactical Feedback loop in Figure 17). It also evaluates whether the organization's products and services meet, or exceed, its customers' needs and requirements, and whether the organization solicits feedback from employees about their experience of working in the organization (level of conflict, pressure, fairness, trust, etc.), and then acts on this information.

Planning and Deployment: This perspective helps assessors to evaluate the degree to which the organization analyzes strategic information about opportunities and threats from industry trends, target markets, and competitors, as well as analyzing the organization's strengths and weaknesses; and then codifies the results of this analysis into a written strategic plan that defines the organization's direction, goals, and objectives. It also evaluates the extent to which broad consensus and commitment are built among managers and key personnel around the overall direction and goals in the strategic plan. The Planning and Deployment perspective enables assessors to evaluate how well the organization implements its strategic goals through operating plans, goals, and budgets in work-groups and organizational units, and through project plans and tasks that have scheduled timetables, milestones, and deliverables.

Strata and Talent: This perspective focuses on the degree to which the organization has purposefully designed the number of managerial layers to handle the complexity of its work and operations (not too few and not too many), and has developed an effective succession management process and an effective method for identifying and attracting top talent. It also evaluates whether managers are perceived as having the expertise, experience, and intellectual horsepower needed to succeed at their assigned organizational level. The Strata and Talent perspective also evaluates the degree to which people are paid for the level of complexity of the work they do and their contribution to the organization, rather than just seniority or job title.

Business Context: This perspective helps assessors to evaluate the degree to which the organization's own perception of its purpose is aligned with the actual needs of market segments and industry trends as shown as the Strategic Feedback loop in Figure 17. It also indicates whether the organization compares its level of performance with its strongest competitors and focuses on identifying new products and services to meet the changing needs and demands of its customers and new market segments. The Business Context perspective also evaluates the extent to which the organization possesses a deep knowledge of emerging industry trends and the needs of market segments in the external environment, and then experiments with multiple lines of action to anticipate changes in the external environment, allowing the results to determine which options are the best alternatives.

The scores on the radar graph in Figure 18 show the averaged responses of all populations at SciTech for the six elements of the Strategic View using the BCI. The radar graph compares the scores of top managers to the scores of all other participants by population.[158] A score of 100 represents excellence. When the scores of top managers and others differ by less than 15 percent, they appear in black indicating that the scores are *aligned* and there is little or no difference in how the populations see this issue. When the difference between the scores of top managers and other populations is between 15 and 30 percent, the score appears in grey signifying that there is a *moderate misalignment* in how the populations see this issue. When the difference between the scores of top managers and other populations differs by more than 30 percent, the score appears in italics signifying that there is a *significant misalignment* between how top managers and the populations see this issue.

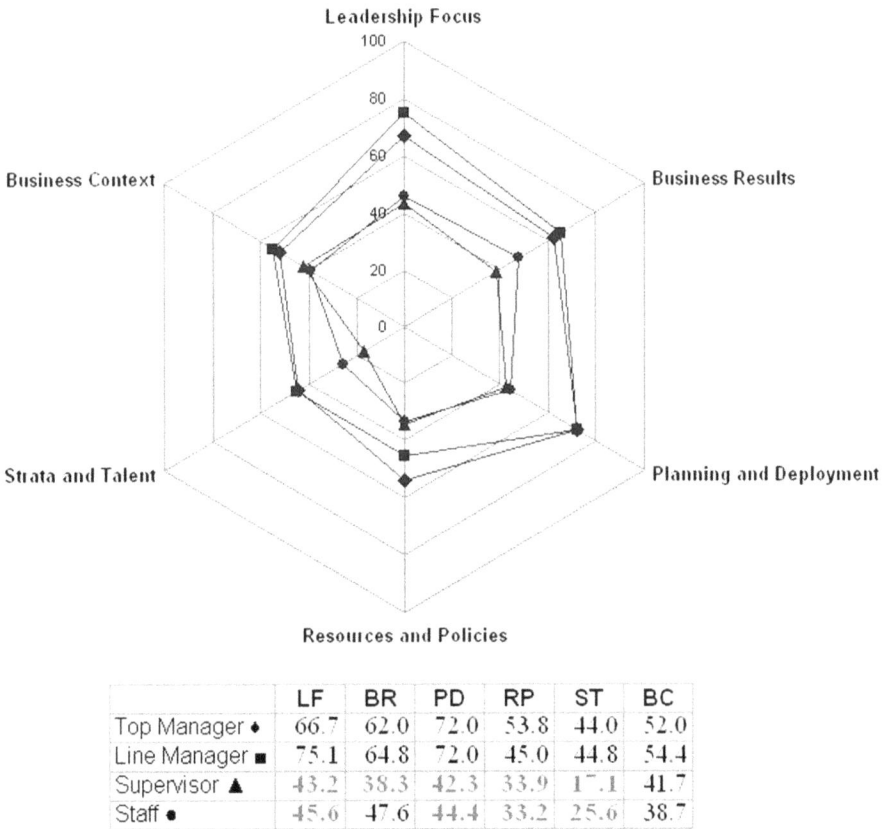

	LF	BR	PD	RP	ST	BC
Top Manager ♦	66.7	62.0	72.0	53.8	44.0	52.0
Line Manager ■	75.1	64.8	72.0	45.0	44.8	54.4
Supervisor ▲	43.2	38.3	42.3	33.9	17.1	41.7
Staff ●	45.6	47.6	44.4	33.2	25.6	38.7

Figure 18

The analysis of the data shown in Figure 18 should begin with the two perspectives positioned at the top and bottom of the radar graph (Leadership Focus and Resources and Policies) which are the critical path of the Strategic View data set. These two perspectives are the key to creating alignment and stability in an organization. The Leadership Focus and Resources and Policies perspectives are high-leverage activities that powerfully shape and define the characteristics of the other four perspectives in the Strategic View data set, and an organization's overall performance. When an organization has a Strength in one (or both) of these areas signified by a High-High scoring pattern, it should be leveraged to improve the other four perspectives of the Strategic View and the performance of work-groups and the overall organization. When an organization Needs Development in one (or both) of these areas signified by a Low-Low scoring pattern, improvement in areas of Leadership Focus and Resources and Policies will positively impact an organization's performance in the other four areas.

The data on the radar graph in Figure 18 shows a High-Low scoring pattern for Leadership Focus which probably indicates that top managers have Blind Spots about the extent to which they are actually providing Leadership Focus for the supervisor and staff levels. Qualitative data gathered in one-on-one interviews and focus groups at SciTech confirm that there is a fairly significant misalignment between how top managers and line managers "see" their ability to provide Leadership Focus for the organization, and the extent to which supervisors and staff members believe they are being led by top managers and line managers. This High-Low scoring pattern is consistent with much of the data gathered at SciTech, which supports the view that communication down through the line organization is a systemic problem that is manifested throughout the BCI data set.

Notice how the Resources and Policies data on Figure 18 reveals a Low-Low scoring pattern which probably indicates a critical path perspective that Needs Development because the scores of all four populations are clustered below 60%. This indicates that the four populations that compose the organization have consensus on the view that the activities and processes associated with this perspective are "broken" and need to be fixed. Qualitative data gathered in one-on-one interviews and focus groups at SciTech confirm that there is a high level of frustration on the part of all employees in the areas described by Resources and Policies. More specifically, top managers and middle managers are frustrated with an overly bureaucratic budgeting process and the inability to obtain timely financial information about the costs associated with projects and ongoing operations. Supervisors and staff members are frustrated by the fact that the inadequate levels of financial, human, and physical resources that they are given undermine their ability to perform their day-to-day work and to achieve their goals and objectives. This consensus can be used to focus the organization's time and energy on creating and sustaining positive change in the area of Resources and Polices.

Figure 19 shows the same data binned by work-group. Notice how low the scores for the Business Development work-group are, especially in the area of Leadership Focus which includes the degree to which top managers have identified the most important sources of revenue that drive financial performance. This is probably a high-leverage area in which to explore the misalignment of scores between top managers and the Business Development work-group in order to determine what is actually occurring in the day-to-day operations of this key organizational function.

	LF	BR	PD	RP	ST	BC
Top Manager	66.7	62.0	72.0	53.8	44.0	52.0
Business Administration	57.8	42.2	51.6	34.8	29.1	46.2
Business Development	40.6	45.7	49.7	25.0	20.0	35.4
Field Operations	46.7	49.6	48.8	36.4	22.4	40.9
Technical Assurance	78.4	60.6	70.0	47.0	47.1	50.9
Technical Services	49.0	49.0	42.6	33.6	32.3	43.8

Figure 19

Also notice that the scores for the Technical Assurance work-group in Figure 19 are aligned with the scores of top managers in all six perspectives of the Strategic View data. Qualitative data gathered in one-on-one interviews and focus groups at SciTech confirm that the manager and supervisors of this work-group are strong supporters of the top manager's leadership style and the overall philosophy and direction that top managers are moving the SciTech organization. This scoring trend appears throughout the data gathered with the BCI assessment. In an organization like SciTech where numerous work-groups are moderately or significantly misaligned with top managers, the commitment of the Technical Assurance managers, supervisors, and staff to support top managers so strongly can (and often does) create destructive conflict and a "we versus they" attitude that is reflected on the organization's Interaction Map.

Execution

The set of benchmarks described in this section enables assessors to evaluate how effectively a client organization can *carry out* and *implement* plans, goals, objectives and the organization's overall strategic direction. These benchmark criteria describe how the organization-wide goals and objectives defined in the Strategic View flow down into the organization and are executed by work-groups. The criteria are based on the principles taught by business experts such as Jim Collins, Dave Hanna, Alec Sharp, Edwards Deming, Thomas Davenport, Paul Harmon, J.M. Juran, Alfie Kohn, Ram Charan, the body of knowledge known as Human Performance Technology, numerous articles in the *Harvard Business Review*, and the Global Organization Design model developed by Elliot Jaques.[159] The right side of Figure 20 shows the six perspectives of Execution, which consist of:

- Decisions

- Rewards

- Structure

- Information

- People

- Processes

An assessor can "see" an organization from any one of these six perspectives, and while all six are important to building a high-performing organization and understanding an organization's culture, the two key elements are Decisions and Rewards because they are the critical path to creating organizational alignment and stability. The six perspectives of Execution map to the context-of-interaction (COI) term of the Breckenridge Equation described in Chapter 2, and provide a view of an organization from the structures-and-systems perspective described in Chapter 1.

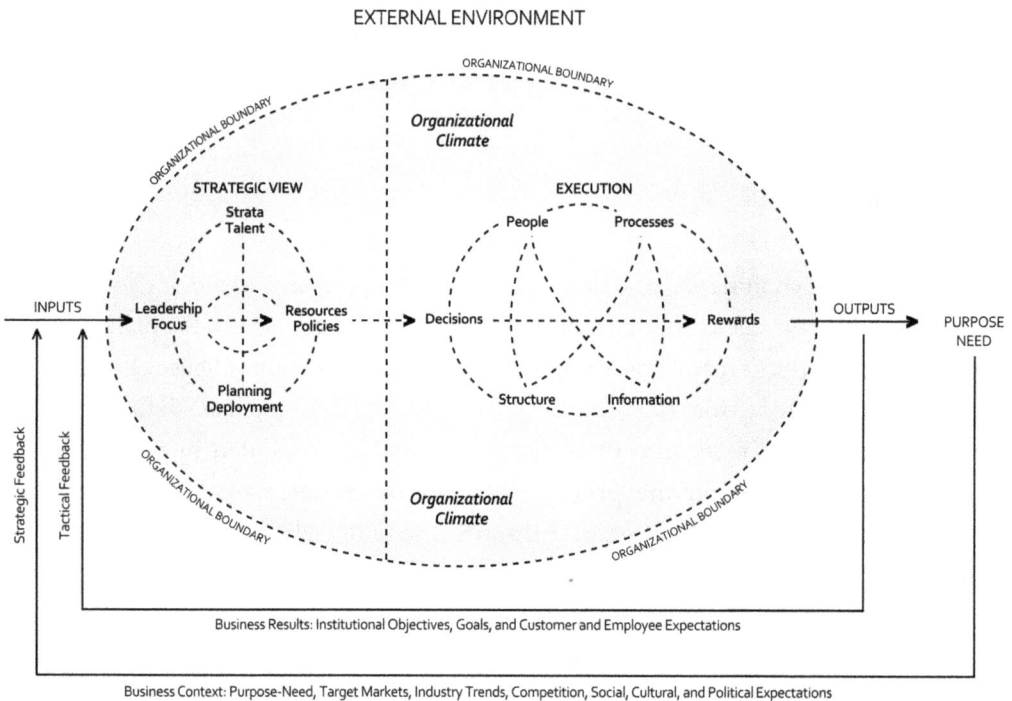

Figure 20

Let's define each of the six perspectives of Execution in more detail, beginning with the two critical path elements: Decisions and Rewards.

Decisions: This perspective helps assessors to evaluate the degree to which an organization's decision-making style has a bias toward action and producing practical solutions (issues don't get "studied to death"), with meetings that are action-oriented and result in task assignments, due dates, milestones, deliverables, and follow-up. Also, managers have an effective method for reaching consensus on important issues, and only support decisions that implement or accelerate achieving the goals in the strategic plan. The Decisions perspective also indicates the extent to which the organization uses fact-based decision-making with quantitative data and scientific analytics, not just business experience and intuition, and whether strategic goals, organizational unit plans, goals, and budgets are used to help direct the organization's week-to-week and month-to-month operations.

Rewards: This perspective focuses on the degree to which managers reward behaviors that implement or accelerate the process of achieving the goals in the strategic plan, and the degree to which they use their own visible behavior to teach employees how to handle problems in ways that reinforce the desired behaviors. The Rewards perspective also evaluates whether the criteria that managers use to allocate rewards and status, and things that managers pay attention to and care about (including their emotional reactions to critical incidents and crises), serve to reinforce the desired behaviors.

People: This perspective focuses on the degree to which people are assigned to work that is consistent with their problem-solving and decision-making abilities; that they have the knowledge and skills to perform that work successfully; and when possible, that they are assigned work and tasks that they are interested in and enjoy. It also indicates whether managers are perceived as having the expertise, experience, and intellectual horsepower needed to succeed at their assigned organizational level, and whether they are able to inspire people with the confidence needed to achieve their goals and objectives. The People perspective also evaluates the extent to which the organization provides the resources for managers and staff members to develop their competencies and skills (on-the-job training, classroom education, mentoring, coaching).

Processes: This perspective helps assessors to evaluate the degree to which an organization's business processes and workflow effectively deliver products and services to customers, with relatively little downtime, work-arounds, and quality issues. It also indicates whether the performance of business processes is regularly analyzed to eliminate unnecessary steps and tasks that negatively impact achieving goals, and whether work assignments and goals are doable to the required level of quality, within the time allowed. The Processes perspective also evaluates the extent to which work assignments and goals are clearly defined and communicated (milestones and deliverables are understood), and whether regular operations reviews of goals and budgets are conducted to keep the outputs of business processes and projects on track.

Information: This perspective focuses on the degree to which people are given the job-related information needed to carry out their work and achieve their goals (procedures, guidelines, manuals). It also indicates whether people receive relevant information and feedback from customers about the organization's performance, and the information needed to understand the impact of their day-to-day decisions on the organization's overall performance. The Information perspective also evaluates the extent to which people communicate and cooperate with other departments so that key information is shared (the left hand knows what the right one is doing), and whether managers explain the reasons behind changes in operating policies and practices.

Structure: This perspective helps assessors to evaluate the degree to which an organization's structures and systems help (rather than hinder) managers and staff members in achieving their goals because they allow the right people to work together on the right tasks to achieve an organization's goals. It also indicates whether responsibilities are clearly defined in order to eliminate confusion about who does what, and whether lines of authority for reporting and decision-making are clearly defined and focused on achieving results. The Structure perspective evaluates the extent to which the lateral working relationships and authority between work-groups is defined; e.g., who can say no to whom and under what circumstances. It also indicates the extent to which the boundaries between work-groups inhibit (or encourage) collaboration and communication, so one department's performance is not optimized at the expense of other departments, or the overall organization.

How effectively the above elements of work are performed powerfully affects the performance of an organization and its work-groups and can create constructive or destructive conflict that frustrates and undermines high-performance. This can positively or negatively affect morale, levels of stress and conflict and the overall working conditions. The Execution data set is also a *window* into the underlying patterns-of-interaction (POI), context-of-interaction (COI), belief structure and repository-of-interaction (ROI) that are key elements of an organization's culture.

The scores on the radar graph in Figure 21 show the averaged responses of all populations at SciTech for the six elements of Execution using the BCI. The radar graph compares the scores of top managers to the scores of all other participants by population.[160] A score of 100 represents excellence. When the scores of top managers and others differ by less than 15 percent, they appear in black indicating that the scores are *aligned* and there is little or no difference in how the populations see this issue. When the difference between the scores of top managers and other populations is between 15 and 30 percent, the score appears in grey signifying that there is a *moderate misalignment* in how the populations see this issue. When the difference between the scores of top managers and other populations differs by more than 30 percent, the score appears in italics signifying that there is a *significant misalignment* between how top managers and the populations see this issue.

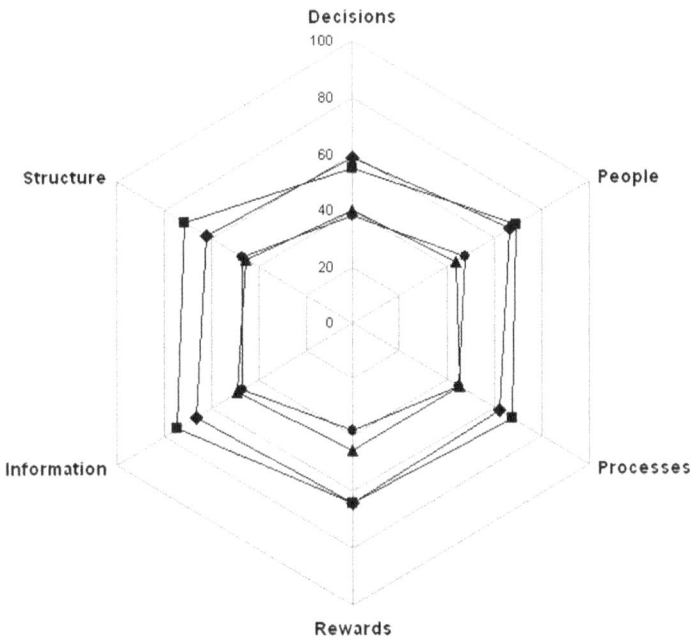

	DEC	PEO	PRO	REW	INF	STR
Top Manager ♦	58.8	66.0	62.0	63.8	66.0	62.0
Line Manager ■	55.0	69.0	67.0	63.8	74.0	71.0
Supervisor ▲	40.0	43.0	45.0	45.0	49.0	46.4
Staff ●	38.0	46.9	44.8	38.3	46.3	46.4

Figure 21

The analysis of the data shown in Figure 21 should begin with the two perspectives positioned at the top and bottom of the radar graph (Decisions and Rewards) which are the critical path of the Execution data set. These two perspectives are the key to creating alignment and stability in an organization. The Decisions and Rewards perspectives are high-leverage activities that powerfully shape and define the characteristics of the other four perspectives in the Execution data set, and an organization's overall performance. When an organization has a Strength in one (or both) of these areas signified by a High-High scoring pattern, it should be leveraged to improve the other four perspectives of the Execution data set and the performance of work-groups and the overall organization. When an organization Needs Development in one (or both) of these areas signified by a Low-Low scoring pattern, improvement in the areas of Decisions and Rewards will positively impact an organization's performance in the other four areas.

The data on the radar graph in Figure 21 shows a Low-Low scoring pattern for Decisions which probably indicates a critical path perspective that Needs Development because the scores of all four populations are clustered below 60%, with the scores of supervisors and staff members being the lowest scores. This indicates that all four populations have consensus that SciTech's decision-making process is "broken" and needs to be fixed. Qualitative data gathered in one-on-one interviews and focus groups confirm that there is a high level of frustration on the part of all employees in the areas described by Decisions. More specifically, decision-making activities in meetings and day-to-day activities lack a bias toward action, with even routine operational matters like standard procurements or changes to business processes being "studied to death." In much the same way, it takes an inordinate amount of time for top managers and line managers to come to consensus on even simple policies and procedures, and once they are finally issued the day-to-day decision-making of line managers and supervisors do not follow the content of these new directives. The consensus of all four populations about the need for improvement regarding SciTech's Decisions can be used to focus the organization's time and energy on creating and sustaining positive change in this critical path area.

Notice that the other critical path perspective in Figure 21, Rewards, also shows a Low-Low scoring pattern, indicating agreement among all four SciTech populations that this area Needs Development, with the scores of supervisors and staff members being the very lowest scores. It's important to remember that the activities associated with Rewards measured by the BCI are not about compensation, or the organization's compensation system as described in the Resources and Policies perspective of the Strategic View. Rather, this perspective evaluates the formal and informal messages sent to employees that reward the desired behaviors, and discourage behaviors that are misaligned with the formal and informal rules for how things are done in the SciTech organization.

Qualitative data gathered in one-on-one interviews and focus groups confirm that the activities associated with this perspective Need Development. For example, there are few consequences for performance (good or bad), even in cases such as managers and supervisors missing established goals, or not delivering on commitments. In addition, the day-to-day actions and interactions of top managers and line managers often violate SciTech's published core values and code of conduct. Also, the formally stated criteria for allocating resources and for advancement are not the way the informal "rules of the game" actually work.

Figure 22 shows the same data binned by work-group. Notice how Field Operations are the lowest scores – a scoring pattern that is seen throughout the SciTech data. This is important because the majority of SciTech's employees are members of this work-group, and the field is the primary place where SciTech's two enterprise-wide operations actually take place; e.g., mining operations and R&D. It is also the primary interface with customers where SciTech's products and services are actually delivered to customers. As shown previously in Figure 15, the Customer perspective is an organizational Strength for SciTech, with a High-High cluster of consensus around the importance of serving customers.

	DEC	PEO	PRO	REW	INF	STR
Top Manager	58.8	66.0	62.0	63.8	66.0	62.0
Business Administration	45.2	54.2	52.0	40.5	57.8	60.4
Business Development	36.1	46.9	49.1	*32.1*	60.6	56.6
Field Operations	35.4	42.1	42.6	36.6	45.9	45.1
Technical Assurance	66.8	68.3	62.9	65.4	68.9	65.4
Technical Services	38.6	52.3	52.0	46.5	50.8	48.3

Figure 22

The combination of the High-High Strength in the customer perspective, and the low scores of the Field Operations work-group, probably indicates that these managers, supervisors, and employees are striving to serve customers despite the ineffective organizational structures and systems within which they are forced to work. This is also reflected in the amount of organizational and psychological energy that is being squandered as indicated in Figures 36, 37, and 38 in Chapter 4, *Governance Issues and Financial Analysis*. Qualitative data gathered in one-on-one interviews and focus groups revealed that a lack of planning on the part of the Technical Services work-group who developed the proposals and project plans for R&D tests, and ineffective support from SciTech's Procurement and Technical Assurance work-groups were important underlying reasons why operations in the field were so problematic. Exploring the underlying causes of the low scores in the Field Operations work-group is probably a high leverage activity for determining

123

the common (systemic) causes of the organization's performance in the structures, systems, and culture.

Organizational Climate

The set of benchmarks described in this section enables assessors to evaluate the nature and characteristics of Organizational Climate. The benchmark criteria are based upon the principles taught by Edgar Schein, John Kotter, David Cooperrider, Terrence Deal and Allan Kennedy, Chris Argyris, Clotaire Rapaille, Alan Wilkins, Howell Baum, William Bridges, Ichak Adizes, Lawrence Miller, Rollo May, Anthony Storr, Arthur Koestler, numerous articles in the *Harvard Business Review*, and the Global Organization Design model developed by Elliot Jaques.[161] Figure 23 shows Organizational Climate as the "atmosphere" within which the Strategic View and Execution perspectives exist. It consists of the six perspectives listed below:

- Just Culture

- Management Philosophy

- Constructive Conflict

- Openness to Change

- Tradition

- Creativity

An assessor can "see" an organization from any one of these six perspectives, and while all six are important to building a high-performing organization and understanding an organization's culture, the two key elements are Just Culture and Management Philosophy because they are the critical path to creating organizational alignment and stability. The six perspectives of Organizational Climate map to the context-of-interaction (COI) term of the Breckenridge Equation described in Chapter 2, and provide a view of the organization from the human-performance perspective described in Chapter 1.

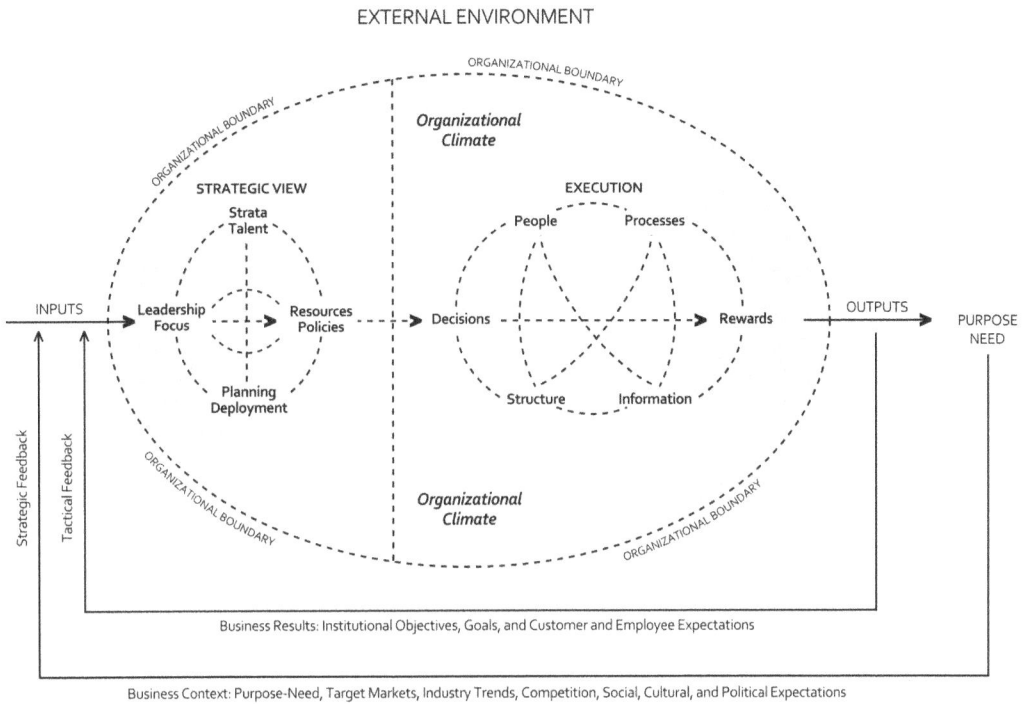

Figure 23

Let's define each of the six perspectives of Organizational Climate in more detail, beginning with the two critical path elements: Just Culture and Management Philosophy.

Just Culture: This perspective helps assessors evaluate the degree to which the organization analyzes the root causes of ineffective organizational performance in the structures, systems, and culture; e.g., managers don't blame individual employees for an organization's performance problems. It also indicates the size of the gap between the formal rules of the game for how things get done (Policies and Procedures) and the informal (unwritten) rules for how things "really" get done. The Just Culture perspective also evaluates whether managers are fair and objective, basing their evaluations on facts and quantitative data, not "politics" or personalities; whether managers and staff members trust the organization to do what it says; and whether people are free to present the unvarnished truth about organizational matters without fear of retribution.

Management Philosophy: This perspective focuses on the degree to which managers are held accountable for the outputs of those who report to them, and for creating and sustaining a team that collaborates and is capable of producing the desired outputs. It also indicates whether managers are held accountable for providing leadership to their team (getting them to move in the same direction), and for adding value to the work of their direct reports. The Management Philosophy perspective also evaluates the extent to which managers have the authority to veto the appointment of new people to their organization, and to decide the kinds of work assignments that their direct reports will carry out. It also indicates whether managers have the authority to conduct personal effectiveness appraisals of their direct reports; to reward the desired performance; and to initiate the removal of a direct report from their role in their organization.

Constructive Conflict: This perspective focuses on the degree to which people are encouraged to challenge the status quo about ineffective organizational structures, systems or ways of doing business; e.g., they can question the reasoning, assumptions, and attitudes that motivate the organization's decisions because the problem-solving process is a matter of public scrutiny. It also indicates the extent to which people participate in power alliances that accumulate power (budgetary resources, knowledge, space, equipment, etc.), and the extent to which they use these resources to oppose the intentions and goals of the larger organization. The Constructive Conflict perspective indicates whether the organization's communication style is open and direct (people go directly to people to discuss problems, rather than involving others and feeding the "grapevine"), and the extent to which managers value self-awareness and emotional intelligence as a key element of handling conflict constructively. It also indicates the degree to which people use their time and energy to do productive work, rather than squandering it on toxic inter-departmental conflicts.

Openness to Change: This perspective helps assessors evaluate the degree to which people openly embrace change that comes from customers and/or the external environment, and allow the organization's policies and decision-making to be influenced by this feedback and input (it's an open system). It also indicates whether managers encourage people to look for new, cutting-edge knowledge to add value to the organization; e.g., reading widely, participating in professional societies, etc. The Openness to Change perspective is an indicator of the extent to which the organization brings in "fresh blood" to stimulate change, innovation and improvement; the degree to which it is comfortable with ambiguity and/or uncertainty in operational matters; and the extent to which people solicit feedback from customers on how to improve, and then act on this information. Openness to Change creates a climate in which *people expect today to be different than yesterday.*

Tradition: This perspective focuses on the degree to which the organization uses its history and culture to teach employees how problems should (or should not) be handled, and to provide a rationale that helps employees identify with an organization's purpose and core values. Consequently, they tend to value a "seasoned" perspective from long-time employees rather than the "fresh" perspective that new employees bring. The Tradition perspective indicates whether the organization celebrates the important events and traditions (stories, heroes, etc.) that have shaped its identity, history, and culture. It also evaluates the extent to which managers use regular operations meetings and periodic events to build group identity (annual planning, team-building sessions, retreats, holiday gatherings, etc.). Tradition creates a climate in which *people expect today to be like yesterday*.

Creativity: This perspective helps assessors evaluate the degree to which the organization invests heavily in product development, creating intellectual property, and R&D activities, and whether people are energized by designing or innovating new products and services to meet the emerging customer needs. It also indicates whether people are encouraged to be creative in solving work-related problems, and whether the organization provides the resources for employees to develop and apply their creative abilities to their work (on-the-job training, classroom education, mentoring). The Creativity perspective also indicates whether people are encouraged to be unconventional, take risks, and use non-traditional approaches to problem-solving (creativity is viewed as an important part of the job), and whether people are encouraged to recognize and explore seemingly contradictory evidence and data that may nonetheless be true.

The organization's climate can powerfully affect the performance of work-groups by creating a constructive or destructive emotional tone and atmosphere which permeates the work-place. This can positively or negatively affect morale, levels of stress and conflict and the overall working conditions in work-groups and the overall organization. Organizational Climate is also a *window* into the underlying patterns-of-interaction (POI), belief structure and repository-of-interaction (ROI) that are key elements of an organization's culture.

The scores on the radar graph in Figure 24 show the averaged responses of all populations at SciTech for the six elements of Organizational Climate using the BCI. The radar graph compares the scores of top managers to the scores of all other participants by population.[162] A score of 100 represents excellence. When the scores of top managers and others differ by less than 15 percent, they appear in black indicating that the scores are *aligned* and there is little or no difference in how the populations see this issue. When the difference between the scores of top managers and other populations is between 15 and 30 percent, the score appears in grey signifying that there is a *moderate misalignment* in how the populations see this issue. When the difference between the scores of top managers and other populations differs by more than 30 percent, the score appears in italics signifying that there is a *significant misalignment* between how top managers and the populations see this issue.

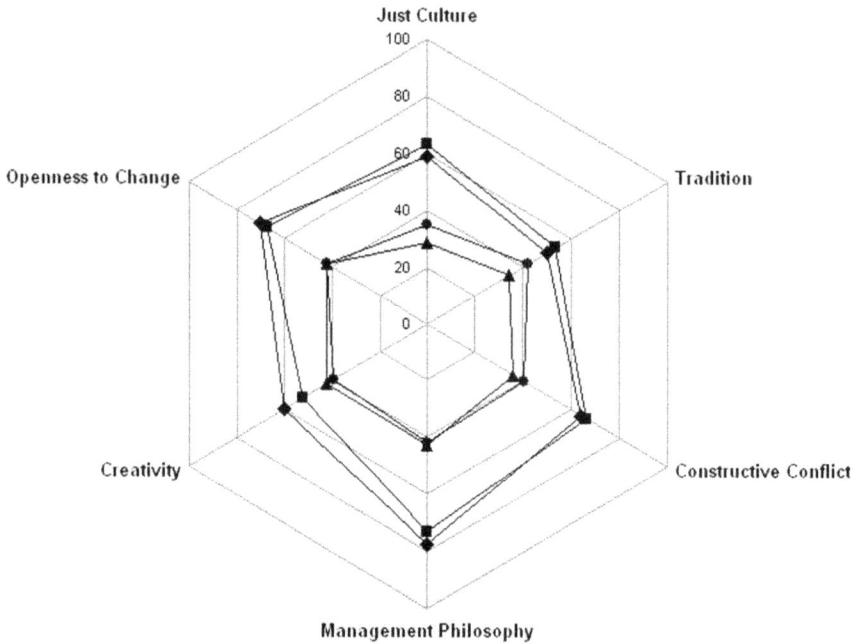

	JC	TR	CC	MP	CR	OC
Top Manager ◆	58.8	50.0	64.0	77.7	60.0	70.0
Line Manager ■	63.0	53.6	66.4	73.2	52.0	67.2
Supervisor ▲	*28.2*	33.7	36.0	*42.9*	41.7	41.9
Staff ●	35.0	42.1	40.4	*41.8*	39.3	41.9

Figure 24

The analysis of the data shown in Figure 24 should begin with the two perspectives positioned at the top and bottom of the radar graph (Just Culture and Management Philosophy) which are the critical path of the Organizational Climate data set. These two perspectives are the key to creating alignment and stability in an organization. The Just Culture and Management Philosophy perspectives are high-leverage activities that powerfully shape and define the characteristics of the other four perspectives of the Organizational Climate data set, and an organization's overall performance. When an organization has a Strength in one (or both) of these areas signified by a High-High scoring pattern, it should be leveraged to improve the other four perspectives of the Organizational Climate radar and the performance of work-groups and the overall organization. When an organization Needs Development in one (or both) of these areas signified by a Low-Low scoring pattern, improvement in the areas of Just Culture and Management Philosophy will positively impact an organization's performance in the other four areas.

The data on the radar graph in Figure 24 shows a Low-Low scoring pattern for Just Culture, which is one of the most problematic sets of scores in the entire SciTech data set. All four populations agree that the activities associated with a Just Culture Need Development, with the scores of top managers and line managers clustering around 60% and the scores of supervisors and staff members clustering around 25-30 points lower. In addition, notice how the scores of supervisors for Just Culture appear in italics because they are significantly misaligned with top managers, which probably has a negative effect on the attitudes and morale of their direct reports through the behaviors they model, the things they reward (and don't reward), and the emotional resonances that the supervisor's actions and interactions set up within their work-group. Qualitative data gathered in one-on-one interviews and focus groups confirm that individual supervisors and staff members are blamed for performance problems that are caused by ineffective organizational structures and systems, and they fear retribution for bringing these matters to the attention of SciTech managers. In addition, qualitative data indicate that there is a significant gap between the formally espoused rules for how things get done in the organization, and the way things "really" get done. The consensus of all four populations about the need for improvement regarding a Just Culture can be used to focus the organization's time and energy on creating and sustaining positive change in this critical path area.

The data on the radar graph in Figure 24 shows a High-Low scoring pattern for Management Philosophy, where top managers' and line managers' scores are clustered at just under 80% and the scores of supervisors and staff members are clustered almost 40 points lower in italics, revealing a significant misalignment between these populations. This is the largest spread of all of SciTech's scores. This may indicate that top managers have Blind Spots about the extent to which managers and supervisors actually have accountability and authority in the way it is defined by the Management Philosophy perspective. Qualitative data gathered in one-on-one interviews and focus groups at SciTech confirm that people who are low performers and who create destructive conflict throughout the organization are not held accountable. More specifically, supervisors do not have the kind of authority defined by the Management Philosophy perspective where they can: a) conduct performance appraisals of direct reports that reward the desired behaviors and discourage behaviors that are misaligned with SciTech's core values, goals, and objectives, and b) initiate the removal of a direct report from their role in the work-group. As mentioned previously, this High-Low scoring pattern is consistent with much of the data gathered at SciTech, which supports the view that top managers and middle managers have a number of Blind Spots about various aspects of their own performance, which may include that there is a systemic problem with ineffective communication down through the SciTech line organization.

Figure 25 shows the same data binned by work-group. Notice how the scores for almost all work-groups are low and misaligned across most of the six perspectives, including significantly misaligned scores in italics in the Management Philosophy perspective. The notable exception is the Technical Assurance work-group – a positive scoring pattern trend that has appeared throughout SciTech's BCI data sample.

	JC	TR	CC	MP	CR	OC
Top Manager	58.8	50.0	64.0	77.7	60.0	70.0
Business Administration	37.3	47.3	46.2	*38.7*	54.2	44.0
Business Development	37.9	36.0	48.0	51.9	34.3	52.6
Field Operations	33.7	41.6	39.1	*46.4*	40.9	41.4
Technical Assurance	68.4	60.6	69.4	71.9	58.0	61.1
Technical Services	39.6	36.2	44.3	*47.3*	35.0	49.0

Figure 25

Also notice the Low-Low scoring pattern in the area of Tradition where all four populations agree that the activities associated with this perspective Need Development. Qualitative data gathered in one-on-one interviews and focus groups at SciTech confirm that seniority, years of service, and a "seasoned" perspective from long-time employees are valued much more highly than the "fresh" perspective that new employees bring to an organization. In addition, SciTech has a rich tradition and history of making contributions since its inception that are not celebrated or used to teach employees how problems should (or should not) be handled, nor are they used to build group identity. Having consensus around the fact that Tradition Needs Development can help SciTech mobilize and focus the time and energy of its employees at all organizational levels.

Four Ways of Working

In Chapter 2 we described how assessors can learn to "see" organizations through the four interdependent lenses of the Four Ways of Working. The four perspectives of the Four Ways of Working map to the context-of-interaction (COI) term of the Breckenridge Equation described in Chapter 2, and provide a view of the organization from both the human-performance perspective, and the structures-and-systems perspective as described in Chapter 1. Let's briefly review each of the four perspectives.

- Type 1 (Production) focuses on *execution* and *what* gets done in an organization. When an organization manifests the Type 1 (Production) way of working, they believe that decisive actions, practical solutions to problems, and a short-term focus on clear, tangible goals will result in improved performance. They have a take-charge attitude, are forceful and direct in getting things done, making decisions and get directly involved in day-to-day operations, focusing on *implementing* the organization's goals and objectives through the teams and individuals in organizational units.

- Type 2 (Connection) focuses on *teambuilding* and *why* things get done in an organization. When an organization manifests the Type 2 (Connection) way of working, they believe that attunement to the external environment; innovation and radical change, exploring options and new ideas, and engaging with and influencing people to work together and collaborate will result in improved performance. They build alliances and cultivate relationships with people *outside* the organization (the public, interest groups, unions, media, and government agencies), and *inside* the organization where managers and staff members are encouraged to align their efforts with the organizational structures and systems in order to achieve the organization's purpose, goals, and objectives.

- Type 3 (Direction) focuses on *leadership* and *how* (that) things get done in an organization. When an organization manifests the Type 3 (Direction) way of working, they believe that defining a long-term direction, with strategic plans, goals and objectives, and creating and maintaining order and efficiency through structures and systems will result in improved performance. Using a quantitative, data-driven, analytical approach to performance, the organization's strategic goals are deployed and monitored through operations plans, goals, and budgets that direct the week-to-week and month-to-month operations of teams and individuals in organizational units to ensure that those goals and objectives are achieved.

- Type 4 (Integration) focuses on *analysis* and *who* gets things done in the organization. When an organization manifests the Type 4 (Integration) way of working, they believe that building the organization's knowledge-base and capabilities, attracting top talent and supporting and encouraging individual contributors, and analyzing how concepts, ideas, and underlying organizational patterns relate to each other will result in improved performance. They help achieve the organization's goals and objectives through inner vision, inspiration, and by integrating the knowledge-base and competencies of human performers with the organization's structures and systems to get the desired results.

Every organization and its work-groups have all Four Ways of Working, but they almost always have a stronger preference for one (or possibly two) of the Four Ways of Working, and rarely does an organization have an equally strong preference for them all. Ideally, a work-group or functional unit should be adaptable enough to refocus their preferences from one combination of the four ways to another depending on the forces and pressures from the external environment and internal pressures and demands. But most times this does not happen because in many organizational functions, the Four Ways of Working reach a state-of-equilibrium that tends to be *imbalanced* in one direction, often at the expense of other seemingly contradictory (but much needed) work practices and beliefs. In other words, they come to "see" some ways of working as more reliable or effective than others through the See-Do-Get Process and then they dismiss other ways of accomplishing goals and improving performance. Figure 26 shows the interrelationship between all Four Ways of Working as a model that assessors can use to "see" invisible aspects of an organization's culture.

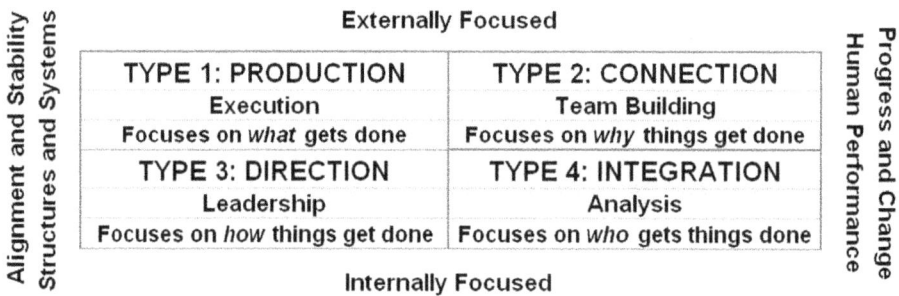

	Externally Focused	
TYPE 1: PRODUCTION Execution Focuses on *what* gets done	**TYPE 2: CONNECTION** Team Building Focuses on *why* things get done	
TYPE 3: DIRECTION Leadership Focuses on *how* things get done	**TYPE 4: INTEGRATION** Analysis Focuses on *who* gets things done	
	Internally Focused	

Left axis: Alignment and Stability / Structures and Systems
Right axis: Progress and Change / Human Performance

Figure 26

Using qualitative data gathered from interviews; on-site observations of business processes and work practices; and quantitative data from the BCI, assessors will begin to see patterns-of-interaction emerge as they analyze and characterize day-to-day operations. Here are some key ways to understand the four quadrants shown above and how the four quadrants relate to each other and might manifest themselves at the organizational and work-group levels.

- *Top Half of the Graph*: Type 1 (Production) and Type 2 (Connection) are externally focused toward the external environment, with a *primary* focus on serving customers as the reason for which an organization exists, and a *secondary* focus on the organization's internal operations.

- *Bottom Half of the Graph*: Type 3 (Direction) and Type 4 (Integration) are internally focused toward the organization's operations, with a *primary* focus on internal operations, and a *secondary* focus on serving customers as the reason for which an organization exists.

- *Left Side of the Graph*: Type 1 (Production) and Type 3 (Direction) tend to see an organization as a mechanistic configuration of structures and systems, with a focus on alignment and stability in both strategic and tactical operations.

- *Right Side of the Graph*: Type 2 (Connection) and Type 4 (Integration) tend to see an organization as an organic network of human performers, with a focus on change and progress at both strategic and tactical levels.

- *Compensatory Opposites*: Type 1 (Production) and Type 4 (Integration) meet only at the center of the graph and are paradoxical opposites that balance each other in a compensatory way, and hold the greatest potential for deep change and growth because they exist in an Essential Tension that drives an organization toward a more well-rounded approach to doing business.

- *Compensatory Opposites*: Type 2 (Connection) and Type 3 (Direction) meet only at the center of the graph and are paradoxical opposites that balance each other in a compensatory way, and hold the greatest potential for deep change and growth because they exist in an Essential Tension that drives an organization toward a more well-rounded approach to doing business.

The left side of Figure 26 tends to be characterized by a culture of *alignment and stability* where people tend to view an organization as a mechanical configuration of structures and systems, which maps to the critical path perspectives on the Strategic View, Execution, and Organizational Climate radar graphs.

- Leadership Focus

- Resources and Policies

- Decisions

- Rewards

- Just Culture

- Management Philosophy

A culture of *alignment* and *stability* allows an organization to act in concert in the face of threat or opportunity. Alignment and stability are key elements of achieving high-performance and are what Jim Collins refers to as "Preserve the Core."[163] This creates high levels of motivation in employees around the organizations core ideology (purpose and core values) and goals. Cultures that are typified by high levels of alignment enable people to *internalize* the organization's direction and core ideology and to provide the structures and systems needed to achieve excellence, without a reliance on the stifling effects of a formal bureaucracy. Aligned cultures can also become too inwardly focused and may lose touch with the changing forces and demands of the external environment. They can also become too focused on the left side of Figure 26; e.g., Type 1 (Production) and Type 3 (Direction).

The right side of Figure 26 is characterized by a culture of *progress and change* where people tend to view the organization as an organic configuration of human performers, which maps to the following perspectives on the Strategic View, Execution, and Organizational Climate radar graphs.

- Business Results

- Business Context

- Information

- Openness to Change

- Creativity

- Constructive Conflict

A culture of *progress* and *change* allows an organization to adapt in the face of threat or opportunity. Progress and change are key elements of achieving high-performance and are what Jim Collins refers to as "Stimulate Progress."[164] In cultures that are typified by progress and change, structures, systems, and cultural norms *morph* to fit the forces and pressures of the external environment. They are created and maintained by top managers who are capable of rapid decision-making, execution of non-traditional strategies, and the ability to redesign (or bypass) formal structures and systems in order to meet the challenges posed by a highly competitive world. Cultures of progress and change can (and sometimes do) become too focused on the right side of Figure 26; e.g., Type 2 (Connection) and Type 4 (Integration).

All Four Ways of Working are required to have an effective organization, but in most organizations the four quadrants reach a state-of-equilibrium that tends to be *imbalanced* in one direction, often at the expense of other seemingly contradictory (but needed) elements. For example, an organization can be so overly focused on external issues of market segments, customer needs and the dynamics of social interaction within the organization (Type 2 Connection) that they under focus on setting organizational direction and building the structures and systems needed to service their customers (Type 3 Direction). The less developed of the Four Ways of Working almost always exist somewhere in the organization, but they are *eclipsed* from the day-to-day reality of operations and are either undeveloped or not seen as viable ways of working. In some organizations, they are marginalized, dismissed, demonized, and consciously repressed – pushed far below the surface of organizational consciousness, so that even the thought of using them as a valid approach to solving problems becomes undiscussible.[165]

High-performing organizations have learned to live in the Essential Tension between all Four Ways of Working and do not seek a "balance" between things like stability and change – rather they relentlessly pursue *both* change *and* stability. While the four quadrants are opposing ways of seeing the world and improving organizational performance, they actually coordinate, support, and complement each other in a synergistic way. The key is to abandon any notion of "balancing" different perspectives like Type 1 Production and Type 3 Direction, and to relentlessly pursue excellence in both. So the most critical piece of the high-performance puzzle is for an organization to learn to: a) relentlessly pursue progress and change, *and at the same time*, b) maintain alignment and stability around their core ideology (purpose and core values). In other words, high-performing organizations strive to develop all Four Ways of Working and are adaptable enough to focus (or defocus) on specific quadrants as the forces and pressures from the external environment change. This enables them to *anticipate* and *adapt* to changes in the external environment, enabling them to obtain (and sustain) high levels of financial and non-financial performance.

The scores shown on the chart in Figure 27 are the averaged responses of all managers and supervisors at SciTech for the quadrants of the Four Ways of

Working using the BCI.[166] A score of 100 represents excellence. Often, the highest score is an indication of an organization's dominant way of working which is powerfully shaped and defined by the working style of the responsible managers and the emotional resonance that they set up in their organization or work-group. The key to high-performance is to have the ability to move seamlessly between all Four Ways of Working as the external forces and pressures of the external environment and the internal demands of day-to-day operations morph over time.

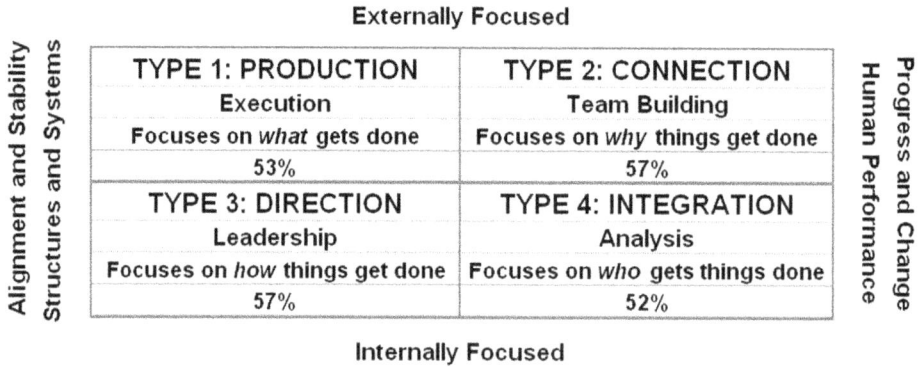

Externally Focused

	TYPE 1: PRODUCTION	TYPE 2: CONNECTION	
Alignment and Stability / Structures and Systems	Execution Focuses on *what* gets done 53%	Team Building Focuses on *why* things get done 57%	Progress and Change / Human Performance
	TYPE 3: DIRECTION	TYPE 4: INTEGRATION	
	Leadership Focuses on *how* things get done 57%	Analysis Focuses on *who* gets things done 52%	

Internally Focused

Figure 27

The scores shown on the chart in Figure 28 show the averaged responses of all managers and supervisors for the Four Ways of Working binned by work-group. When the scores of top managers and other managers and supervisors differ by less than 15 percent, they appear in black indicating that the scores are *aligned* and there is little or no difference in how the populations see this issue. When the difference between the scores of top managers and other managers and supervisors is between 15 and 30 percent, the score appears in grey signifying that there is a *moderate misalignment* in how the populations see this issue. When the difference between the scores of top managers and other managers and supervisors differs by more than 30 percent, the score appears in italics signifying that there is a *significant misalignment* between how top managers and the populations see this issue.

	TYPE 1	TYPE 2	TYPE 3	TYPE 4
Top Manager	63.0	61.3	64.5	58.0
Business Administration	42.9	57.5	35.0	45.5
Business Development	31.4	32.5	43.8	23.6
Field Operations	46.5	56.9	57.9	51.9
Technical Assurance	69.3	66.3	72.5	64.5
Technical Services	41.2	45.2	40.9	42.0

Figure 28

Notice that almost all of the scores are at or below the 60% level, signifying that all Four Ways of Working probably Need Development, with some work-groups showing lower scores and moderate misalignment – most notably the Business Development group's scores are consistently misaligned with the scores of top managers. There is solid agreement that the activities associated with Type 1 and Type 3 are the most problematic and since these are the functions that create alignment and stability in organizations like SciTech, they are probably the two areas that the organization should begin with. In addition, the alignment of scores for Type 2 combined with the low scores of the Business Development group probably makes Type 2 another area of Low-Low consensus that could be leveraged to drive organizational improvement. The scoring pattern for Type 2 is consistent with the High-High scoring pattern for customers in Figure 15 (Focus on Key Stakeholders).

Emotional Messages

In this section, assessors will learn to "see" conflict between managers and staff members as underlying patterns-of-interaction that can frustrate and undermine effective performance and morale. This includes one-on-one conflict between individuals, and conflicts between small-groups of 2s, 3s, and 4s which are the building blocks of organizational culture.

The See-Do-Get Process described in Chapter 2 is a powerful way of explaining how our knowledge and beliefs are shaped by our experience, background, education, disciplinary paradigm, and our personality. We see the world a certain way and specific behaviors and emotions naturally flow from that worldview because we believe that it is "reality." When we act, people read our body language and respond to the message they see in us. Their responses reinforce how we see them. We see, we do, we get. Because each of us learns to see the "reality" of life differently through the See-Do-Get Process, conflict in relationships is inevitable, so the question is not, do people experience conflict in personal and professional relationships, but rather to what extent is their conflict *constructive* or *destructive*. It's ironic – it's the same world out there, but so often people see it very differently.

After 20 years of research on the relationships of thousands of couples, John Gottman discovered four *destructive* emotional messages that people convey to each other through body language, tone of voice, and word choice. The emotional messages are criticism, contempt, defensiveness, and stonewalling.[167] These same messages are used in the workplace and manifest themselves in e-mails, work-group meetings, small-group meetings, power struggles between Border Guards, project reviews, one-on-one interactions, passing remarks to others, indirect communication where people vent about real or perceived wrongs done to them by group members, and other day-to-day interactions.[168] The four emotional messages are a *window* into the destructive conflict caused by ineffective autopilot operations, the Red Flags, and Invisible Bureaucracy as shown on the Interaction Map and different ways of "seeing" that emerge from our personality. Over time, conflicts between managers and staff members form definable patterns-of-interaction (POI) that are clusters of habitual behaviors and emotional messages that coworkers send to each other.

The list below shows the eight emotional messages, with four being destructive (deficiency-driven) as defined by Gottman, and four being constructive (growth-motivated) as defined by the Breckenridge Institute.

Destructive (Deficiency-Driven)	Constructive (Growth-Motivated)
Criticism	Empathy
Contempt	Respect
Defensiveness	Trust
Stonewalling	Direct Contact

Each of the destructive emotional messages along with its constructive counterpart is described in detail below.

Criticism: Criticism is the act of passing judgment on the merits of a person, object, activity or critiquing and faultfinding. Criticism is present in an interaction when people analyze others' personality, character and philosophy of life in a disapproving manner. Rather than focusing on the specific behaviors that caused the situation at hand, Gottman describes how people who use criticism tend to comment on general themes using statements like "You're the type of person who…."[169] In addition, criticism is evident when people focus on *who* is at fault rather than describing which actions and interactions are ineffective. They tend to use generalizations like "you never" or "you always" rather than focusing on the specific behaviors and processes that caused the conflict and they do not show empathy by understanding others' positions. When expressing criticism has become an autopilot pattern-of-interaction (POI), people: a) continue criticizing others despite the fact that it escalates the level of destructive conflict, b) find it increasingly difficult to back down and stop criticizing once conflict has started, and c) find it more and more difficult to express constructive emotional messages even when objective evidence would support doing so.

Empathy: Empathy is present in an interaction when we identify with (and understand) another person's situation, context, emotions, concerns, thoughts, motives, and limitations. We can empathize with someone else to the point that we vicariously experience many of the same emotions that they do and sometimes even respond physically, as when we spontaneously give someone who is mourning a hug or put a hand on their shoulder in order to comfort them. Empathy counteracts the destructive effects of criticism because it seeks to understand the perspective of the other person – to see the world the way they see it and experience what they experience. When expressing empathy has become an autopilot pattern-of-interaction (POI), people: a) listen empathically, b) seek to understand the other person's frame of reference, worldview, and how they have learned to see the world through the See-Do-Get Process, c) offer advice only when asked or prompted to do so, and d) focus on the specific behaviors that are involved in the situation rather than giving commentary on (or critique about) the other's personality, character, or philosophy of life.[170]

Contempt: We show contempt when we view someone as being despised, disdained, worthless, or vile. Contempt is present in an interaction when people intentionally take their anger out on others because they are disgusted with them and they purposely insult others because they have lost respect for them.[171] In addition, they do not show respect for others' views, opinions, and positions and they try to turn the tables on others to retaliate for how they have been offended. When we are contemptuous we exhibit facial expressions that indicate that we have negative thoughts running through our minds during the conflict, thus sending the emotional message that we see the other person as being repulsive, stupid, disgusting, incompetent, etc. When we are contemptuous of another, we tend to disconfirm, rather than confirm (or even reject) the value and worth of another individual as a person.[172] When expressing contempt has become an autopilot pattern-of-interaction (POI), people: a) continue showing contempt toward others despite the fact that it escalates the level of destructive conflict, b) find it increasingly difficult to back down and stop being contemptuous once conflict has started, and c) find it more and more difficult to express constructive emotional messages even when objective evidence would support doing so.

Respect: Respect is when we esteem another person and acknowledge their worth, value, capabilities, qualities, traits, character, abilities, and natural talents. We give deference to people we respect in the sense of showing them proper courtesy and acceptance and we confirm (rather than disconfirm) the person they present themselves to be.[173] Respect counteracts the destructive effects of contempt because it communicates a sense of honor, privilege, deference, and esteem to the other person. When expressing respect has become an autopilot pattern-of-interaction (POI), people: a) try to support one another rather than trying to turn the tables on each other to retaliate, b) exhibit facial expressions that communicate an emotional message of admiration, recognition, regard, and interest in what the other person is saying or trying to communicate non-verbally, c) grow in self-awareness as a result of working-through issues in the relationship, and d) learn from how the other person sees themselves, others, and the world around them.

Defensive: Being defensive is when people are excessively concerned about guarding against the real (or perceived) embarrassment and threat of having their shortcomings, inadequacies, failures, mistakes, or Blind Spots revealed by others. Being defensive is often caused by a lack of self-esteem and a lack of trust in ourselves, others, and the world. Defensiveness is present in an interaction when people try to make excuses when others complain about something they have done; they deny their responsibility for the things that caused the conflict and develop counter arguments to others' complaints about them that put the blame back on others; e.g., "Yes-But-You…."[174] They also try to second-guess others' true feelings and motives; e.g., "You did that because you really think…" and rarely trust others to do what is appropriate and fair. When being defensive has become an autopilot pattern-of-interaction (POI), people: a) continue being defensive with others despite the fact that it escalates the level of destructive conflict, b) find it increasingly difficult to back down and stop their defensiveness once conflict has started, and c) find it more and more difficult to express constructive emotional messages even when objective evidence would support doing so.

Trust: Trust is when we have confidence in (and can rely on) another person to deal with us honestly, fairly, with integrity, and to have our best interest in mind. People who encourage trust in others often exhibit six key characteristics, they: speak the unvarnished truth; have integrity by doing what they say (their deeds follow their words); use power fairly and without self-interest; demonstrate authentic competency in their personal and professional lives; model ethics and values even in difficult situations where it would be in their best interest to do otherwise; see us for who we really are.[175] Trust counteracts the destructive effects of defensiveness because there is no need to defend ourselves against people who demonstrate the six characteristics of trust over time. When expressing trust has become an autopilot pattern-of-interaction (POI), people: a) accept personal responsibility for their mistakes, shortcomings, and failures, b) don't blame others for problems and situations they have created, c) don't try to second-guess others true feelings and motives as a way of excusing their own behavior, and d) generally trust others to do what is appropriate and fair in a given situation.

Stonewalling: When people stonewall, they intentionally block, stall, resist, obstruct, hinder, or passively undermine decisions, actions, or interactions while trying to appear that they are not doing so. Stonewalling is present in an interaction when people show their disapproval with others by just walking away, leaving the room, or by letting others talk on-and-on and just "tuning out" what they are saying.[176] They try not to show any reaction at all, even though they know that others are upset with them. When people stonewall others, they just bite their tongue rather than respond to others' complaints about them, and they do not communicate directly and openly about situations so many things are left unsaid and many issues remain unsolved. When stonewalling has become an autopilot pattern-of-interaction (POI), people: a) continue stonewalling others despite the fact that it escalates the level of destructive conflict, b) find it increasingly difficult to stop stonewalling and communicate directly once conflict has started, and c) find it more and more difficult to express constructive emotional messages even when objective evidence would support doing so.

Direct Contact: Direct contact is when people are straightforward, frank, candid, open, and transparent about dealing with a situation or interaction that is frustrating and undermining the relationship. Rather than defer an open discussion with another person (even if it involves conflict), people who practice direct contact like to get things out on the table, especially in close relationships. Direct contact counteracts the destructive effects of stonewalling because it acknowledges the reality of the situation and its effect on the other person and the importance of dealing with problematic situations as quickly as possible. When direct contact has become an autopilot pattern-of-interaction (POI), people: a) make eye contact in face-to-face discussions and situations that frustrate and undermine the relationship, b) focus on (and tune into) what others are trying to say and communicate in order to move beyond the impasse, c) show honest reactions and give frank feedback to others to communicate their perspective, and d) do not leave issues unsettled or things unsaid lest they accumulate, fester, and escalate destructive conflict over time.

Long-Term Effects of Destructive Conflict: There are a number of long-term effects of *destructive* conflict in organizations. Managers and staff members remain unchanged and do not grow professionally or personally, and sometimes things get worse – much worse. In addition, decision-making is often ineffective and sometimes decisions are not made at all because people evoke explicit or implicit rules to prevent an organization or work-group from working through the impasse, which is a form of Organizational Entrapment.[177] Enormous amounts of time and energy are squandered on destructive conflict (precious resources that become unavailable to achieve an organization's goals and objectives), and the morale and self-esteem of managers and staff members are frustrated and undermined. Over time, destructive conflict creates division and polarization between managers and staff members who tend to become galvanized into conflicting and competing coalitions of 2s, 3s, and 4s.

Long-Term Effects of Constructive Conflict. When the conflict in an organization is *constructive*, people are positively changed, they grow professionally and personally and decision-making becomes action-oriented and highly effective. In addition, an organization develops confidence and a track record for facing and moving past the most problematic situations "as a group" which builds teamwork, group learning, and group identity. The time and energy of managers and staff members are focused on achieving an organization's goals, rather than being derailed by destructive patterns-of-interaction. Consequently, involvement, morale, and the self-esteem of managers and staff members are increased because their work becomes part of the solution to life's issues, rather than one more problem to face. Managers and staff members develop positive synergy in units of 2s, 3s, and 4s by using constructive conflict to build a common vision, unity, identity, and direction.

The scores on the radar graph in Figure 29 show the averaged responses of all populations at SciTech for the four elements of the Emotional Messages using the BCI. The radar graph compares the scores of top managers to the scores of all other participants by population.[178] It's important to note that the <u>higher</u> the score shown the more prevalent this destructive emotional message is in SciTech's interactions. Unlike any other radar graph described thus far, a higher score is worse, not better. When the scores of top managers and others differ by less than 15 percent, they appear in black indicating that the scores are *aligned* and there is little or no difference in how the populations see this issue. When the difference between the scores of top managers and other populations is between 15 and 30 percent, the score appears in grey signifying that there is a *moderate misalignment* in how the populations see this issue. When the difference between the scores of top managers and other populations differs by more than 30 percent, the score appears in italics signifying that there is a *significant misalignment* between how top managers and the populations see this issue. The four perspectives of the radar shown in Figure 29 map to the context-of-interaction (COI) term of the Breckenridge Equation described in Chapter 2, and provide a view of an organization from the human-performance perspective described in Chapter 1.

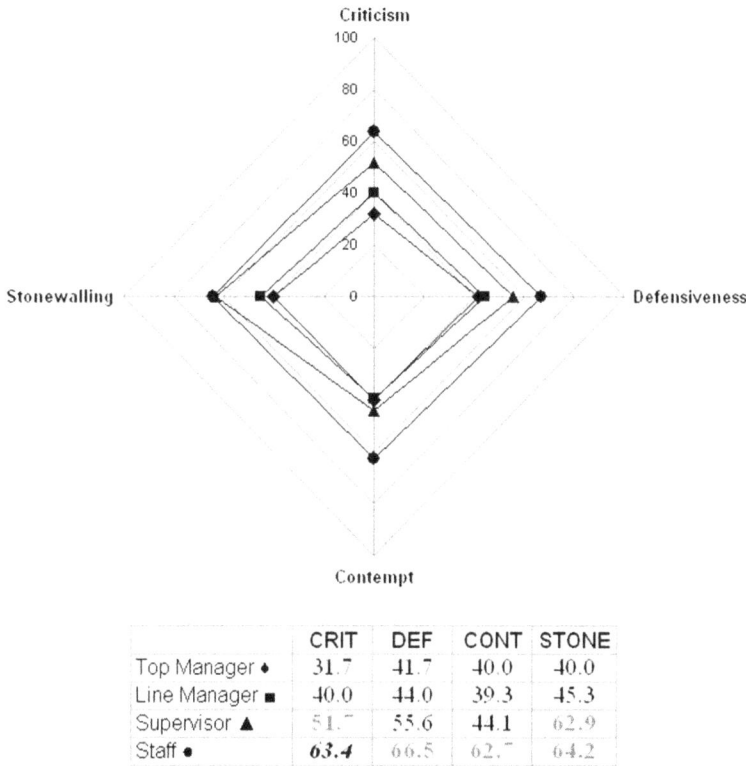

	CRIT	DEF	CONT	STONE
Top Manager ♦	31.7	41.7	40.0	40.0
Line Manager ■	40.0	44.0	39.3	45.3
Supervisor ▲	51.7	55.6	44.1	62.9
Staff ●	*63.4*	66.5	62.7	64.2

Figure 29

The analysis of the data shown in Figure 29 should begin with the two perspectives positioned at the top and bottom of the radar graph (Criticism and Contempt) which Gottman's research has shown are the most serious and damaging of the destructive emotional messages. The Criticism and Contempt perspectives powerfully shape and define the characteristics of the other two perspectives in this data set, and the overall climate and culture in organizations. When an organization has a Strength in one (or both) of these areas signified by a Low-Low scoring pattern, it should be leveraged to improve the other two perspectives and the performance of work-groups and the overall organization. When an organization Needs Development in one (or both) of these areas signified by a High-High scoring pattern, improvement in the areas of Criticism and Contempt will positively impact the organizational climate in the other two areas.

The pattern of low scores for supervisors and staff members shown in Figure 29 is reflected throughout the BCI data discussed thus far. Notice that the overall scores of staff members are the highest, indicating the most pronounced presence of destructive emotional messages, with Defensiveness being the highest score. Notice that the score for Criticism appears in italics, indicating a significant misalignment between top managers and staff members; e.g., almost a 32-point difference. As reflected in other BCI data to this point, the overall scores of top managers and line managers are better than the rest of the organization, indicating that a culture of negativity may be present from the supervisor level down to staff members.

Figure 30 shows the same data binned by work-group. Notice how the scores for the Field Operations work-group are high (indicating more destructive conflict) and the scores for Criticism and Defensiveness appear in italics (indicting a significant misalignment with top managers). The scores for Business Administration are also high and show a fair degree of misalignment with top managers – a trend that is revealed throughout the scoring patterns of the BCI data for this work-group.

	CRIT	DEF	CONT	STONE
Top Manager	31.7	41.7	40.0	40.0
Business Administration	60.3	65.5	51.8	63.6
Business Development	42.9	45.7	46.7	54.3
Field Operations	*67.0*	*73.2*	68.8	69.9
Technical Assurance	37.1	40.0	26.9	38.3
Technical Services	29.0	26.7	24.2	29.6

Figure 30

Shifting the ratio from destructive to constructive by using the emotional messages of empathy, respect, trust, and direct contact is the most effective way to build *trust* between coworkers. In most situations, managers and staff members can begin to shift the overall balance of the repository-of-interaction (ROI) from destructive to constructive using the four *constructive* emotional messages shown above. Remember that the level of *rigidity* with which a person holds to their way of seeing the world is often directly proportional to their tendency to practice *either-or-thinking*, rather than *both-and-thinking*. In fact, the crucial test of how solidified and fixated the patterns-of-interaction are in this relationship is to begin using the constructive messages to shift the distribution in the repository-of-interaction to reflect the 80-20 Rule, and to evaluate the degree to which these conscious attempts are *derailed* by the destructive forces in the organization.

Organizational Trust Index

The set of benchmarks described in this section enables assessors to evaluate the level of trust in an organization. The degree to which managers or staff members either *trust* the structures, systems, and culture of the organization they work in, or *fear* them, is a *window* into the underlying patterns that constitute an organization's culture. The Organizational Trust Index™ is an indicator of the degree to which an organization's culture is *driven by fear* or *motivated by trust*. The Organizational Trust Index quantitatively characterizes what people have come to believe about an organization with regard to the six perspectives listed below.

- Truth

- Integrity

- Power

- Competency

- Values

- Recognition

An assessor can "see" an organization from any one of these six perspectives, and while all six are important to building a high-performing organization and understanding an organization's culture, the two key elements are Truth and Integrity because they are the critical path to creating organizational alignment and stability. The six perspectives of the Organizational Trust Index are a key link between the day-to-day reality of Organizational Climate shown in Figure 31, and the tacit, unquestioned, taken-for-granted assumptions and beliefs of organizational culture. The six perspectives also map to the context-of-interaction (COI) term of the Breckenridge Equation described in Chapter 2, and provide a view of an organization from the human-performance perspective described in Chapter 1.

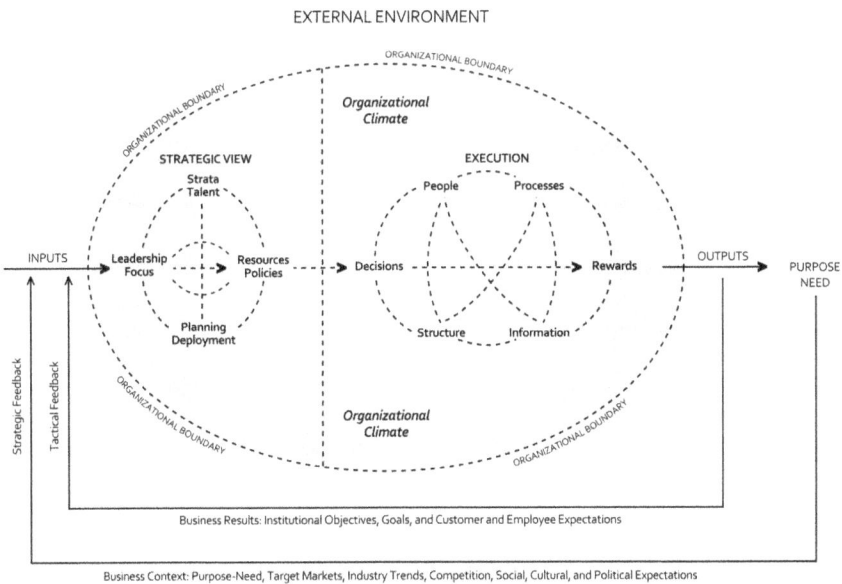

Figure 31

Let's define what each of the six perspectives of the Organizational Trust Index means in more detail, beginning with the two critical path elements: Truth and Integrity.

- *Truth*: An organization has a deep commitment to establishing "organizational truth" (what's really going on in the organization), so employees are free to present the unvarnished truth about organizational matters and question the reasoning, assumptions, and attitudes that motivate the organization's decisions.

- *Integrity*: An organization has integrity (it does what it says), it practices "fair process" (it's fair and objective) and it bases its evaluations of people and issues on facts and quantitative data, not "politics" and personalities.

- *Power*: Managers in an organization use their power fairly and effectively to achieve the organization's purpose and goals and to positively influence people (not out of self-interest).

- *Competency*: An organization is competent to overcome the challenges it faces and it makes decisions that will ensure the achievement of its strategic and tactical goals (this company knows what it's doing).

- *Values*: An organization has a well-defined set of core values that it communicates to all employees, that it authentically lives by (even in difficult situations), and that are consistent with the personal values of managers and staff members.

- *Recognition*: An organization recognizes (notices) the contributions that managers and staff members make in the workplace and confirms their own views about their professional abilities. Consequently, people believe that they have a future in the company.

Let's explore the issue of organizational trust in more detail. Trust is the foundation of all human interactions, and the cornerstone upon which high-performing organizational cultures are built. The Organizational Trust Index was developed by the Breckenridge Institute as a method for measuring the level of trust in an organization and the degree to which an organization's culture is either *motivated* by trust or *driven* by fear. Managers have two choices. They can either consciously build organizational trust as the foundation of an Intended Culture, or they can allow day-to-day issues, ineffective communication, and misperception to erode trust and develop an Unintended Culture that is based on fear. The six perspectives of the Organizational Trust Index can help managers evaluate the level of trust in their organization, determine the degree to which their culture is either *motivated* by trust or *driven* by fear, and provide a step-by-step process for consciously building a culture that is based on trust.

Trust is often thought of in terms of individual people and one-on-one relationships, for example we trust our coworkers, direct reports, or our boss – most notably, Stephen M.R. Covey's book, *The Speed of Trust.*[179] Unlike trusting individuals, the interdependent actions and interactions of structures, systems, and culture can reach a level of combinatorial complexity where the "system" takes on a life of its own and almost no one can change it. As one manager remarked to a direct report's request for more resources to better serve customers, "I know you're disappointed with this decision Jane, but our system just doesn't allow us to do what you want." Stop reading this section, and personalize the material by asking yourself the following question, "Can you really trust the organization you work in?" Now get more specific by reflecting on the six perspectives of the Organizational Trust Index listed below.

- *Truth*: Does your organization have a deep commitment to establishing "organizational truth" (what's really going on in the organization), so employees are free to present the unvarnished truth about organizational matters and question the reasoning, assumptions, and attitudes that motivate the organization's decisions?

- *Integrity*: Does your organization have integrity (does it do what it says), does it practice "fair process" (is it fair and objective) and does it base its evaluations of people and issues on facts and quantitative data, not "politics" and personalities?

- *Power*: Do managers in your organization use their power fairly and effectively to achieve the organization's purpose and goals and to positively influence people, not out of self-interest?

- *Competency*: Is your organization competent to overcome the challenges it faces and can leaders make decisions that will ensure the achievement of its strategic and tactical goals (does your organization know what it's doing)?

- *Values*: Does your organization have a well-defined set of core values that it communicates to all employees, does it authentically live by those values (even in difficult situations), and are those values consistent with your own personal values?

- *Recognition*: Does your organization recognize (notice) the contributions that you make in the workplace and does it confirm your own views about your professional abilities? Do you have a future in this organization?

As a general rule, managers and staff members do not consciously think about the six issues listed above rather their beliefs about these issues are *tacit* and emerge naturally regardless of whether they work in for-profit, non-profit, or government organizations. Beliefs about the six issues emerge slowly over time in long-term emotional memory through an accumulated process of group-learning and group-experience which creates important aspects of an organization's culture and sub-cultures; e.g., its belief structure, tacit assumptions, "folk wisdom," unspoken rules, and prohibitions. In other words, the answers to these questions exist invisibly just below the surface of consciousness, and can be *made visible* by repetitively asking the question "why" in the face of organizational issues. For example, "Why do managers consistently fail to share information, so the left hand does not know what the right hand is doing, even though they know that it negatively affects the overall performance of the organization?" The answer might be that managers are territorial so they don't share information easily. The next question might be, "But why are managers territorial and why do they fail to share information even when they *know* it's in the best interest of the organization? Is it because they want to retain their own power? Do they view others as being incompetent to get the job done? Do they have different core values than their coworkers?" And so on. The underlying causes and motivations of ineffective organizational performance are often traceable to an interlocking set of beliefs, tacit assumptions, and patterns of human interaction that emerge from the six perspectives of the Organizational Trust Index. The answers that groups of managers and staff members give to the six questions are indicative of their level of trust in the organization and the degree to which the culture is either *motivated* by trust or *driven* by fear.

While some managers believe that fear is a necessary part of achieving goals and objectives, researchers from Abraham Maslow to W. Edwards Deming have warned against the subtle, but profound, effects of management-by-fear (rather than trust) and the devastating effects that fear can have on establishing or maintaining a high-performing organizational culture. Deming argues that fear makes people afraid to share their best ideas; expand their capabilities and skills; admit mistakes; suggest process improvements; question the underlying purpose and reasoning of decisions or procedures; or even to act in the best interest of the company.[180] Managers and staff members fear: a) being the object of real or perceived retribution, b) being passed over for promotion, c) receiving lower performance ratings, d) looking uninformed or like a trouble-maker, e) being assigned to "grunt" work, rather than the more visible projects, and f) being seen as not having sufficient intellectual horsepower to advance beyond one's current position. Fear ultimately leads to padded figures, distorted measures of performance, and the tendency to sanitize, spin, and reinterpret what's really going on in an organization as information moves up through organizational levels to top management.

Maslow argues that while each of us has a deep need to know the truth about our capabilities, strengths, areas for improvement, and Blind Spots, many people fear (or even evade) knowing the truth about themselves. Fear undermines our courage to speak up, our confidence in our professional abilities, and over time fear erodes our self-esteem. While most managers want to know the truth about what's really going on in their organization in terms of milestones, processes, delivering on commitments to customers, and employee perspectives, these same managers often fear, resist, and evade knowing the truth (the brutal facts) about the underlying causes of these same issues. Maslow argues that enlightened managers genuinely *want* their employees to know the truth about what's going on in the workplace (everything relevant to their situation), and that, "…knowing is good for them, that the truth, the facts, and honesty tend to be curative, healing, to taste good, to be familiar…."[181]

It's not just a fear of discovering our negative traits and characteristics, as Maslow explains, "To discover in oneself a great talent can certainly bring exhilaration, but it also can create a fear of the dangers and responsibilities and duties of being a leader and of being all alone."[182] The bottom line is that *fear* kills curiosity, exploration, innovation, creativity, growth, high-performance, synergy, teamwork, and morale in organizations. Fear negatively impacts organizational performance in ways that are difficult or impossible to discover because it operates on autopilot, below the surface of organizational awareness, as undiscussible Invisible Bureaucracy.

The scores on the radar graph in Figure 32 show the averaged responses of all populations at SciTech for the six elements of the Organizational Trust Index using the BCI, and compare the scores of top managers to the scores of all other participants by population.[183] A score of 100 represents excellence. When the scores of top managers and others differ by less than 15 percent, they appear in black indicating that the scores are *aligned* and there is little or no difference in how the populations see this issue. When the difference between the scores of top managers and other populations is between 15 and 30 percent, the score appears in grey signifying that there is a *moderate misalignment* in how the populations see this issue.

When the difference between the scores of top managers and other populations differs by more than 30 percent, the score appears in italics signifying that there is a *significant misalignment* between how top managers and the populations see this issue.

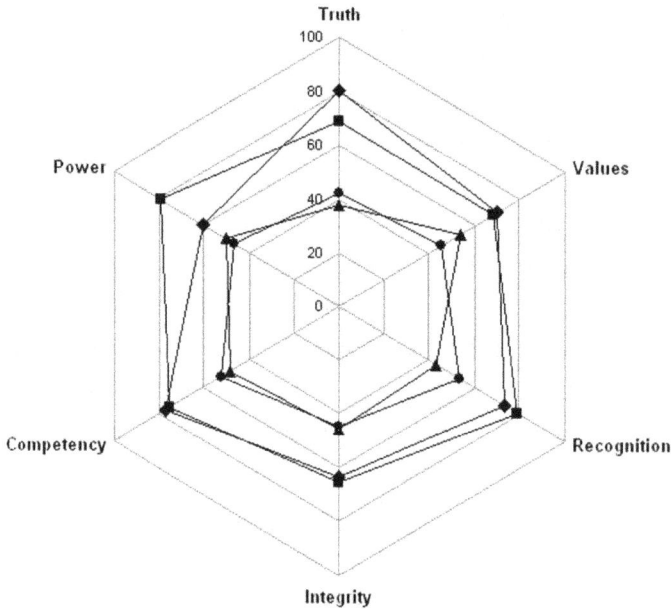

	TRU	VAL	REC	INT	COMP	POW
Top Manager ♦	80.0	70.0	73.3	63.3	76.7	60.0
Line Manager ■	68.8	68.0	78.7	65.3	74.7	78.7
Supervisor ▲	*37.7*	53.3	*42.9*	45.6	48.0	46.4
Staff ●	*42.2*	45.3	53.1	44.6	51.8	46.4

Figure 32

The analysis of the data shown in Figure 32 should begin with the two perspectives positioned at the top and bottom of the radar graph (Truth and Integrity) which are the critical path of the Organizational Trust Index data set. These two perspectives are the key to creating alignment and stability in an organization. The Truth and Integrity perspectives are high-leverage activities that powerfully shape and define the characteristics of the other four perspectives of the Organizational Trust Index data set, and an organization's overall performance. When an organization has a Strength in one (or both) of these areas signified by a High-High scoring pattern, it should be leveraged to improve the other four perspectives of the Organizational Trust Index radar and the performance of work-groups and the overall organization. When an organization Needs Development in one (or both) of these areas signified by a Low-Low scoring pattern, improvement in the areas of Truth and Integrity will positively impact an organization's performance in the other four areas.

The data on the radar graph in Figure 32 shows a High-Low scoring pattern for Truth which probably indicates that top managers have Blind Spots about the extent to which they are perceived as having a deep commitment to establishing "organizational truth" and what's really going on in the SciTech organization. The scores are shown in italics, indicting a significant misalignment between supervisors and staff managers, and the top managers and line managers – with the scores of supervisors being even lower than those of staff members. Qualitative data gathered in one-on-one interviews and focus groups at SciTech confirm that supervisors and staff members do not believe that they are free to present the unvarnished truth about organizational matters, nor do they believe that they can question the underlying motivations, reasoning, and assumptions of decisions that affect their day-to-day operations without fear of retribution. This High-Low scoring pattern is consistent with much of the data gathered at SciTech, which supports the view that effective communication down through the line organization is a systemic problem that is manifested throughout the BCI data set.

Notice how the Integrity data on Figure 32 reveals a Low-Low scoring pattern which probably indicates a critical path perspective that Needs Development because the scores of all four populations are clustered at and below 60%. Qualitative data gathered in one-on-one interviews and focus groups at SciTech confirm that the organization does not practice "fair process" and the evaluations of people and issues are often based on politics and personalities, rather than facts and quantitative data. The consensus among all four populations about this area Needing Development can be used to focus SciTech's time and energy on creating (and sustaining) positive change.

Figure 33 shows the same data binned by work-group. The BCI measures the level of trust at both the organizational and work-group levels because while employees may not trust the structures, systems, and culture of the overall organization, they may trust their work-group manager because he/she functions as a Border Guard who mitigates (absorbs) the negative impacts that the organizational culture has on direct reports. In much the same way, the overall culture of an organization may be constructive and effective, but the sub-culture created by a work-group manager may produce a destructive and ineffective climate within that work-group.

	TRU	VAL	REC	INT	COMP	POW
Top Manager	80.0	70.0	73.3	63.3	76.7	60.0
Business Administration	58.2	69.1	70.9	44.8	58.2	52.1
Business Development	50.3	59.0	64.8	72.4	62.9	66.7
Field Operations	42.2	44.4	48.9	43.7	53.2	45.8
Technical Assurance	68.3	71.4	71.4	67.6	67.1	72.9
Technical Services	41.0	46.4	57.1	47.0	54.8	60.6

Figure 33

151

Notice that the most significant misalignments are in the Truth perspective, especially with the Field Operations and Technical Services work-groups which execute SciTech's enterprise-wide business processes. This is one of the most serious issues revealed by the BCI data set, and is a high-leverage area for improvement where the alignment between supervisors, staff members, and the two other groups of managers could be significantly improved. Also note how many of the scores appear in black, signifying a high level of consensus on numerous other areas of the Organizational Trust Index, especially the perspective of Power which could be used to leverage change in the other five perspectives.

Corporate Life Cycle Analysis

This section will teach assessors how to "see" organizations within the context of Corporate Life Cycles. It uses Lawrence Miller's model of the corporate life cycle and the Four Ways of Working to evaluate how the elements of organizational culture unfold over-time.[184] All living things exhibit definable patterns of growth, aging, and decline that ultimately lead to death. As open systems, organizations are man-made entities, *goal-seeking organisms* that pass through the six definable life cycle phases shown in Figure 34; e.g., birth, infancy, adolescence, maturity, stagnation, decline, and death. As evidenced by the fact that many of the companies that were listed on the *Fortune 500* just ten years ago no longer exist, organizations are born, they grow, and then they die.

The model shown in Figure 34 is a simple, yet powerful, description of the *normal* evolution of an organization's structures, systems, and culture over the entire corporate life cycle. However, this normal pattern of growth and decline can be powerfully shaped by the forces and pressures that the external environment exerts on an organization, as well as the actions and interaction of the organization itself in response to the external environment. This is why it is important for assessors to carefully reconstruct an organization's history using *kairos* events on a timeline as described in Chapter 3 as a way of identifying disruptions and perturbations in the normal evolutionary patterns shown in Figure 34. Often the degree to which an organization's culture is chronically dysfunctional (and even neurotic) is directly proportional to the degree of ongoing, repetitive crisis that it has been forced to respond to over the course of the organization's history.

Miller's Corporate Life Cycle

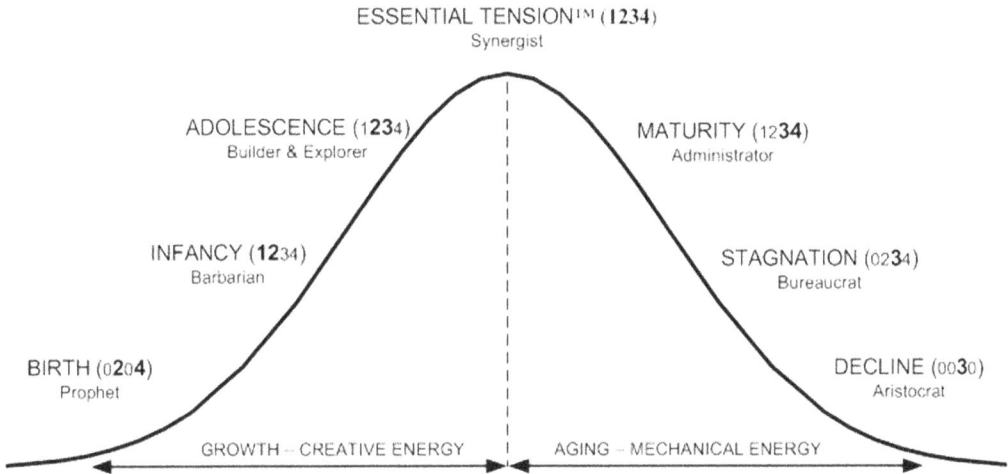

Figure 34

The large bolded numbers on the above diagram indicate which of the Four Ways of Working is normally *dominant* during this stage of the corporate life cycle and this indicates the primary focus of organizational and psychological energy. By way of review, the Four Ways of Working are shown below.

- Type 1: Production (What Things Get Done)

- Type 2: Connection (Why Things Get Done)

- Type 3: Direction (How Things Get Done)

- Type 4: Integration (Who Gets Things Done)

The small un-bolded numbers indicate which of the Four Ways of Working exist in the organization during that phase, but are not the primary focus of organizational and psychological energy. The absence of a number for one of the Four Ways of Working (indicated by a zero) indicates that this element has been repressed below the surface of organizational consciousness. While it may still exist somewhere in the organization, it has been eclipsed from the day-to-day reality of operational life. Often a strategy can become marginalized and dismissed to the point where even the thought of using it as a valid approach to problem-solving becomes undiscussible.

The descriptions of the life cycle phases listed below echo the leadership styles that Miller claims are needed at each stage in the life cycle. At each phase, the organization's leader must assume a new role with a different set of personal, professional, and social competencies, or be replaced by someone who can take the organization to the next level. It is not uncommon for a person to morph from one role to the next, but it is unlikely that people can span more than two phases in the corporate life cycle.

- **Birth**: the *prophet* has the vision (external or inner) to create the breakthrough and the passion and energy to codify the product, service, or intellectual property and move the organization forward. They manifest the creative process (creative ideas + the creative act = true creativity) and begin to build a group of people around them that shares their vision and subsequently they become the core of the new organization by the unfolding of the corporate life cycle process shown in Figure 34. The people who are involved focus almost exclusively on the human performance aspects of the product, service, and customers and are not really a formal organization in the sense of formal structures and systems; e.g., accounting system, planning, goals, records, policies, procedures, and formal human resource development and management. The code for this phase in the life cycle shown in Figure 34 is 0204, where Type Two (Connection) and Type Four (Integration) are the dominant focus of the organization's time and energy.

- **Infancy**: the *barbarian* adopts the prophet's vision and takes the new organization from birth through infancy by dominating the organization and the external environment with a command-and-control style and the force-of-will to drive the new company toward rapid growth. There is little or no sharing or delegating of power, and decisions tend to be unilateral and are rarely collaborative. The barbarian style of leadership appears in the Infancy phase of the life cycle, and when the company is trying to move *from* the downhill slide of aging *to* new growth, creative energy, and the kind of culture change described in this book. Regardless of what one calls it, this kind of deep change follows the elements of the Breckenridge Equation. The code for this phase in the life cycle shown in Figure 34 is **1234**, where Type One (Production) and Type Two (Connection) are the dominant focus of the organization's time and energy.

- **Adolescence**: the *builder-explorer* has a dual role, where the *builder* role concerns itself with defining the organization's overall strategic direction and at the same time builds the structures, systems, and specialized functions needed to support rapid growth and efficiency. The *explorer* aspect of the role pushes outward into the external environment, connecting with people and technologies to build alliances, relationships, collaborations and external networks that they subsequently link to the overall direction of the organization. By this phase of the corporate life cycle, decision-making becomes more decentralized through delegation because the internal and external environments have become too complex for the kind of centralized decision-making that typifies the Infancy stage. Because they are experts in developing the infrastructure and the specialized skills needed to support production and sales, leaders who exemplify the builder-explorer are the key element to building a large corporation. The code for this phase in the life cycle shown in Figure 34 is 1**23**4, where Type Two (Connection) and Type Three (Direction) are the dominant focus of the organization's time and energy.

- **Maturity**: the *administrator* develops integrated, enterprise-wide structures, systems, and functions and shifts the organization's focus from growth and expansion to security. The goals in this phase are producing quality products and services reliably and predictably, so the unpredictability and creative spirit typified during the growth phase are not valued, and may even be avoided. As work-groups become increasingly solidified with well-defined sub-cultures based on function and disciplinary paradigms (silos), the challenges that must be faced come primarily from within the organization rather than from the external environment. The focus on meeting needs in the external environment is eclipsed by inter-departmental conflict as work-groups tend to optimize their own performance and sub-optimize the performance of other work-groups and the entire organization. Integration of these various work-groups becomes a key competency where managers must resolve inter-departmental conflicts between work-groups and the Border Guards that head them who sometimes "see" the world from entirely different perspectives. Despite the fact that top managers often become detached from (or disinterested in) the core operation of the company during this phase of the corporate life cycle, the organizations they lead often accumulate enormous material wealth and success. The code for this phase in the life cycle shown in Figure 34 is 12**34**, where Type Three (Direction) and Type Four (Integration) are the dominant focus of the organization's time and energy.

- **Stagnation:** the *bureaucrat* imposes an iron grip of control on all levels of the organization and marginalizes, dismisses, and even demonizes the roles played by the *prophet, barbarian,* and *builder-explorer.* Creativity, production, and expansion cease, and the tail of organizational structures, systems, and functions wags the dog of the purpose, objectives, and goals. The organization is typified (at all levels) by self-interest rather than the organization's purpose of meeting needs in the external environment, and it squanders enormous amounts of time and energy on internal battles and struggles for power. Relationship building is primarily meant to create: a) symbols of authority that affirm their identity (buildings, offices, etc.), b) obligation from others, c) a language that symbolizes the culture, and d) a tacit commitment to resist any change that threatens people's power and privilege, rather than increasing production or sales. Organizations that are entrenched in this way of doing business often require an extensive deconstruction (and reconstruction) of their structures, systems, and culture. The code for this phase in the life cycle shown in Figure 34 is 0234, where Type Three (Direction) is the dominant focus of the organization's time and energy.

- **Decline:** the *aristocrats* are the leaders and managers who inherit the wealth, infrastructure, and client portfolios from those who have gone before them. They are significantly misaligned from the people who perform productive work and have an attitude of entitlement, privilege, and status that is based on status symbols like the size and décor of office space, executive dining rooms, and well-defined body language and deference shown to them in meetings and public interactions. Eventually, employees, customers, suppliers, or other groups associated with this kind of organizational culture rebel and ultimately withdraw the last vestiges of their support. The code for this phase in the life cycle shown in Figure 34 is 0030, where Type Three (Direction) is the sole focus of the organization's time and energy.

- **Essential Tension:** a *synergist* lives in the Essential Tension and constructive conflict of all of the life cycle stages, which allows them to maintain the forward motion of large and complex organizations by valuing the unique contributions of the *prophet, barbarian, builder-explorer,* and *administrator.* The code shown in Figure 34 is **1234**, where the dominant focus of the organization's time and energy can be shifted to meet the changing demands of the internal and external environments in order to achieve an organization's goals and objectives.

Organizations that are newly founded and growing (left side of Figure 34) are usually under the control of their founders and the cultural norms that are established in these organizations are adhered to by employees out of a sense of loyalty and identification with the founder's vision. Organizations that reach mid-life and are stabilizing (top of Figure 34) have had several generations of professional managers appointed by boards, with organizational cultures that have evolved into sub-cultures based on function, product lines, technologies, markets, and geography. This stage requires accurate cultural assessment in order to maintain the parts of the culture that are working for the organization as defined by the Breckenridge Equation, and to change those cultural elements that are not producing the desired results. This stage is particularly important when navigating the issues associated with mergers and acquisitions.

Maturing, Stagnating, and Declining organizations (right side of Figure 34) must often evolve, adapt, and change elements of their structures, systems, and culture, or they will not be able to adapt to a changing external environment. The tendency is for managers and staff members to cling to whatever made them successful (POI, COI, and ROI) and this often precludes them from seeing their Blind Spots and the need for change. As the organization's configuration of structures, systems, and culture solidifies into a state-of-equilibrium and a specific way of "seeing" emerges, the field of options is narrowed, and this creates decision-making bias and predictable errors in judgment in terms of strategies, goals, and ways of working. This level of organizational "fixation" often requires a massive transformation in organizational structures, systems, and culture combined with enormous time-pressure to avoid serious economic damage. The change process is much the same as the one used in midlife organizations, but the *amount* of change needed, and the *short time frames* often demand drastic measures.

It is important to distinguish between the growth and decline of *material assets* (right side of Figure 34) as opposed to the growth and decline of the *creative energy* (left side) within an organization. They are not the same thing and often change independently or inversely to one another. On the one hand, a spirit of creativity and innovation can *increase* sharply in an organization, while its material assets substantially *decrease*. This is often a predictor of future growth in material assets. On the other hand, a loss of creative energy and innovation combined with the emergence of tight controls and destructive conflict are almost always indicators that an organization is aging and in decline. Let's explore the ways in which the focus of time and energy on financial management shifts during the life cycle in more detail.

Income Statement and Cash Flow: The primary focus of time and energy in organizations on the left side of the curve shown in Figure 34 will tend to be growth and the *Income Statement*, as well as the focus of *Cash Flow* being on reinvesting capital into the company with the goal of future growth and expansion. This will include differing assumptions and beliefs about:

- How to generate revenue.

- Underlying patterns of spending and budgeting.

- Reinvesting capital into the company through R&D, facilities upgrades, etc. to invest in the future.

Balance Sheet and Cash Flow: The primary focus of time and energy in organizations on the right side of the curve shown in Figure 34 will tend to be on assets and the *Balance Sheet*, as well as the focus of *Cash Flow* being on maintaining optimal cash flow in the present and building assets. This will include differing assumptions and beliefs about:

- How to accumulate human, material, and financial assets.

- The accumulation of debt, obligations, and the level and use of lines of credit.

- Building cash reserves.

Notice that the options under the headings above are opposed to each other, and are based largely on where an organization is in its life cycle. More specifically, generating revenue is the opposite of underlying patterns of spending and budgeting; accumulating assets is the opposite of accumulating debt; and reinvesting in a company is the opposite of maintaining an optimal amount of cash for the future. The leadership styles of managers based on the tacit assumptions, beliefs, and preferences toward these six items will determine how well that manager "fits" within an organization during a given life cycle phase and how prepared they are to lead the organization at that particular time in its corporate history. These six areas are shown in Figure 35 in a matrix with the six phases of the corporate life cycle. The chart uses the following rankings: a) high focus of time and energy = 10, b) medium focus of time and energy = 7, c) low focus of time and energy = 3, and d) no focus of time and energy = 0.

	BIRTH	INFANCY	ADOLESCENCE	MATURITY	STAGNATION	DECLINE
Revenue	3	7	10	10	7	3
Spending	3	7	10	10	7	3
Assets	3	3	7	10	7	3
Debt/Obligations	3	7	10	7	3	0
Reinvest	0	3	10	7	3	0
Cash Reserve	0	0	3	7	10	7

Figure 35

As described previously, the *Birth* phase is one of "ideas and creativity" where a founder assembles a team of people who are devoted to their vision (getting the right people on the bus) and therefore all of the financial indicators shown in Figure 35 will tend to be Low or non-existent. The *Infancy* phase is a period of "taking over new territory and tilling-planting the soil" and requires mostly Medium financials (assets are few and cash reserves are non-existent since revenues that would be invested here are being plowed back in to the company). The *Adolescence* phase is a time of "building internal capability and growth-expansion," so most of the financial indicators are rated as High with assets being built to a significant level. The *Maturity* phase reflects a state of "building enterprise-wide structures-systems and management controls" where the categories are about half High, and half Medium – assets and cash reserves have been accumulated and increasing them dominates the focus of the organization's time and energy. The *Stagnation* phase is a time of "bureaucracy and self-interest" where revenue, spending, and reinvestment are waning, assets are Medium and debt is Low. The *Decline* phase is characterized by "misalignment with workers and entitlement and complacency" accompanied by the status symbols of power and privilege. Revenue, assets, and cash reserves are diminishing and unless the company is turned around, over time the matrix shown in Figure 35 will show even further declines.

Assessors should note that the culture in most organizations is not homogeneous across the entire institution, but is an emergent phenomenon that is defined by the interaction between the sub-cultures of work-groups and the Border Guards that head them as shown on the Interaction Map. In addition, different work-groups can be at different stages of the corporate life cycle at the same time because: a) they do not all "age" at the same rate, b) some functions and disciplines are administrative by nature and more easily migrate to the aging side of the life cycle, and c) the personality types of the Border Guards and people in a work-group combined with their ability to practice *both-and-thinking* powerfully affect the characteristics of that sub-culture. For example, the finance and accounting department may be in the Stagnation stage with excessive controls, while the marketing and sales department and process-improvement groups are in the Builder-Explorer stage trying to grow and expand the organization's client portfolio and build the infrastructure to support that growth.

Gap Analysis and Validating Assessment Results

This section teaches assessors how to perform a high level gap analysis that compares the qualitative and quantitative data gathered during the assessment with the facts and realities of day-to-day operations, using objective, verifiable evidence. The key is to establish the degree to which the documents, processes, actions, and interactions gathered during the assessment process are a vital, living part of day-to-day life in the organization. The line of inquiry that assessors might use is as follows:

- Do the appropriate documents, processes, actions, and interactions actually *exist* in the organization and are they oral, written, or IT automated?

- Are the documents, processes, actions, and interactions a part of the day-to-day operations, or are they window dressing that "sits on the shelf"?

- Are the documents, processes, actions, and interactions known, understood, and used uniformly across the organization?

- To what extent are the profile scores in these areas an accurate reflection of the day-to-day operational actions, interactions, and realities of organizational life?

Although the assessor could attempt to validate the data from every radar graph and chart described in this book as part of a gap analysis and validation process, the key items listed below will help to *link* the qualitative data from interviews and the quantitative scores from the BCI (what the organization "says" about itself), to the day-to-day realities of organizational life (what it actually does) in terms of things that are objectively verifiable. Assessors should evaluate the extent to which the following areas manifest themselves in the organization.

Leadership Focus
- Set of "vital few" performance measures.

- Well-defined economic driver.

- Written strategic plan and annual operating plans for work-groups with goals and objectives.

Resources and Policies

- Adequate (understandable) budgets that are aligned with achieving the organization's strategic goals and objectives and send right signals.

- High-level policies that are aligned with achieving strategic goals and objectives.

- A compensation system that motivates people and the use of effective performance appraisals.

Decisions

- Action-oriented meetings that result in assigned tasks, deliverables, and in follow-up.

- Use of fact-based decision-making (quantitative data, scientific analytics), not just intuition and business experience.

- Use of strategic goals and annual plans to direct weekly/monthly operations.

- Well-defined method for reaching consensus on important issues.

Rewards

- Managers pay attention to (and care about) things that reinforce the desired behaviors.

- Managers reward behaviors that implement (accelerate) achieving goals.

- Managers use their own visible behavior to reinforce the desired behaviors.

Just Culture

- Analyze root causes of performance problems in structures and systems (not blame individuals).

- There is little or no gap between the formal and informal rules of the game.

- People trust the organization to do what it says (organizational integrity).

Management Philosophy

- Managers are held accountable for four elements.

- Managers have (and can exercise) the four authorities.

Emotional Messages

- Meetings (decision-making) are typified by constructive-destructive emotional messages.

- Employees' actions-interactions are typified by constructive-destructive emotional messages.

Four Ways of Working

- The organization is primarily on the left or right side of the graph.

- The organization is primarily at the top or bottom of the graph.

Life Cycle Analysis

- The qualitative data from interviews and quantitative data from the BCI and additional financial analysis can help to establish which phase of the corporate life cycle that an organization is in.

The line of questioning that assessors can use for other on-site interviews that are conducted as part of an assessment is more open-ended, with questions such as, "What results is the organization getting that it wishes it wasn't getting?" These open-ended questions are designed to allow underlying patterns and cultural themes to emerge from the interview process. The line of questioning described above as part of the gap analysis and verification process is designed to allow assessors to compare the quantitative scores of BCI with the facts and realities of day-to-day operations using objective, verifiable evidence. The goal is for assessors to establish the degree to which documents, processes, actions, and interactions are a vital, living part of day-to-day life in the organization and not just "window dressing." The ultimate goal is to *link* the quantitative data from the BCI (what the organization "says" about itself) to the day-to-day realities of organizational life (what it actually does) in terms of things that are objectively verifiable, and can function like a baseline for organizational performance and improvement.

CHAPTER 4
GOVERNANCE ISSUES AND FINANCIAL ANALYSIS

Perhaps the single most important part of evaluating an organization's culture is gaining a clear understanding of the nature, viability, and sustainability of its revenue and funding streams, and the expectations and pressures that are exerted on an organization by customers, competitors, suppliers, regulators, taxpayers, and other forces in the external environment. This chapter helps assessors understand the ways in which an organization's governance and corporate structure can powerfully shape and define its culture. It also describes how the BCI measures the amount of time and energy that are squandered in organizations.

Governance Issues

When assessors look beyond an organization's Internal Revenue Service (IRS) non-profit status as reported on their IRS 990 Form, many of the distinctions between *For-Profit* and *Non-Profit* corporations become operationally meaningless when viewed from the structures-and-systems perspective. As Peter Drucker states, "The differences between managing a chain of retail stores and managing a Roman Catholic Diocese are amazingly fewer than retail executives or bishops realize. The differences are mainly in the application rather than the principles."[185] Many of the timeless principles that produce sustained financial and non-financial performance in high-performing For-Profit companies can also be applied to Non-Profit corporations, as described by Collins in his monograph, *Good to Great and the Social Sectors*.[186] In fact, contrary to the view taught in many business schools, recent studies such as Collins and Porras' *Good to Great* have shown that profit and wealth are not the driving force or primary objective of truly visionary For-Profit companies. Rather, For-Profit companies have a larger purpose in life, and this purpose becomes the focal point on the business horizon, guiding every decision they make. Generating revenue becomes a means to an end for truly visionary For-Profit companies, not an end in itself.[187]

The Breckenridge Institute has identified two kinds of Non-Profit organizations that powerfully shape and define an organization's culture based on how they generate the majority of their revenue:

- Type 1 Non-Profits

- Type 2 Non-Profits

While Type 1 Non-Profits may generate some of their financial resources through endowments, fund-raising, and gifts from donors, most of their revenue comes from providing products and services to customers and work performed for funding agencies and grantee organizations; e.g., the results of clinical trials, applied R&D, basic research, or the development of new technologies. Operationally, they function much like their For-Profit counterparts – they have standard business and work processes, proposal writing functions, marketing and sales goals, suppliers, inventory, customers or clients to satisfy, and competitors in both the Non-Profit and For-Profit arenas. Examples of Type 1 Non-Profit organizations include: hospitals, medical clinics, convalescent care facilities, agricultural organizations, retail operations (Goodwill has over 1,900 stores), some contract research organizations, research institutes that do applied R&D, and educational organizations.

While Type 2 Non-Profits may generate some of their financial resources by providing products and services to those outside of their organization, most of their revenue comes from grants, awards, funding agencies, endowments, fund-raising, membership dues, and gifts from donors. Operationally and culturally, these organizations are more complex than their For-Profit counterparts and function very differently. For example, rather than customers or clients in the traditional sense of the words, Type 2 Non-Profits serve two major constituencies: a) the needs of the public and society at large, academia and furthering the arts and sciences as a legacy for future generations, and b) the demands of funding agencies, grantors, sponsors, members, and donors for fiscal and programmatic responsibility. Ultimate responsibility for compliance with federal, state, and local requirements, public relations, fund-raising, and overall fiscal and programmatic effectiveness and stewardship lies with the Type 2 institution. The institution's administrative staff uses standard business and work processes to support a scientific, technical, or artisan staff that often has joint appointments with other institutes or collaborating universities, so the people who produce the core contribution to the Type 2 organization's purpose and strategic objectives may not be full-time employees of that institution. Examples of Type 2 Non-Profit organizations include: a) institutes and universities that conduct research in the physical, biological, ecological, political, social, and computing sciences, b) organizations that distribute food and medical care to the needy, and c) museums, art institutes, and schools of music that create and sustain artistic expression and culture.

The revenue for most government organizations at the federal, state, county, and municipal levels comes from appropriations granted by legislative bodies (like the U.S. Congress), and this appropriated revenue stream powerfully shapes and defines the culture of government organizations. This is because the basis for increasing or decreasing revenue from appropriated funds is driven largely by political issues, not the actual performance of the government organization. One of the best ways to characterize these differences is to compare the key elements that drive For-Profit companies in industry, with government entities. More specifically, there are four drivers in For-Profit organizations: a) business results, b) customer satisfaction, c) consequences for performance (good and bad), and d) the leadership and management needed to enact and energize the first three. Like the wind in the sails of a boat, business results and customer satisfaction are the driving forces that link For-Profit companies to the business environment outside the organization, as shown in the open systems diagram in Figure 1. Consequences for performance are the indispensible drivers that enable managers to oversee day-to-day operations within the context of the organization's structures, systems, and culture. Consequences are the equivalent to accountability and authority as measured by the Management Philosophy perspective in Figure 24.

Our experience of working with government organizations up to the Under Secretary level has shown that there are *no real equivalents* to business results, customer satisfaction, and consequences for performance (good or bad) in most government agencies. The notable exception is "hybrid" organizations like SciTech that receive a portion of their revenue from providing products and services to customers. For example, in industry, if a company is not profitable it goes out of business. In government agencies, organizations and projects sometimes continue to exist long after their purpose is questionable, often for political reasons. In industry, customer satisfaction is a bulwark of business results and process improvement. If customers are not satisfied, they buy elsewhere, the company's profits decline, and eventually the company goes out of business. In many government agencies, managers and staff members have endless debates about whether they even have customers other than the ephemeral "taxpayer" or "future unborn generations." In industry, if a worker's performance is exemplary they are rewarded, and if performance is inadequate, the company can fire them. There are consequences for performance – good and bad. In most government agencies, the difference between the raises and rewards given to high-performers and those given to low-performers is often a few dollars a month. An unwritten cultural norm in many government agencies is that it's not appropriate for managers to give marginal ratings for fear that even the most incompetent workers will take retribution by filing grievances against a manager who dares to tell the truth about their level of performance. More importantly, even the remaining industry-type driver of leadership and management is undermined when top managers cannot openly demonstrate that there are consequences for performance because the system within which they are embedded does not provide them with accountability and authority.

Assessors should note that in the absence of revenue streams that are linked to an organization's actual performance, the currency that "trades" in government organizations is *power-through-visibility*. In other words, if a government organization or a manager is involved with an "initiative" or "program" that is well received by the agency leaders, the media, or the public; this creates the currency of positive visibility. If the organization or manager is associated with actions and interactions that are frowned on by agency leaders, the media, or the public; this creates the currency of negative visibility. As a general rule, all sectors of government are increasingly under pressure to demonstrate the applicability and value-added results of their services to meet public needs and this scrutiny generates either positive or negative currency in visibility. But when an organizational unit within a government entity is responsible for the active enforcement of laws and regulations, their purpose, strategic objectives, goals and day-to-day interaction with the public are often subject to more intense scrutiny by the public and the media so the issues associated with power-through-visibility are more intense because these constituencies function more like actual customers. Government entities are also under constant pressure to demonstrate that their operations are efficient and that they are using publicly generated funds responsibly, despite the absence of the four drivers mentioned above, which increases the importance of creating the currency of positive visibility. The tacit, unexamined, taken-for-granted currency of power-through-visibility is one of the most powerful forces in the world of government entities, and assessors should help their clients recognize this reality and actively manage it through key performance indicators.

Financial Analysis

Kotter and Heskett performed the first systematic study that demonstrated a cause-and-effect relationship between the characteristics of an organization's culture and sustainable financial and non-financial performance.[188] Their research showed that high-performing organizations are able to internally adapt *and* respond to a constantly changing external environment – to be influenced by business realities, and at the same time maintain a deep sense of organizational identity. Their research showed that achieving this kind of interdependent balance produces long-term, superior financial performance; e.g., net revenue growth, net income growth, return on investment, return on assets, sales growth, and market share. Collins and Porras' studies confirmed a link between organizational culture and outstanding performance.[189] They demonstrated that truly visionary companies develop organizational cultures that are built around timeless principles of leadership and management, along with a deep commitment.

Despite the evidence of these research projects, I remain skeptical about attempts to systematically link organizational culture to the kinds of financial indicators used in such studies; e.g., net revenue growth, net income growth, return on investment, return on assets, sales growth, and market share. Often the statistical correlations between culture and these financial indicators are weak, and even where the correlations appear to be strong, there are too many unmeasured and unknown parameters and contextual factors to make a convincing case for a cause-and-effect relationship.

But a cause-and-effect relationship between organizational culture and financial measures can be established by examining an organization's tacit, unquestioned, taken-for-granted patterns of spending; attitudes toward generating revenue; and their overall philosophy about the allocation of (and investment in) financial, physical, and human resources. At a strategic level, the cultural dimension of financial performance manifests itself as having a primary focus of organizational time and energy on either the earning side of the equation (income statement and growth), or the spending side of the equation (balance sheet), which is related to where an organization is in its corporate life cycle. For example:

Income Statement and Cash Flow: The primary focus of time and energy in these organizations tends to be growth and the *Income Statement*, as well as the focus of *Cash Flow* being on reinvesting capital into the company with the goal of future growth and expansion. An organization's cultural norms will be manifested as tacit, unquestioned, taken-for-granted assumptions and beliefs about:

- How to generate revenue.

- Underlying patterns of spending and budgeting.

- Reinvesting capital into the company through R&D, facilities upgrades, etc. to invest in the future.

Balance Sheet and Cash Flow: The primary focus of time and energy in these organizations tends to be on assets and the *Balance Sheet*, as well as the focus of *Cash Flow* being on maintaining optimal cash flow in the present and building assets. An organization's cultural norms will be manifested as tacit, unquestioned, taken-for-granted assumptions and beliefs about:

- How to accumulate human, material, and financial assets.

- The accumulation of debt, obligations, and the level and use of lines of credit.

- Building cash reserves.

At a tactical level, tacit, unquestioned, taken-for-granted assumptions and beliefs are often revealed by a systematic analysis of an organization's revenue portfolio, labor costs, and operating expenses. More specifically, organizational functions and work-groups that are "seen" as being most important to the business will tend to receive larger allocations of human, physical, and financial resources. A bias toward viewing organizations from either the structures-and-systems perspective or the human-performance-perspective may be evidenced in a distribution of resources for labor and operating expenses that focuses on either "hard" quantitative budget line items like IT and equipment, versus "soft" qualitative initiatives like training and development. An organization's revenue portfolio is often a Pareto distribution where 80% of its revenue comes from 20% of its customers which may indicate biases in the organization's strategy. In fact, tacit, unquestioned, taken-for-granted assumptions and beliefs have a powerful shaping and defining effect on organizational strategy. As Schein points out, "We tend to think that we can separate strategy from culture, but we fail to notice that in most organizations strategic thinking is deeply colored by tacit assumptions about who they are and what their mission is."[190] Ultimately, strategic thinking defines and drives the allocation of the human, material, and financial resources needed to execute a given strategy. While these ways of "seeing" the budgeting process and the allocation of resources are often espoused as being "organizational truth" that is based on quantitative measurements and business experience, they are often the product of the kind of active, tacit, and disciplinary cultural teaching described in Chapter 2 – "the way it's done around here."

So it's important for assessors to help clients understand the tacit, unexamined assumptions, beliefs, and models upon which their budgeting process and resource allocations are based by evaluating them against criteria like those listed below:

- *Reliability*: To what extent are the client's budgeting process and resource allocations based on an underlying theoretical model of organizations, work-groups, human interaction, cognitive operations-preferences, and a well-defined portfolio of key performance indicators that is *reliable*; e.g., it describes and predicts the actions, interactions, and overall performance of organizations, work-groups, and the people in them?

- *Validity*: To what extent are the reasoning and assumptions that underlie the budgeting process and resource allocations *valid* in the sense that they have been reflected on, made explicit, and subject to public tests and scrutiny to deconstruct organizational defense routines, control for the self-interest of Border Guards, and to establish the "organizational truth" of what's really going on in the situation?

- *Being Actionable*: To what extent are the client's budgeting process and resource allocations *actionable* in the sense that: a) they outline detailed concrete budget-related actions that will produce the desired results, b) they can be crafted so managers and staff members can implement the budget-related actions required to produce the desired results, and c) the implementation of budget-related actions will not be frustrated and/or undermined (overtly-covertly, intentionally-unintentionally) by the organizational context and cultural norms within which they are embedded?

Assessors should evaluate the revenue, labor, and operating data for the entire organization, by population, and by work-group using a *spreadsheet* that maps to the structure of the BCI Report. More specifically, the number of populations and work-groups that are defined in a BCI Report on the radar graphs and the charts should be mirrored in the structure of the spreadsheet. For example, revenue, labor and operating costs should be defined by population (how much do middle managers cost the organization), and by organizational work-group (how much does a specific work-group cost the organization). If the software program Excel® is used, the assessor should create five sheets that can be linked through equations and macros including: a) key performance indicators, b) summary sheet, c) revenue, d) labor costs, e) and operating expenses. The kinds of data that appear in the spreadsheet will reflect the organization's form of governance and legal structure; e.g., For-Profit, Non-Profit, or government as shown in the examples below.

Once the spreadsheet has been populated with data, assessors should analyze the financial and non-financial data to identify underlying (tacit) *patterns* in an organization's: a) revenue streams and revenue portfolio, b) spending, budgeting, and expenses, c) labor costs and distribution, and d) the overall allocation of human, financial, and physical resources. These patterns of revenue, labor, and operating costs become "windows" into the tacit beliefs and assumptions of the organization's history, identity, and culture. The data in the spreadsheet can also be used to help assessors determine which phase in the corporate life cycle an organization is in, as described in Chapter 3. Let's describe some suggested elements that should be included in a spreadsheet for For-Profit, Non-Profit, and government organizations.

For-Profit Spread Sheet. With For-Profit companies, assessors should include the following items in the spreadsheet, and add others that are relevant to the business and industry that the client is in.

Key Performance Indicators Sheet: Key performance indicators (KPIs) can be either financial or non-financial and can be developed at the organizational and work-group levels. When possible, they should be goals, measures, and targets with measurable outcomes. In some instances, 0/1 goals can be developed to baseline an organization's actual performance, but this should be avoided unless necessary.

Summary Sheet: The summary sheet should contain a number of key measurements, including:

- Total Revenue
- Total Expenses
- Cash Paid Out
- Gross Margin
- Cost Reductions
- Return on Assets
- Return on Sales
- Backlog (Recurring Income)

Revenue Sheet: The revenue sheet should be used to evaluate the robustness of an organization's revenue streams at the organizational and the work-group levels. The goal should be to have diversity in an organization's revenue portfolio.

- Revenue from Services
- Revenue from Products
- Revenue from Investments
- Top Ten Customers
- Other Revenue

Labor Cost Sheet: The labor sheet should show the cost of labor by population and by work-group. Each population or work-group should be broken out by the number of FTEs, the cost based on the mid-range of the job description, and the percent of the total cost of labor for the entire organization. This should be mapped to the structure of the BCI assessment. For example:

- Top Managers: a) number of FTE, b) FTE$ as mid-range of job description, and c) percent of total employees.

- Middle Managers: a) number of FTE, b) FTE$ as mid-range of job description, and c) percent of total employees.

- Supervisors: a) number of FTE, b) FTE$ as mid-range of job description, and c) percent of total employees.

- Staff Members: a) number of FTE, b) FTE$ as mid-range of job description, and c) percent of total employees.

- Cost of Employee Turnover: This includes items like the cost of advertizing, screening, hiring, orienting, training and developing new employees. It also includes the cost of severance pay, lost sales, moving expenses paid, the cost of interim workers, and the cost of travel for interviewers and interviewees. These data should be gathered for the entire organization, a population, or by work-group.

Operating Expenses Sheet: The operating expenses sheet should show the non-labor-related cost to operate the organization by population and work-group. These costs should be broken out by one time (episodic) costs, and ongoing costs.

One Time Costs

- Facilities and Buildings
- IT Hardware and Software
- Vehicles and Equipment
- Attorney Fees
- Outsourcing
- Legal Settlements
- Training Materials
- Product Development
- Service Development
- Section 179 Depreciation
- Top Ten One Time Costs
- Other

On-Going Costs

- Travel
- Communication
- Office Supplies
- Advertising
- Annual Planning Meeting
- Insurance
- Interest
- Utilities
- IT Licenses
- Local Meals and Entertainment for Clients and Prospects

- Rent
- Repairs
- Depreciation
- Professional Fees
- Outsourcing
- Taxes
- Top Ten On-Going Costs
- Other

The financial and non-financial measures that are listed in this section can powerfully shape, define, and reflect the characteristics of the structures, systems, and culture in For-Profit organizations. Assessors need to factor these into the process of assessing and changing organizational culture.

Non-Profit Spread Sheet: With Non-Profit corporations, assessors should include the following items in the spreadsheet, and add others that are relevant to the business and industry that the client is in.

Key Performance Indicators Sheet: Key performance indicators (KPIs) can be either financial or non-financial and can be developed at the organizational and work-group levels. When possible, they should be goals, measures, and targets with measurable outcomes. In some instances, 0/1 goals can be developed to baseline performance, but this should be avoided unless necessary.

Summary Sheet: The summary sheet should contain a number of key measurements, including:

- Total Revenue
- Total Expenses
- Cash Paid Out
- Excess
- Cost Reductions

- Administrative Ratio
- Fund Raising Ratio
- Program Ratio
- Backlog (Recurring Income)

Revenue Sheet: The revenue sheet should be used to evaluate the robustness of an organization's revenue streams at the organizational and the work-group levels. The goal should be to have diversity in an organization's revenue portfolio.

- Corporate Contributions
- Individual Contributions
- Top Ten Contributors
- Sales of Services to Customers
- Sales of Products to Customers
- Top Ten Customers
- Grants
- Investments

Labor Cost Sheet: The labor sheet should show the cost of labor by population and by work-group. Each population or work-group is broken out by the number of FTEs, the cost based on the mid-range of the job description, and the percent of the total cost of labor for the entire organization. This should be mapped to the structure of the BCI assessment. For example:

- Top Managers: a) number of FTE, b) FTE$ as mid-range of job description, and c) percent of total employees.

- Middle Managers: a) number of FTE, b) FTE$ as mid-range of job description, and c) percent of total employees.

- Supervisors: a) number of FTE, b) FTE$ as mid-range of job description, and c) percent of total employees.

- Staff Members: a) number of FTE, b) FTE$ as mid-range of job description, and c) percent of total employees.

- Cost of Employee Turnover: This includes items like the cost of advertizing, screening, hiring, orienting, training and developing new employees. It also includes the cost of severance pay, lost sales, moving expenses paid, the cost of interim workers, and the cost of travel for interviewers and interviewees. These data should be gathered for the entire organization, a population, or by work-group.

Operating Expenses Sheet: The operating expenses sheet should show the non-labor-related cost to operate the organization by population and work-group. These costs should be broken out by one time (episodic) costs, and ongoing costs.

One Time Costs

- Facilities and Buildings
- IT Hardware and Software
- Vehicles and Equipment
- Attorney Fees
- Outsourcing
- Legal Settlements
- Training Materials

- Product Development
- Service Development
- Top Ten One Time Costs
- Other

On-Going Costs

- Travel
- Communication
- Office Supplies
- Advertising
- Annual Planning Meeting
- Insurance
- Interest
- Utilities
- IT Licenses
- Local Meals and Entertainment for Clients and Prospects

- Rent
- Repairs
- Depreciation
- Professional Fees
- Outsourcing
- Taxes
- Top Ten On-Going Costs
- Other

The financial and non-financial measures that are listed in this section can powerfully shape, define, and reflect the characteristics of the structures, systems, and culture in Non-Profit organizations. Assessors need to factor these into the process of assessing and changing organizational culture in Non-Profit organizations.

Government Spread Sheet. With government entities, assessors should include the following items in the spreadsheet, and add others that are relevant to the kinds of products and services that are provided at the federal, state, county, or local government levels.

Key Performance Indicators Sheet: Key performance indicators (KPIs) can be either financial or non-financial and can be developed at the organizational and work-group levels. When possible, they should be goals, measures, and targets with measurable outcomes. In some instances, 0/1 goals can be developed to baseline performance, but this should be avoided unless necessary. One of the most important KPIs for government organizations to track is power through visibility.

Summary Sheet: The summary sheet should contain a number of key measurements, including:

- Total Revenue
- Total Expenses
- Cash Paid Out
- Cost Reductions
- Backlog (Carry Over Revenue)

Revenue Sheet: The revenue sheet should be used to evaluate the robustness of an organization's revenue streams at the organizational and the work-group levels. It's important to analyze trends in funding levels, and the use of visibility as an economic driver to increase an organization's appropriation level. If possible, the goal is to have diversity in the revenue portfolio as with "hybrid" government organizations that have multiple revenue streams, not just funding from appropriations.

- Revenue from Appropriations
- Revenue from Work for Others
- Revenue from Projects
- Top Ten Customers/Projects
- Other Revenue

Labor Cost Sheet: The labor sheet should show the cost of labor by population and by work-group. Each population or work-group is broken out by the number of FTEs, the cost based on the mid-range of the job description, and the percent of the total cost of labor for the entire organization. This should be mapped to the structure of the BCI assessment. For example:

- Top Managers: a) number of FTE, b) FTE$ as mid-range of job description, and c) percent of total employees.

- Middle Managers: a) number of FTE, b) FTE$ as mid-range of job description, and c) percent of total employees.

- Supervisors: a) number of FTE, b) FTE$ as mid-range of job description, and c) percent of total employees.

- Staff Members: a) number of FTE, b) FTE$ as mid-range of job description, and c) percent of total employees.

- Cost of Employee Turnover: This includes items like the cost of advertizing, screening, hiring, orienting, training and developing new employees. It also includes the cost of severance pay, lost sales, moving expenses paid, the cost of interim workers, and the cost of travel for interviewers and interviewees. These data should be gathered for the entire organization, a population, or by work-group.

Operating Expenses Sheet: The operating expenses sheet should show the non-labor-related cost to operate the organization by population and work-group. These costs should be broken out by one time (episodic) costs, and ongoing costs.

One Time Costs

- Facilities and Buildings
- IT Hardware and Software
- Vehicles and Equipment
- Attorney Fees
- Outsourcing
- Legal Settlements

- Training Materials
- Product Development
- Service Development
- Top Ten One Time Costs
- Other

On-Going Costs

- Travel
- Communication
- Office Supplies
- Advertising
- Annual Planning Meeting
- Insurance
- Interest
- Utilities

- IT Licenses
- Rent
- Repairs
- Depreciation
- Professional Fees
- Outsourcing
- Top Ten On-Going Costs
- Other

The financial and non-financial measures that are listed in this section can powerfully shape, define, and reflect the characteristics of the structures, systems, and culture in government organizations. Assessors need to factor these into the process of assessing and changing organizational culture in government organizations.

Squandered Time and Energy

This section will help assessors and their clients begin to quantify the financial impact of ineffective autopilot operations, the Red Flags, and Invisible Bureaucracy. These items are commonly called "hidden" costs because they do not directly show up in traditional financial accounting systems like budget statements or balance sheets. In some cases where an organization's performance is dominated by Invisible Bureaucracy, the hidden costs of squandered time and energy can be a substantial part of the total cost of doing business.[191] Let's discuss the characteristics of squandered time and energy in more detail.

Squandered Organizational Energy

The data shown on the chart below indicates the amount of dollars in cost inefficiencies that ineffective work processes are causing in the SciTech organization for the current year and two subsequent years, should these issues remain unresolved.

Squandered Organizational Energy							
Population	FTE $/Hr	Hrs/Day	# of Emp	Lost $/Yr 1	Lost $/Yr 2	Lost $/Yr 3	Total
Top Manager	$125	0.75	2	$37,500	$37,500	$37,500	$112,500
Line Manager	$94	1.70	5	$159,800	$159,800	$159,800	$479,400
Supervisor	$75	2.79	7	$292,950	$292,950	$292,950	$878,850
Staff	$47	2.21	56	$1,163,344	$1,163,344	$1,163,344	$3,490,032
Total			70	$1,653,594	$1,653,594	$1,653,594	**$4,960,782**

Figure 36

As part of the BCI assessment question set, participants were asked to estimate how many hours per day they spend on work-process-related inefficiencies (for example, rework, poor or inconsistent quality and service, work-arounds, timeliness, downtime, etc.).[192]

Squandered Psychological Energy

The data shown on the chart below indicates the amount of dollars in cost inefficiencies that ineffective communication and destructive conflict are causing in the SciTech organization for the current year and two subsequent years, should these issues remain unresolved. As part of the BCI assessment question set, participants were asked to estimate how many hours per day they spend on interpersonal conflict (for example, poor or ineffective communication, exchanges of negative energy, people frustrating or undermining positive change, fear of retribution, power struggles between managers and coworkers).

Squandered Psychological Energy							
Population	FTE $/Hr	Hrs/Day	# of Emp	Lost $/Yr 1	Lost $/Yr 2	Lost $/Yr 3	Total
Top Manager	$125	1.75	2	$87,500	$87,500	$87,500	$262,500
Line Manager	$94	1.10	5	$103,400	$103,400	$103,400	$310,200
Supervisor	$75	2.21	7	$232,050	$232,050	$232,050	$696,150
Staff	$47	1.67	56	$879,088	$879,088	$879,088	$2,637,264
Total			70	$1,302,038	$1,302,038	$1,302,038	$3,906,114

Figure 37

It's important to note that organizational and psychological energy are some of the most valuable resources that an organization has. When used ineffectively, the time and energy shown in Figure 36 and Figure 37 are unavailable to help an organization fulfill its purpose and achieve its goals and objectives. The data shown in Figure 38 is the total three-year financial impact of squandered organizational energy and squandered psychological energy for the SciTech organization.

Total 3-Year Financial Impact	
Organizational Energy	$4,960,782
Psychological Energy	$3,906,114
Total	**$8,866,896**

Figure 38

Given the fact that these ineffective structures, systems and patterns-of-interaction tend to be habitual and on autopilot, it is unlikely that this negative financial impact can be mitigated without a sustained commitment of time and resources to corrective action on the part of management.

CHAPTER 5
IMPROVING ORGANIZATIONAL PERFORMANCE

One of the problems with identifying and eliminating the kind of Invisible Bureaucracy that frustrates and undermines organizational performance is that managers and staff members are actively involved in the patterns-of-interaction that create and sustain this bureaucracy and don't recognize it because these day-to-day operations are on autopilot. This chapter describes how assessors can help their clients: a) take these patterns-of-interaction off autopilot and raise them back into personal and organizational awareness, b) reconfigure ineffective processes and behaviors to get different results, c) migrate new more effective patterns-of-interaction back to autopilot operation, and d) define a path forward for achieving an organization's goals and objectives. Learning and internalizing the principles and practices described in this chapter will enable managers (at all organizational levels) to consciously create, manage, or deconstruct organizational culture as a way of improving its performance. Assessors will learn how to help their clients use their culture *as a powerful resource* that facilitates, rather than opposes, achieving their organization's purpose and goals. This is the key to becoming an Island of Excellence® in a sea of mediocrity.

Recognizing the Problem

Deep sustainable change in organizations almost always requires a burning platform and there are two kinds of burning platforms: reactive and proactive. The *reactive* kind is when managers wait until a situation has gone critical to seek help or try to alter destructive patterns-of-interaction. Alternatively, managers who adopt the *proactive* kind of burning platform realize that while the situation may not be critical right now, it probably *will be* if they allow destructive patterns-of-interaction to continue frustrating and undermining their work-group. Managers and their staff need to ask the question, "How bad are we hurting?" If the answer is, "Not that bad," then things normally go on as they are, until the next destructive conflict

179

raises its ugly head – normally when they least expect it. So how do managers and staff members who "see" the world so differently come to see the world otherwise? Edgar Schein's model for raising organizational awareness (described below) is a powerful tool for changing how managers and staff members see themselves, others, and the world around them.[193]

- The ***first step*** is to use objective data from the organization's actual performance, and the BCI Report to begin to cast doubt on an organization's ways of doing business and cultural norms; e.g., how managers and staff members "see" themselves, coworkers, and the external environment.

- The ***second step*** requires managers and staff members to begin to see themselves as being partly *responsible* for causing an organization's performance problems and issues. Once this sense of personal responsibility sufficiently penetrates a person's denial and defense routines, they begin to experience *survival anxiety* or *guilt* about the "truth" that they really need to change. In the final analysis, organizations are collective-cultural entities that are led, managed and changed one person at a time.

- As their awareness increases, the ***third step*** is for individuals to allow *their* contributions to the day-to-day problems in an organization to function as additional *disconfirming evidence* that further convinces them that things cannot continue the way they are. When the weight of evidence of these three steps *combines*, this becomes a powerful motivation for managers and staff members in an organization to change.

But Schein points out that as soon as managers and staff members accept the need to change, they begin experiencing *learning anxiety*; e.g., the fear of doing things differently, changing the patterns-of-interaction in relationships (POI), and reconfiguring the world (reality) in which the work-group operates (COI). This creates both cognitive and emotional dissonance. In fact, the level of rigidity with which a person holds to their way of seeing the world is often directly proportional to their tendency to practice *either-or-thinking*, rather than *both-and-thinking*.

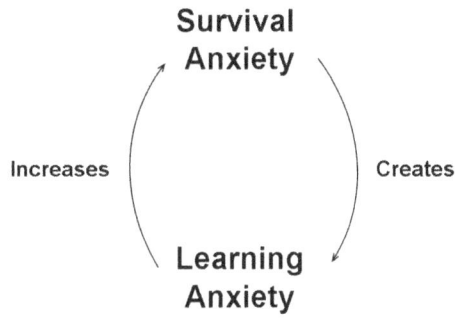

Figure 39

As shown in Figure 39, the self-reinforcing loop of survival anxiety, creating learning anxiety, and in turn increasing survival anxiety, is why most people actually maintain organizational and interpersonal interactions that are dominated by destructive conflict. Schein claims that there are two principles that summarize a process for moving beyond this self-defeating cycle.[194]

- Initially, survival anxiety and/or guilt must be greater than the learning anxiety on the part of managers and staff in order to penetrate their defenses and begin the process of recognizing and changing destructive patterns-of-interaction.

- Creating change requires that learning anxiety be *reduced* by creating a climate of psychological safety for managers and staff members, rather than increasing survival anxiety for the people involved.

One of the best ways to decrease learning anxiety in the face of survival anxiety is to depersonalize the issues and conflict, which mitigates or eliminates blame. This is one of the greatest values of the data presented by the BCI – they *depersonalize* conflict by showing that the vast majority of destructive conflict or ineffective communication is not the result of intentional behavior. Rather, destructive conflict is often the product of an organization's structures, systems, culture, and the autopilot responses of the personalities of managers and staff members. Managed properly, the interaction between learning anxiety and survival anxiety can be used to create deep, profound, sustainable change in work-groups and entire organizations.

Deep Learning Requires Unlearning

As outlined in Chapter 2, the See-Do-Get Process is a meta-model that describes how organizational culture is created, reinforced, and maintained. More specifically, the purpose of culture (any culture) is to teach people how to see the world. Understanding the See-Do-Get Process will reveal underlying patterns of behavior that happen all around you, but are not well-understood or seen to be what they are. Let's return to the example of Curt, Sarah, and Jeff where a customer (Curt) walks into a store and a new sales person (Sarah) and her manager (Jeff) are standing at the register checking an order. Jeff comments quietly about Curt, "He always gives us a hard time," so they ignore him, trying to avoid conflict. Curt reads this emotional message in their behavior and actually feels ignored. After a few minutes of just standing around, Curt snaps critically, "Hey, young lady! I need some help over here!" Sarah looks at Jeff and thinks to herself,

See – You said he'd give me a hard time!

The See-Do-Get Process is a way of describing how our knowledge and beliefs are shaped by how we see ourselves, other people, and the world around us (see Figure 40). First, we are taught to see the world a certain way and specific behaviors and emotions naturally flow from that worldview because we believe that it is "reality." When we act out these behaviors in relationships, people read our body language and respond to the message they see in us. Their response then reinforces how we see them, how they see us, and it begins to create patterns-of-interaction in the relationship.

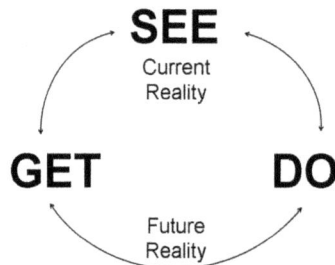

SEE
Current
Reality

GET

DO

Future
Reality

Figure 40

Managers and staff members are actively taught how to see themselves, coworkers, customers, suppliers, competitors, and the external environment in which they are embedded. Recall the example of John and Sally, where John starts a new job as an Account Executive in the Sales Department at SciTech and as he begins calling on his new accounts, his manager Sally says, "That's not how we do it around here. Let me show you how we want you to see our customers, and the people in the Production Department." The Active Teaching Process is one of the primary ways that organizational and work-group culture is passed on to both new and existing employees. So work-groups actively teach employees to see the world a certain way with the goal that specific actions and interactions will naturally flow from that worldview. When an experienced manager or more seasoned employee models (acts out) the cultural norms they teach as a problem-solving strategy or in response to day-to-day operations, new or less experienced employees take note of their actions, interactions, and body language. If they are more or less successful in getting the desired results, this reinforces the cultural norm and creates a shared understanding that this is how things are done in that work-group or the entire organization.

It is important to note that deep learning almost always requires us to "unlearn" other ways of seeing ourselves, others, and the world around us. The process of unlearning happens when we run the See-Do-Get Process backwards in the counter-clockwise direction with the goal of developing a different future reality for our organizations, our work-groups, and our relationships (see Figure 40). It is also important to remember the Individual-Collective Paradox; e.g., that *organizations are collective-cultural entities that are led, managed, and changed one person at a time.* So whether an assessor is working with an individual; small-groups of 2s, 3s, or 4s; a work-group; or with an entire organization, they should begin by leading their clients through a series of questions that will take them backwards through the See-Do-Get Process. Notice that the steps listed below are mapped to the Breckenridge Equation described in Chapter 2.

- *Get (Results)*: What results are we getting that we wish we weren't getting (Current Results)?

- *Do (Patterns-of-interaction)*: In what ways are the current results linked to (and created by) the "gap" between the formal organization's structures, systems, and culture (COI) and the informal structures, systems, and culture (POI) as manifested in the Interaction Map?

- *See (Repository-of-interaction)*: What are the underlying beliefs and tacit assumptions (ROI) that allow the current patterns-of-interaction to continue (POI), despite the fact that the organization or work-group is not achieving its goals and objectives (COI)?

- *Do (Patterns-of-interaction)*: How do we reconfigure the formal structures and systems (COI) and informal structures, systems, and patterns-of-interaction (POI) to reflect new ways of seeing ourselves, others, and the world (ROI) that will give us the results we want? What changes can we predict in the results we're currently getting that can be empirically verified to prove that we are making progress toward our goals and that improvement has actually occurred?

- *Get (Results)*: Over time, positive changes will begin to *disconfirm* the old ways of seeing, previous patterns-of-interaction, and ways of doing business (Desired Results).

While the above process is presented in a sequential order, the key to using the See-Do-Get Process in the counter clockwise direction is: a) to work on the See and Do steps at the same time, and b) to embed changes in the day-to-day realities of life until the new more effective ways of doing business happen as automatically as the old ineffective ones once did. When new results emerge from the See-Do-Get Process, they will confirm the fact that change has actually occurred, which will reinforce a new view; e.g., "See, we can improve our performance."

So what happens when individuals don't want to accept organizational and cultural change and are either overtly or covertly opposed to the personal and/or group change process? Employees in organizations normally fall into a well-defined distribution that follows a 20-60-20 Rule. In any given situation where change is initiated, about 20% of the people will be strong supporters of the change and about 20% will be strongly opposed, as shown in Figure 41. The 20% groups on both ends of the distribution are normally so firmly set in their ways of seeing that no amount of persuasion will change their views. The remaining 60% tend to align with whichever end of the distribution gains control.

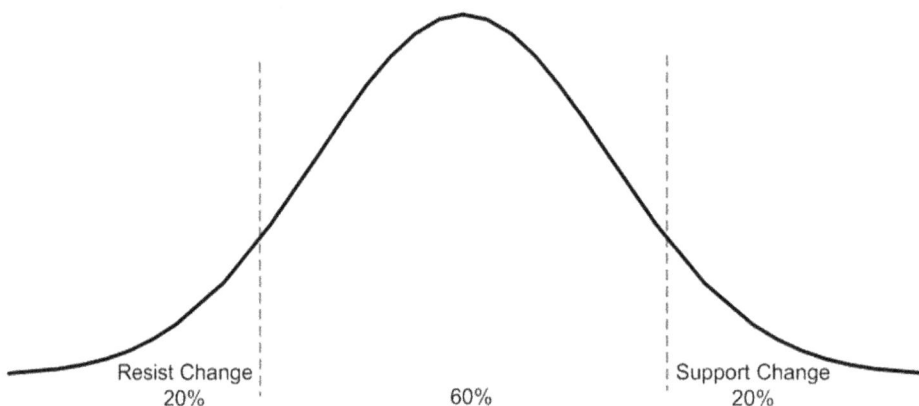

| Resist Change | 60% | Support Change |
| 20% | | 20% |

Figure 41

The most difficult issue is when high-performing individuals do not (or will not) accept change that top managers or middle managers believe is in the best interest of the organization. When otherwise productive employees resist change in unproductive or destructive ways, the goal should be to migrate them to the right side of the distribution shown in Figure 41 if at all possible. Often times, the new social norms make the pressure to conform so powerful that people who don't buy in (or won't buy-in) *self-select* out of a work-group or organization.

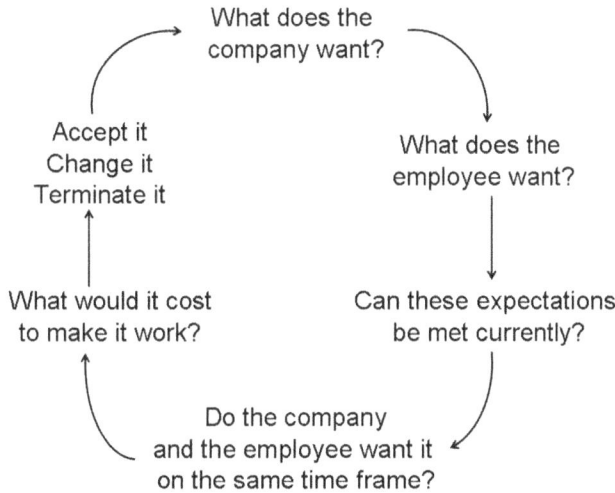

Figure 42

When people will not *self-select* out and they continue to frustrate and undermine the organization's performance through destructive conflict, managers need to follow Jim Collins advice and get the right people on the bus and the wrong people off the bus.[195] The diagram above shows a Six-Step Decision Making Process for doing this.

The six questions listed below can be used to evaluate employee issues regardless of whether they are top managers, middle managers, front-line supervisors, or staff members. The responsible manager and the employee must ask:

- What does the company really want from the employee?

- What does the employee really want from the company?

- Can these expectations be met in the current situation?

- Do the company and the employee want it on the same time frame?

- What would it cost to make it work (time, money, energy, etc.)?

- Three choices: accept it, change it, or terminate the relationship

Sometimes an organization wants very different levels of performance and attitudes from an employee than a manager or staff member wants to give. Sometimes the company and the employee both want the same things, but they can't make it happen in the present context. For example, the company and the employee agree that the person is best suited for a sales position, but the organization does not have an opening for the person at the appropriate organizational and salary levels. Maybe the organization and the employee want the same things, and even want them within the present context, but they want them on very different time frames. For example, the organization wants the employee to move from a front-line supervisor to a middle manager, but they don't have the budget to support the promotion until the next fiscal year and the employee has a job offer from another company and needs to make a decision now. Sometimes organizations and employees want the same things in the work relationship, on the same time frame, but one or the other may be unwilling to pay the price it would take to make the professional relationship work. Based on these questions, the responsible manager and the employee always have three choices:

- They can *accept* the situation (do nothing)

- They can try to *change* the situation

- They can *terminate* the work relationship

When properly understood and validated, the data provided in the BCI provide a shorthand way of understanding and more effectively managing the differences between people at the individual, small-group, work-group, and organizational levels and for making these kinds of staffing decisions.

The Path Forward to Desired Results

Once assessors help their client organization identify what they want their desired results to be using the process described in the previous section, the Breckenridge Change Equation™ (described below) can be used to identify corrective actions and define a path forward toward achieving those desired results. There are two key principles that must be kept in mind whenever change is introduced into an organization.

- First, focus on improving the configuration of the organizational structures, systems, and culture, *not* blaming individuals for organizational performance problems.

- Second, when you change the configuration of the structures, systems, and culture, assessors and their clients should ensure that they do not frustrate or undermine things that are working now; e.g., they don't optimize one part of the configuration, and sub-optimize the performance of another work-group or the overall organization.

Remember that organizational structures and systems are either *consciously* defined with purpose and intent around a strategic direction yielding an Intended Culture, or they *emerge naturally* from the operational and relational patterns-of-interaction of group members (POI) within a specific organizational context (COI) as an Unintended Culture. Unintentionally designed structures, systems, and culture often create contention between managers and staff and are the single biggest cause of destructive conflict and decreased levels of performance in work-groups. Using the Breckenridge Change Equation allows work-groups to consciously reconfigure their day-to-day operations to get the results they want. The Breckenridge Change Equation is as follows:

$$POI \leftrightarrow COI \leftrightarrow ROI \text{ X } EOI = \textbf{Desired Results}^{\text{TM}}$$

The goal is to: a) raise the ineffective operational (work processes) and relational (2s, 3s, and 4s) POIs and problematic elements of the COI back into organizational consciousness, b) reconfigure them to get the desired results, c) migrate them back to autopilot operations by embedding these changes through repetition (EOI), until d) the organization achieves the desired results, and e) the new ROI and POI happen as unconsciously as the old ineffective ones did. This can be viewed as a seven-step process.[196]

- Step 1: Define the desired results, including both quantitative and qualitative measures of performance (key performance indicators). Quantify what the return on investment will be if these changes are made in terms of improved performance, decreased conflict, increased revenue, and/or decreased labor and operating costs.

- Step 2: Identify ineffective POI, COI, and ROI that are preventing the work-group from getting these results and then take them off autopilot through careful analysis, scrutiny, measurement, and evaluation of enterprise-wide business processes and the associated support processes. These are the ineffective autopilot operations, Red Flags, and Invisible Bureaucracy described throughout this book.

- Step 3: Reconfigure as many of the ineffective elements of COI as possible; e.g., structures, systems, policies, processes, facilities, locations, etc. Build alliances and partnerships with other work-groups to reconfigure ineffective elements of COI that cross organizational and functional boundaries.

- Step 4: Disrupt and reconfigure the ineffective operational (work processes) and relational (2s, 3s, and 4s) POIs to achieve the desired results.

- Step 5: Use the quantitative and qualitative measures of performance defined in Step 1 to: a) measure the rate and characteristics of change, b) disconfirm previous ways of seeing and working, c) reinforce the fact that change is actually happening, and d) increase the momentum and support for change.[197]

- Step 6: Identify and implement embedding processes that will institutionalize change and make it sustainable through repetition (EOI); e.g., build change into the organization's compensation system and ensure that managers reward change by what they pay attention to and focus on, etc. It's important to remember that ROI emerges naturally (indirectly) from the interaction of POI and COI, not through direct action and activities.

- Step 7: Migrate the new POI, COI, and ROI back to autopilot through repetition (EOI) until the new ways of seeing and working, and the desired results, happen as automatically as the old ineffective ones did. This creates *effective* autopilot operations, and minimizes or eliminates the Red Flags and Invisible Bureaucracy.

Whether a leader is the founder of a new company or a top, line or middle manager in a well-established company, one of their most important tasks is to *create*, *manage*, and (if necessary) to *destroy* organizational culture in order to get the desired results for a work-group or organization. The precise definition of culture presented in the Breckenridge Equation and the embedding mechanisms described below give leaders and managers a powerful set of tools for doing this.[198]

An organization's existing culture is solidified and reinforced by four things: a) *primary* embedding mechanisms that solidify and reinforce an organization's existing culture by rewarding the actions and interactions that should *actually* get done (POI), b) *secondary* embedding mechanisms composed primarily of elements of the organization's COI, c) *tertiary* embedding mechanisms for "managing meaning" about what the primary and secondary embedding mechanisms mean within that cultural setting, and d) repetition that reaffirms the view that the organization's reality is *the* reality. In culture change initiatives, the same four embedding mechanisms are used, but they must be: a) taken off autopilot, b) reconfigured to get the desired results, and c) intentionally migrated back to autopilot operations through repetition (EOI) until the new more effective results happen as automatically as the former ineffective ones did. The embedding mechanisms are described in more detail below:

- *Primary Embedding Mechanisms*: Rewards and Decisions are a vital part of, and primary embedding mechanism for, reinforcing cultural change because they define what actions and interactions should *actually* get done; e.g., what people should focus their time, energy, and resources on. These are measured by the Execution radar shown in Figure 21 as well as other BCI perspectives.

- *Secondary Embedding Mechanisms*: These include organizational design; geographic location; physical space, décor, and facilities; equipment; procedures; formal statements about core ideology (purpose, core values) and philosophy; structures and systems that are consciously designed to reinforce (reward) the desired behaviors and send a consistent set of signals that narrow the gap between the POI and the COI. These are measured by the Strategic View radar shown in Figure 18, the Execution radar shown in Figure 21, the Organizational Climate radar shown in Figure 24, as well as other aspects of the BCI assessment and the day-to-day realities of organizational life.

- *Tertiary Embedding Mechanisms*: This is about "managing meaning" at the organizational, work-group, small-group, and individual levels by interpreting what primary and secondary embedding mechanisms and other aspects of the organization's actions and interactions *mean* (ROI) within the context of the organization's history and culture. It also involves consciously creating organizational rituals, ceremonies, traditions, heroes, and stories that reinforce the primary and secondary embedding mechanisms and in turn become part of the organization's identity and history.

- *Repetition:* This is the migrating function that solidifies a new organizational reality where over time the desired more effective results begin to happen as automatically as the former ineffective ones did.

Here are ten guidelines for the managers who attempt to make the kinds of changes described in this chapter and throughout the contents of this book.[199]

- Make sure that the changes you propose are in the best interest of the overall organization, not the self-interest of your work-group.

- Solve your own work-group's problems first and become an example of change.

- Create your own organizational "space" and obtain additional resources based on the value you add.

- Align your work-group's vision with other work-groups, departments, and functional units by focusing on the things you hold in common and contribute to achieving the purpose and goals of the overall organization.

- Communicate the trade-offs of actually accomplishing change to work-group members.

- Manage meaning for people both in and out of your work-group so changes are interpreted through the "lens" of your work-group's vision.

- Only engage in constructive conflict with other work-groups or managers, and only do this when you have to for the best interest of the overall organization.

- Cultivate allies who will support the change and form open coalitions to ensure that change is sustainable.

- Create a concrete, tangible path forward with credible next steps and a well-defined picture of the value-added that the change will bring to the overall organization.

- Find and use exemplars (measurements) to *reinforce* the fact that change is actually happening and also to *accelerate* change.

The bottom-line in considering whether an organization should embark on a cultural change process is that culture change is extremely difficult to make and sustain, so managers should count the cost before embarking on the journey. Cultural change requires a sustained investment of resources as well as an enormous amount of psychological and organizational energy. This type of deep change will disrupt an organization's status quo and challenge its tacit assumptions, belief structure and ways of doing business, so an organization must really want to change badly in order to endure the chaos that the process will create. Schein argues that the intensity of disruption of cultural change is *the organizational equivalent of psychotherapy for individuals.*[200] The difficulty of deconstructing an individual's personality fixations pales in the light of creating and sustaining that kind of change for hundreds (or even thousands) of people. In many cases, it challenges and undermines employees' professional identities and the way they've done their jobs for years, so they overtly or covertly push back on change with enormous force of will.

Schein reminds us that the popular notion that learning is "fun" does not apply to cultural change because the profound deconstruction of organizational culture is coercive and produces anxiety and fear that is not unlike what happens during *brainwashing.* Consequently, an organization should not underestimate the enormous levels of fear and powerful defense routines that will mobilize to resist even the constructive conflict that is required for cultural change. This is why most cultural change initiatives fail. Owners and managers wade into the deep waters of the change process, get in over their heads, and then decide they don't want change *that* bad! Obtaining sustainable cultural change will require your organization to tolerate the uncertainty that deconstructing brings *long enough* for new cultural norms to emerge and replace the old ones.

John Kotter and James Heskett liken the resistance to cultural change to a mattress or sofa with inner springs. When you sit on a sofa, the force of your body-weight changes the sofa's shape, but the springs are designed to return to their original position once the force is removed.[201] In much the same way, leaders use the force of their authority to change the "shape" of organizational culture, but like a sofa it resists. When employees *say* they will support change, but *do* things to undermine and frustrate it, leaders and managers normally increase the amount of force proportionally and this becomes increasingly difficult to sustain over long periods of time. A practical example of the "sofa effect" is the use of software packages to change the way work is performed. In most cases, leaders and managers don't have to apply increasing levels of pressure to enforce changes to work processes because the new software won't allow employees to work in the old way – they're forced to adopt the change. But despite this, some employees will circumvent change by spending days, weeks, or even months using peripheral software packages to make the new system look and feel like the old one; e.g., they download data from the new accounting software into a spreadsheet then format it to work like the old process. In other words, they create *shadow systems*. When leaders diminish, remove, or inconsistently apply organizational force, the culture migrates back to its original shape just like a sofa. Often, employees passively resist the changes and eventually the initiative loses steam and dies. Each time employees succeed in derailing a change initiative the culture of ineffective autopilot operations, Red Flags, and Invisible Bureaucracy becomes more robust and more difficult to change the next time. The Breckenridge Institute normally advises clients that it's better *not* to undertake a process of cultural transformation at all than to begin, fail, and fatigue your organization with yet one more "flavor of the month."

As described earlier in this chapter, Schein explains that the most effective way to mitigate the fear and *learning anxiety* that are associated with cultural change is to create a sense of organizational and psychological safety for people undergoing the change. He suggests a number of ways for approaching culture change initiatives. The list below echoes his suggestions as well as others from Collins' book, *Good to Great*.[202]

- Have an inspiring and compelling vision that people resonate with.

- Educate the organization about the concept of culture and what is involved in cultural change.

- Clearly identify which cultural elements will aid in the change effort and which will hinder it.

- Use measurement and quantitative data to *disconfirm* information that creates learning anxiety.

- Conduct formal training and workshops on the new skills, behaviors, or attitudes.

- Involve the learners in shaping the training process.

- Conduct informal training of sub-groups and teams.

- Create a temporary (parallel) learning system where new skills and assumptions can be learned and tested.

- Provide resources, time, coaching, mentoring, and feedback on the performance of new tasks.

- Use positive role models that people can imitate and identify with to concretize new behaviors.

- Form support groups for people to talk about how they feel about the change.

- Help people connect new meanings to old concepts and practices (manage meaning).

- Ensure that communication about the change sends a consistent set of signals.

- Create new standards of performance evaluation that align with and reinforce the change.

- Adopt the Stockdale Paradox as a creed: never give up hope of prevailing *and* face the brutal facts.

So moving beyond the "sofa effect" and actually changing an organization's culture requires a climate of organizational and psychological safety that gives employees time to internalize and adopt these changes *as their own*. As William Bridges points out, this transition happens slowly, over time, as people discover that the *new* ways of working are more effective than the *old* ones and only then can they rationally relate the new ways of working to the ones used previously.[203] Even when the change has a profoundly *positive* impact on an organization's work process, efficiency, and overall performance; if employees can't make psychological sense out of the change it will not be sustainable.

How long does it take to make this type of deep cultural change? Realistically, it takes as long as it takes. In fact, some studies show that a cultural change initiative requires years and that the momentum is lost at least once because many employees prefer that the change not happen. In many of these cases, visionary leaders intervened personally to get the change process back on track, and publicly reaffirm their commitment to staying the course. Studies and extensive experience have shown that in a mature organization where the culture is well solidified, even when substantial resources are *dedicated specifically* to the change process it takes at least eighteen months to two years per level of organizational management changed. In other words, if an organization's structure has three levels – top, middle, and front line managers – deep cultural change may take about eight years. Schein reminds us that with major cultural transformations (like Procter & Gamble's conversion to a new manufacturing system) the process took over fifteen years.[204]

The approach to assessing and changing organizational culture described in this book will help assessors and their clients transform an organization's culture into a powerful resource that *effectively* performs day-to-day operations on autopilot; e.g., effectively and seamlessly without thinking about them. When done *effectively*, autopilot operations can be an organization's greatest ally because they increase its ability to compete and achieve its goals and objective. But in most cases they are self-defeating because they perpetuate problems with work performance, communication, interpersonal conflict, and decision-making and then derail attempts to create positive change. This unique approach to organizational culture helps managers take ineffective operations off autopilot, *reconfigure* them, and then *migrate* them back to autopilot operations that produce the desired results. Understanding how Invisible Bureaucracy actually works allows an organization to transform its culture into a more reliable resource that can be used to achieve its goals, objectives, and organizational purpose.

I'd like to end this book by reaffirming my conviction that the process of assessing and changing organizational culture must be focused on business problems and issues that matter to managers. It's a mistake for assessors to lead with cultural analysis and cultural change because such activities are of little value unless they are linked to one or more of the six interdependent dimensions of organizational life: a) generating and retaining revenue, b) the effectiveness and cost of labor, human capital, c) the effectiveness and cost of operating an organization, d) key performance indicators that measure an organization's performance with high-precision, e) the identification and reduction of squandered time and energy, and f) a focus on sustainability and making long-term investments in human, material, and financial resources. If the activities associated with assessing and changing organizational culture cannot be meaningfully linked to one or more of these six dimensions, then they should probably not be done. Diagnosing and changing organizational culture for its own sake provides little or no value to organizations and the managers who lead them. Rather, if an organization needs to develop a new strategy or strategic plan; improve its execution and day-to-day operations; implement new IT infrastructure; seamlessly integrate business systems; or improve the decision-making and consensus process for the allocation of human, material, and financial resources; then understanding how its culture positively and negatively impacts these (and other) issues is not only value-added, it's necessary.

ABOUT THE AUTHOR

Mark Bodnarczuk is the Executive Director of the Breckenridge Institute®, a research and consulting firm that focuses on organizational development and organizational culture based in Boulder, Colorado. He was on the staff in the Director's Office at Fermi National Accelerator Laboratory (Fermilab) from 1980 through 1992, and the National Renewable Energy Laboratory from 1992 until 1996 when he founded the Breckenridge Institute®. While at the University of Chicago, his research focused on the sociology and culture of large physics collaborations at Fermilab.

He is an author, researcher, consultant, teacher, and facilitator with more than twenty years of experience working with companies in the area of high-tech, basic and applied research, pharmaceuticals, health care, retail as well as government and non-profit organizations. Mark has published widely in the areas of corporate culture and leadership development and is the author of a number of books including, *The Breckenridge Enneagram: A Guide to Personal and Professional Growth*, and *Diving In: Discovering Who You Are In the Second Half of Life*. Mark has published numerous articles on the leadership and management of science and the cultural dimensions of laboratory life.

Mark is also the author of a number of psychometrically validated instruments including, the *Breckenridge Culture Indicator™ (BCI™)* which provides a quantitative and qualitative measure of organizational culture with high levels of reliability, validity and overall statistical precision, and the *Breckenridge Type Indicator™ (BTI™)* which is the most valid and reliable on-line Enneagram assessment instrument available.

Mark is a professional-level member of the International Society for Performance Improvement (ISPI) and the Institute of Management Consultants (IMC). He has a BA from Mid-America University, an MA from Wheaton College, and an AM from the University of Chicago.

FOR MORE INFORMATION

The Breckenridge Institute® offers on-line and workshop-based training on the principles and practices described in this book and the Breckenridge Culture Indicator™ (BCI™) for professionals who want to use this approach in their consulting practice. Typical business applications of *Making Invisible Bureaucracy Visible* and the BCI are:

- *Changes in Leadership or Management*: The BCI gives new senior or middle managers the operational and cultural information they need to get "up to speed" more quickly.

- *Mergers and Acquisitions*: When two companies are merged, or when one company purchases another, the BCI can help identify misalignments between the cultural characteristics and ways of working in both entities, thus facilitating the integration process.

- *Declining or Plateaued Organizational Performance*: Senior or middle managers can use the BCI to identify the root causes and underlying patterns of ineffective organizational behaviors that stifle growth and prevent organizations from achieving their goals.

- *Business Process Improvement*: The BCI identifies the cultural context within which business processes operate so process owners can develop more effective solutions to problems like rework, poor or inconsistent quality and service, work-arounds, timeliness, downtime, ineffective communication, interpersonal conflict, and lack of employee motivation.

- *Organizational Growth*: Proactive companies can use the BCI as a tool for creating the new organizational structures, systems, and competencies needed to manage growth.

- *Management Reviews*: The BCI can be used by a Board of Directors or senior managers to obtain an outside, "third party" perspective on a project's status, or an organization's or work-group's level of performance relative to its goals and objectives, within the context of its unique configuration of structures, systems, and culture.

- *Change Management*: When implementing a new IT system, reorganizing work-groups, or implementing new business processes, the BCI can provide penetrating insight into the underlying assumptions, beliefs, values, and cultural issues that can frustrate, undermine and ultimately derail the implementation of structures and systems designed to improve organizational performance.

- *Strategic Planning*: The BCI provides quantitative input into a company's strategic planning process by indicating the organization's Strengths and Weaknesses and the ways in which they act interdependently with Opportunities and Threats in the business environment (SWOT analysis).

- *Leadership Development*: The BCI can be used to develop leadership skills within the context of an organization's structures, systems, and culture. It can also be used as a more effective alternative to 360-degree reviews which often become "finger-pointing" exercises.

- *Teambuilding*: Used with teams of managers or work units, the BCI helps create common purpose and goals for work units that might otherwise operate as functional "silos," thus undermining the objectives of the overall organization.

For information go to
http://www.breckenridgeinstitute.com/online-assessments.htm,
or contact the Breckenridge Institute at the address below.

Breckenridge Institute®
PO Box 7950
Boulder, Colorado 80306
Phone: 1-800-303-2554; Fax: 1-888-745-1886
info@breckenridgeinstitute.com
www.breckenridgeinstitute.com

END NOTES AND RESOURCES

[1] The notion of "Invisible Bureaucracy" was first used in Howell Baum, *The Invisible Bureaucracy: The Unconscious in Organizational Problem Solving*, (New York: Oxford University Press, 1987).

[2] Deming claims that 94% of organizational performance problems are attributable to "common causes" in the structures, systems, and culture that are the responsibility of "management" and only 6% are due to the performance of individual employees (local causes), see W. Edwards Deming, *Out of Crisis*, (Cambridge, MA: Massachusetts Institute of Technology Center for Advanced Engineering Study, 1992), p. 314 ff. Juran claims that 85% of performance problems are attributable to root causes in the structures, systems and culture, see J.M Juran (ed.), *Quality Control Handbook*, 3rd edition, (New York: McGraw-Hill Book Company, 1979) p. 2/20 ff. In the area of safety investigation and risk analysis, James Reason attributes about 80% of all human errors and safety incidents to latent conditions (latent organizational weaknesses) in an organization's structures, systems, and culture, see James Reason, *Managing the Risks of Organizational Accidents*, (Burlington, VT: Ashgate, 1997), p. 10 ff.

[3] See Edgar Schein, *Process Consultation Revisited*, (New York: Addison-Wesley, 1999).

[4] See Harry Levinson, *Organizational Assessment*, (Washington, DC: American Psychological Association, 2002).

[5] See Chris Argyris, Robert Putnam, and Diana McLain Smith, *Action Science: Concepts, Methods, and Skills for Research and Intervention*, (San Francisco: Jossey-Bass Publishers, 1985).

[6] See Chris Argyris, *Flawed Advice and the Management Trap: How Managers Can Know When They're Getting Good Advice and When They're Not*, (New York: Oxford University Press, 2000).

[7] See Argyris, *Flawed Advice and the Management Trap*, 2000, pp. 3-4.

[8] Edgar Schein describes difficulties that he had in two different client organizations where the interventions he was leading "were not working." He reflected on these experiences, stating, "I did not really understand what happened in either of these cases until I began to examine *my own assumptions* about how things should work in these organizations and began to test whether my assumptions fitted those operating in my client systems." See Edgar Schein, *Organizational Culture and Leadership*, 2nd edition, (San Francisco, CA: Jossey-Bass, 1992), p. 7.

[9] This extended quote comes from James C. Collins and Jerry I Porras, *Built to Last: Successful Habits of Visionary Companies*, (New York: Harper Business, 1994), pp. 43-44 ff.

[10] The view that the yin and yang principles are opposite, but mutually complementary is discussed in more detail in Alfred Huang, *The Complete I Ching*, (Rochester, VT: Inner Traditions, 1998), p. 43 ff. Covey refers to this as Synergy – learning how to value the differences in others, see Stephen R. Covey, *The 7 Habits of Highly Effective People*, (New York: A Fireside Book, 1990), p. 261 ff. Carl Jung discusses the essential tension and ultimate union of opposites as one of the central problems in both individual and collective (social) psychology, see C.G. Jung, "Mysterium Coniunctionis" 2nd edition in, *The Collected Works of C.G. Jung*, volume 14, (Princeton, NJ: Princeton University Press, 1989), p. 3 (par. 1), and p. 457 (par. 654).

[11] See David Sibbet, "75 Years of Management Ideas and Practice" in the *Harvard Business Review*, September-October 1997, Reprint 97500.

[12] See Alfred Chandler, *Strategy and Structure*, (Cambridge, MA: MIT Press, 1970).

[13] See Alfred Chandler, *The Visible Hand*, (Cambridge, MA: Harvard University Press, 1977).

[14] See Jay Galbraith, *Organization Design*, (New York: Addison Wesley Publishing Company, 1977).

[15] See Raymond Miles and Charles Snow, *Organizational Strategy, Structure, and Process*, (Stanford, CA: Stanford Business Classics, 1978).

[16] See Michael Porter, *Competitive Strategy*, (New York: Free Press, 1980).

[17] See Deming, *Out of Crisis*, 1982.

[18] See Michael Porter, *Competitive Advantage*, (New York: Free Press, 1985).

[19] David Hanna, *Designing Organizations for High Performance*, (New York: Addison-Wesley Publishing Company, 1988).

[20] See C.K. Prahalad and Gary Hamel, "Core Competence of the Corporation" in *Harvard Business Review*, May-June, 1990, Reprint 90311.

[21] See Henry Mintzberg, "The Manager's Job: Folklore and Fact" in the *Harvard Business Review*, March-April, 1990, Reprint 90210.

[22] See Robert Kaplan and David Norton, *The Balanced Scorecard*, (Boston: Harvard Business School Press, 1996).

[23] See Thomas Davenport, *Process Innovation: Reengineering Work through Information Technology*, (Boston: Harvard Business School Press, 1992).

[24] See Michael Hammer and James Champy, *Reengineering the Corporation*, (New York: Harper Business, 1994).

[25] See Bob Filipczak, "I Have to What?" in *Training*, Volume 32, No. 12, pp. 30-34.

[26] See Thomas Davenport, "Why Reengineering Failed: The Fad that Forgot People" in *Fast Company*, Premiere Issue, p. 72.

[27] See David Noer, *Healing the Wounds: Overcoming the Trauma of Layoffs and Revitalizing Downsized Organizations*, (San Francisco: Jossey-Bass, 1993), p. 20.

[28] See Carol J. Loomis, "AT&T has No Clothes" in *Fortune*, February 5, 1996, p. 78 ff.

[29] See Thomas Davenport, "Why Reengineering Failed: The Fad that Forgot People" in *Fast Company*, Premiere Issue, pp. 71-72; and Noer, *Healing the Wounds*, 1993, p.88.

[30] See Larry Bossidy and Ram Charan, *Confronting Reality: Doing What Matters to Get Things Right*, (New York: Crown Books, 2004); W. Chan Kim and Renee Mauborgne, *Blue Ocean Strategy: How to Create Uncontested Market Space and Make the Competition Irrelevant*, (Boston: Harvard Business School Press, 2005); Alec Sharp and Patrick McDermott, *Workflow Modeling: Tools for Process Improvement and Application Development*, (2001); Bennet Lientz and Kathryn Rea, *Breakthrough IT Change Management*, (New York: Elsevier Butterworth Heinemann, 2004); and John Hayes, *The Theory and Practice of Change Management*, 2nd edition, (New York: Palgrave Macmillian, 2007).

[31] Some of the books that have been written subsequently include the following: Terrence Deal and Allan Kennedy, *The New Corporate Cultures*, (Cambridge, MA: Perseus Publishing, 2000); Edgar Schein, *The Corporate Culture Survival Guide*, (San Francisco: Jossey-Bass, 1999); Kim Cameron and Robert Quinn, *Diagnosing and Changing Organizational Culture*, (New York: Addison-Wesley, 1999); Andrew Brown, *Organisational Culture*, (New York: Prentice Hall, 1998); Gerald Driskill and Angela Laird Brenton, *Organizational Culture in Action*, (Thousand Oaks, CA: Sage Publications, 2005); and Joanne Martin, *Organizational Culture: Mapping the Terrain*, (Thousand Oaks, CA: Sage Publications, 2002).

[32] See Charles Handy, *Understanding Organizations*, 4th edition (New York: Penguin Global, 2005).

[33] See Geert Hofstede, *Culture's Consequences: Comparing Values, Behaviors, Institutions, and Organizations across Nations*, 2nd edition, (New York: Sage Publications, 2003).

[34] See Terrence Deal and Allen Kennedy, *Corporate Cultures: The Rites and Rituals of Corporate Life*, (Menlo Park, CA: Addison-Wesley Publishing Company, 1982).

[35] See Thomas Peters and Robert Waterman, *In Search of Excellence*, (New York: Time Warner Books, 1982).

[36] See Rosabeth Moss Kanter, *The Change Masters: Innovation & Entrepreneurship in the American Corporation*, (New York: A Touchstone Book, 1983).

[37] See Schein, *Organizational Culture and Leadership*, 1992.

[38] See Argyris, *Action Science*, 1985.

[39] See Ralph Kilmann, Mary Saxton, Roy Serpa (eds.), *Gaining Control of the Corporate Culture*, (San Francisco, CA: Jossey-Bass, 1985).

[40] Baum, *The Invisible Bureaucracy*, 1987.

[41] Ichak Adizes, *Corporate Life Cycles*, (Paramus, NJ: Prentice Hall, 1988).

[42] See Lawrence Miller, *Barbarians to Bureaucrats*, (New York: Fawcett Columbine, 1989).

[43] See Alan Wilkins, *Developing Corporate Character: How to Successfully Change an Organization without Destroying It*, (San Francisco, CA: Jossey-Bass, 1989).

[44] See Peter Senge, *The Fifth Discipline*, (New York: Currency Doubleday, 1990).

[45] John Kotter and James Heskett, *Corporate Culture and Performance*, (New York: Free Press, 1992).

[46] See Collins and Porras, *Built to Last*, 1994.

[47] See Robert Barnhart (ed.), *Chambers Dictionary of Etymology*, (New York: H.W. Wilson Company, 2003), p. 241; N.J. Rengger, *Retreat from the Modern: Humanism, Postmodernism, and the Fight from Modernist Culture*, (London: Bowerdean Publishing Limited, 1996), p. 9 and ff.; and William Wordsworth, *Prelude*, (New York: W.W. Norton & Company, 1978).

[48] See Matthew Arnold, *Culture and Anarchy and other Writings*, edited by Stefan Collini, (New York: Cambridge University Press, 1993).

[49] See Raymond Williams, *Culture and Society 1780-1950*, (New York: Columbia University Press, 1983); Raymond Williams, *Keywords: A Vocabulary of Culture and Society*, (New York: Oxford University Press, 1985); John Storey, *Cultural Theory and Popular Culture*, 3rd edition, (Atlanta, GA: University of Georgia Press, 2001); and Raymond Betts, *A History of Popular Culture*, 1st edition, (New York: Routledge, 2004).

[50] See Allan Bloom, "Commerce and Culture," in *Giants and Dwarfs*, (Simon and Schuster: Touchstone, 1990); Immanuel Kant, *Perpetual Peace, and Other Essays on Politics, History, and Morals*, (New York: Hackett Publishing Company, 1983); Jean-Jacques Rousseau, *A Discourse on the Origin of Inequality and A Discourse on Political Economy*, (London: Neeland Media, LLC, 2007); and Jean-Jacques Rousseau, *Rousseau: "The Social Contract" and Other Later Political Writings (Cambridge Texts in the History of Political Thought)*, (New York: Cambridge University Press, 1997).

[51] See Arnold, *Arnold: "Culture and Anarchy" and Other Writings*, 1993; and T.S. Eliot, *Notes Towards a definition of Culture*, (New York: Faber and Faber, 1973).

[52] See Raymond Williams, *The Sociology of Culture*, (Chicago: The University of Chicago Press, 1995), p. 10; Johann Gottfried von Herder, *Herder: Philosophical Writings (Cambridge Texts in the History of Philosophy)*, (New York: Cambridge University Press, 2002); and the earlier work of Giambattista Vico, *New Science*, (Penguin Classics, 3rd edition, 2000).

[53] See The American Heritage College Dictionary 3rd edition, (New York: Houghton Mifflin Company, 1997), p. 337. The 19th Century philosopher and historian of culture Wilhelm Dilthey made a subsequent distinction between the "cultural" sciences and the "natural" sciences as did Emile Durkheim who was instrumental in forming the disciplines of sociology and anthropology. See Wilhelm Dilthey, *Introduction to the Human Sciences: Selected Works*, (Princeton, NJ: Princeton University Press, 1989). Durkheim insisted that society and culture were more than the sum of their parts which included "social facts" which were socio-cultural phenomena that had an objective existence and were not bound by, or reducible to, the actions of individuals. See Emile Durkheim, *The Division of Labor in Society*, (New York: Free Press, 1997); and Emile Durkheim, *Rule of Sociological Method*, (New York: Free Press, 1982).

[54] Elliot Jaques was the first person to coin the phrase "corporate culture" in his 1951 Ph.D. dissertation at Harvard that was subsequently published as, Elliot Jaques, *The Changing Culture of a Factory: A Study of Authority and Participation in an Industrial Setting*, (London: Tavistock, 1951). It should also be noted the analysis of organizational "climate" began with Lewin's notion that human behavior was the product of "individuals in context" and was solidified by a number of subsequent studies of organizational climate in the late 1960s as described in Daniel Denison, *Corporate Culture and Organizational Effectiveness*, (Denison Consulting, 1990), p. 22 ff.

[55] See Hofstede, *Cultures Consequences*, 2001; and Geert Hofstede, *Cultures and Organizations: Software of the Mind*, (New York: McGraw-Hill Book Company, 1991).

[56] For another extensive study on the topic of values across cultures within this time frame see, H. Andrew Michener, John Delamater, Shalom Schwartz, and Robert Merton, *Social Psychology*, 2nd edition, (1990).

[57] This fifth dimension was not part of the original IBM study. This new dimension was developed when Michael Harris Bond (a Canadian located in the Far East for many years) studied people's values around the world from an Asian (Chinese) perspective. This reinforced the fact that researchers had to identify and control for their own cultural biases. See Hofstede, *Cultures and Organizations: Software of the Mind*, 1991, pp. 14-15.

[58] See Hofstede, *Cultures Consequences*, 2003.

[59] The notion of symmetric versus complementary relationships is described in, Paul Watzlawick, *Pragmatics of Human Communication*, (New York: W.W. Norton & Company, 1967), pp. 51-54, and pp. 67-71.

[60] "Corporate Culture: The Hard-to-Change Values That Spell Success or Failure," in *Business Week*, October 27, 1980, pp. 148-160.

[61] See Deal and Kennedy, *Corporate Cultures*, 1982.

[62] See Deal and Kennedy, *Corporate Cultures*, 1982, p. iv.

[63] The eight basic findings were: a) a bias for action, b) staying close to the customer, c) autonomy and entrepreneurship, d) productivity through people, e) hands-on, values-driven, f) stick to the knitting, g) simple form, lean staff, and h) simultaneous loose-tight properties. See Peters and Waterman, *In Search of Excellence*, 1982, Front Matter.

[64] The McKinsey 7-S Framework© includes: a) structures, b) strategy, c) systems, d) shared values, e) skills, f) style, and g) staff. See Thomas Peters and Robert Waterman, *In Search of Excellence*, 1982, p. 10.

[65] See Peters and Waterman, *In Search of Excellence*, 1982, pp. 75-76.

[66] See Hofstede, *Cultures and Organizations: Software of the Mind*, 1991, p. 180.

[67] See Schein, *Organizational Culture and Leadership*, 1992, p. 3.

[68] See Schein, *Organizational Culture and Leadership*, 1992, p. 4.

[69] See Schein, *The Corporate Culture Survival Guide*, 1999, p. 86.

[70] Kotter and Heskett, *Corporate Culture and Performance*, 1992.

[71] Kotter and Heskett, *Corporate Culture and Performance*, 1992, p. 15 ff.

[72] See Collins and Porras, *Built to Last*, 1994, p. 17 ff.

[73] See Collins and Porras, *Built to Last*, 1994, p. 89.

[74] See Collins and Porras, *Built to Last*, 1994, p. 54.

[75] See Collins and Porras, *Built to Last*, 1994, pp. 82-83.

[76] Capra argues that all of life and living systems can be organized into interdependent patterns, structures, and processes. See Fritjof Capra, *The Web of Life: A New Scientific Understanding of Living Systems*, (New York: Anchor Books, 1997).

[77] Much of the information about open systems that appears in this section echoes the work of David Hanna in Hanna, *Designing Organizations for High Performance*, 1988, p. 8 ff. For other views on Open Systems Theory see, Ludwig von Bertalanffy, *General Systems Theory*, revised edition, (New York: George Braziller, 1969); W. Richard Scott and John Meyer, *Institutional Environments and Organizations: Structural Complexity and Individualism*, (Thousand Oaks, CA: Sage Publications, 1994); Capra, *The Web of Life*, 1997); Barry Oshry, *Seeing Systems: Unlocking the Mysteries of Organizational Life*, (San Francisco: Berrett-Koehler Publishers, 1996); and Gerald Weinberg, *An Introduction to General Systems Thinking*, (New York: Dorset House Publishing, 2001).

[78] Capra, *The Web of Life*, 1997, p. 159 ff.

[79] This view is espoused by the following writers: Kotter and Heskett, *Corporate Culture and Performance*, 1992; Hanna, *Designing Organizations for High-Performance*, 1988; Collins and Porras, *Built to Last*, 1994. Miller, *Barbarians to Bureaucrats*, 1989.

[80] The notion of organizations having an "implicit contract" with the external environment is described in Hanna, *Designing Organizations for High Performance*, 1988, p. 10 ff.

[81] See Hanna, *Designing Organizations for High Performance*, 1988, p. 36.

[82] See Schein, *Organizational Culture and Leadership*, 1992.

[83] Hanna, *Designing Organizations for High Performance*, 1988.

[84] Kotter and Heskett, *Corporate Culture and Performance*, 1992.

[85] As mentioned previously, Deming claims that 94% of organizational performance problems are attributable to "common causes" in the structures, systems, and culture and only 6% are due to the performance of individual employees (local causes), see Deming, *Out of Crisis*, 1992, p. 314 ff. Juran claims that 85% of performance problems are attributable to root causes in the structures, systems, and culture, see Juran, *Quality Control Handbook*, 1979, p. 2/20 ff. In the area of safety investigation and risk analysis, Reason attributes about 80% of all human errors and safety incidents to latent conditions (latent organizational weaknesses), see Reason, *Managing the Risks of Organizational Accidents*, 1997, p. 10 ff.

[86] The metaphor of organizational culture as a "stage" is used very effectively in, Driskill and Brenton, *Organizational Culture in Action*, 2005.

[87] See Daniel Wegner, "Transactive Memory: A Contemporary Analysis of the Group Mind" in Brian Mullen and Georg Goethals, (eds.), *Theories of Group Behavior*, (New York: Springer-Verlag, 1987), p. 187-208; and D. M. Wegner, T. Giuliano, and P. Hertel, "Cognitive Interdependence In Close Relationships" in W.J. Ickes (ed.), *Compatible and Incompatible Relationships*, (New York: Springer-Verlag, 1985).

[88] See David Reiss, *The Family's Construction of Reality*, (Cambridge, MA: Harvard University Press, 1987).

[89] Another important component of how we "see" our selves and how others "see" us is our physical appearance. This includes our gender, race, color, size, looks, and other physical characteristics or natural abilities (multiple intelligences) that are either valued, or not valued within a specific cultural setting. This line of inquiry is associated with Implicit Personality Theory where the first traits that we recognize in others influence the interpretation and perception of subsequent ones; e.g., how we see them. Frequent instances include false beliefs such as; attractive people have a more desirable personality and intelligence than people with average appearance. Some times physical appearance can be misaligned with our personality; e.g., type Eights who see themselves as being powerful, but who are smaller-than-average in size or who belong to a demographic segment in society that is not seen as being powerful, for example children or the elderly. In addition, the traits associated with our socialized-self can powerfully influence the interpretation and perception of subsequent information (how people see us) through stereotypes and assumptions of which personality traits go together. More specifically, we are biased toward seeing positive characteristics as going along with other positive traits. Instances include false beliefs such as, happy people are friendly, quiet people are timid, intelligent people are arrogant, aggressive people are stupid, and polite and attentive people can be trusted. For a more complete discussion of Implicit Personality Theory see, Craig Anderson, "Implicit Personality Theories and Empirical Data" in *Social Cognition*, Volume 13, Number 1, 1995, pp. 25-48; and Craig Anderson and B. Weiner, "Attribution and Attributional Processes in Personality" in Gian Vittorio Caprara and Daniel Cervone (eds.), *Personality: Determinants, Dynamics, and Potentials*, (New York: Cambridge University Press, 2000), pp. 295-324.

[90] See Argyris, *Overcoming Organizational Defenses*, (Upper Saddle River, NJ: Prentice Hall, 1990).

[91] See Argyris, *Flawed Advice and the Management Trap*, 2000, p. 22 ff.

[92] See Argyris, *Overcoming Organizational Defenses*, 1990), p. xii ff.

[93] The notion of a disciplinary paradigm is used by Thomas Kuhn as a way to characterize the nature of scientific disciplines, but his model has broader applications to any group of workers, tradesmen, business functions, or professionals. A disciplinary paradigm includes scientific laws and theories, applications and technologies, tools and problem-solving methodologies, professional associations, technical standards, a common discipline-related language and models from which emerge traditions, stories, heroes, symbols and cultural norms. See Thomas Kuhn, *The Structure of Scientific Revolutions*, (Chicago: The University of Chicago Press, 1996).

[94] See, Hammer and Champy, *Reengineering the Corporation*, 1993, p. 11. Also see, Michael Hammer, *Beyond Reengineering*, (New York: Harper Business, 1996).

[95] The distinction between what, why, how, and who gets things done in organizations was suggested in Adizes, *Corporate Life Cycles*, 1988.

⁹⁶ The Jungian type codes that map to Type 1 (Production) are: ENFJ, ENTJ, ESTJ, and ESTP.

⁹⁷ The Jungian type codes that map to Type 2 (Connection) are: ENFP, ENTP, ESFJ, and ESFP.

⁹⁸ The Jungian type codes that map to Type 3 (Direction) are: INFJ, INTJ, ISTJ, and ISTP.

⁹⁹ The Jungian type codes that map to Type 4 (Integration) are: INFP, INTP, ISFJ, and ISFP.

¹⁰⁰ See G.E.R Lloyd, *Early Greek Science: Thales to Aristotle*, (New York: W.W. Norton & Company, 1970); and S. Sambursky, *The Physical World of the Greeks*, (Princeton, NJ: Princeton University Press, 1987).

¹⁰¹ See John Locke, *Two Treatises of Government and A Letter Concerning Toleration*, edited by Ian Shapiro, (New Haven, CT: Yale University Press, 2003); and Jean-Jacques Rousseau, *The Social Contract and other later political writings*, edited by Victor Gourevitch, (New York: Cambridge University Press, 2006).

¹⁰² See William Bridges, *Transitions: Making Sense of Life's Changes*, (Cambridge, MA: Perseus Books, 1980), and William Bridges, *Managing Transitions*, (New York: Addison-Wesley Publishing Company, 1991).

¹⁰³ Chris Argyris, *Knowledge for Action: A Guide to Overcoming Barriers to Organizational Change*, (San Francisco: Jossey-Bass Publishers, 1993), p. 20.

¹⁰⁴ Argyris, *Knowledge for Action*, p. 52.

¹⁰⁵ See, John Gottman, *Why Marriages Succeed or Fail and How You Can Make Yours Last*, (New York: Simon & Schuster, 1994), and John Gottman, *The Marriage Clinic: A Scientifically Based Marital Therapy*, (New York: W.W. Norton & Company, 1999).

¹⁰⁶ Paul Watzlawick argues that it is impossible for people *not* to communicate see, Watzlawick, *Pragmatics of Human Communication*, 1967, p. 48 ff.

¹⁰⁷ See the discussion and commentary on Gottman's research in Malcolm Gladwell, *Blink*, (New York: Little, Brown, and Company, 2005), pp. 18-23.

¹⁰⁸ The concepts of Tacit Creeds, Growth Motivators, Deficiency Drivers, and Somatic Instincts link the patterns-of-interaction between coworkers shown in Figure 4 to the Breckenridge Enneagram theory of personality that is described in, Mark Bodnarczuk, *The Breckenridge Enneagram: A Guide to Personal and Professional Growth*, (Boulder, CO: Breckenridge Press, 2009).

¹⁰⁹ The notion of symmetric versus complementary relationships is described in, Watzlawick, *Pragmatics of Human Communication*, 1967, pp. 51-54, and pp. 67-71.

¹¹⁰ The content versus relationship distinction is described in, Watzlawick, *Pragmatics of Human Communication*, 1967, pp. 51-54, and pp. 67-71.

¹¹¹ This is an adaptation of a model presented in, Kerry Patterson, Joseph Grenny, Ron McMillan, and Al Switzler, *Crucial Confrontations*, (New York: McGraw-Hill, 2005), p. 32 ff.

¹¹² For a discussion of the problem of Group Entrapment, see Joseph Luft, *Group Processes: An Introduction to Group Dynamics*, 3ʳᵈ edition, (San Francisco: Mayfield Publishing Company, 1984), p. 174 ff.; and Watzlawick, *Pragmatics of Human Communication*, 1967, p. 187 ff.

¹¹³ See Robin Dunbar, *Grooming, Gossip, and the Evolution of Language*, (New York: Farber and Farber, 1996), p. 69 ff.

¹¹⁴ Daniel Wegner's research focuses on the point that we don't have to know everything necessary to do our work in our brains; we just need to know where to find what we need to do our work. In work-groups, this becomes a kind of collective memory system called Transactive Memory that develops when people work closely together. It's like an invisible memory network that managers and staff are connected to where people just know who is best suited to remember what kind of things and who is best able to solve which kind of problems. See Daniel Wegner, Paula Raymond, and Ralph Erber, "Transactive Memory in Close Relationships" in *Journal of Personality and Social Psychology*, 1991, Volume 61, Number 6, 923-929; Daniel Wegner, "Transactive Memory: A Contemporary Analysis of the Group Mind" in Brian Mullen and George Goethals (eds.), *Theories of Group Behavior*, (New York: Springer-Verlag, 1987), p. 5 ff.; Monique Lambert and Ben Shaw, *Transactive Memory and Exception Handling in High-Performance Project Teams*, Center for Integrated Facility Engineering, Stanford University, July 2002, CIFE Technical Report #137; and Malcolm Gladwell, *The Tipping Point: How Little Things Can Make a Big Difference*, (New York: Little, Brown, and Company, 2002), p. 187-191.

[115] Elliot Jaques argues that natural laws of organizational structure exist that are based on the structure and processing capabilities of the human mind. He calls this a "requisite" organizational structure. Jaques' notion of a requisite organization echoes the interdependent connection between the human brain and its context proposed by Bruce Wexler and Clotaire Rapaille. See Elliot Jaques, *Requisite Organization*, revised 2nd edition memorial, (Baltimore, MD: Cason Hall & Co, 2006); Elliot Jaques and Kathryn Cason, *Human Capability*, (Falls Church, VA: Cason Hall & Co, 1994); Bruce Wexler, *Brain and Culture*, (Cambridge, MA: A Bradford Book, 2006); and Clotaire Rapaille, *The Culture Code*, (New York: Broadway Books, 2006).

[116] The four accountabilities and authorities discussed in this section are based on the principles taught in, Elliot Jaques and Stephen Clement, *Executive Leadership: A Practical Guide to Managing Complexity*, (Arlington, VA: Cason Hall & Co, 1994); and Jaques, *Requisite Organization*, 2006.

[117] The two other things that help to limit the tendency for personality to rule are: a) quantitative measures of performance and summary data, and b) processes that are shaped by IT infrastructure.

[118] Alan Wilkins describes a "Border Guard" as any person who has responsibility for (and defends) a distinct sub-group (departments, teams, divisions, etc.) that has human, financial, and material resources and exists within a larger organizational structure. Sometimes, these sub-groups may not appear on the formal organization chart and may not be part of the formal organizational structure; e.g., they may be based on disciplinary paradigms that cross traditional organizational boundaries. Border guards consciously (or unconsciously) recruit or enroll employees by explicitly or implicitly promising to meet their needs and to get them the results they want within the context of the organization's structures, systems, and culture, see, Wilkins, *Developing Corporate Character*, 1989, p. 123 ff.

[119] Wexler, *Brain and Culture*, 2006, p. 27.

[120] Rapaille, *The Culture Code*, 2006, p. 17 ff.

[121] Communication theorists like Paul Watzlawick argue that when people send emotional messages about: a) how they see themselves, b) how they see others, and c) how they see situations in the world around them, that there are three possible responses that are critical to forming both constructive and destructive patterns of communication. The first response is *confirmation*; e.g., where people affirm the fact that they see themselves, others, and the world in very similar (or identical) ways. The second response is *rejection*; e.g., where people do not necessarily negate the reality of the other's point of view, but they may disagree with definitions, semantics, examples, assumptions, data, facts, observations or other things that support how they "see" – their point of view. The third response is *disconfirmation*; e.g., where people are no longer concerned with establishing truth or falsity, but rather they negate the reality of the other's way of seeing themselves, others, and the world around them. See Watzlawick, *Pragmatics of Human Communication*, 1967, p. 83 ff.

[122] The concepts of Tacit Creeds, Growth Motivators, Deficiency Drivers, and Somatic Instincts link the patterns-of-interaction between coworkers shown in Figure 5 to the Breckenridge Enneagram theory of personality that is described in, Bodnarczuk, *The Breckenridge Enneagram*, 2009.

[123] Daniel Goleman, *Social Intelligence: The New Science of Human Relationships*, (New York: Bantam Books, 2006), p. 109 ff.

[124] Watzlawick makes the distinction between the *content* element of communication which conveys information and is largely cognitive, and the *relationship* element of communication which is related to the emotional part of the brain; e.g., the Amygdala. He likens the content element to digital (verbal) communication, and the relationship element to analogue (non-verbal) communication. Trying to resolve destructive conflict that exists at the relationship-emotional level by interacting at the content-cognitive level tends to increase the amount of destructive conflict, and the level of cognitive dissonance in the interaction. See Watzlawick, *Pragmatics of Human Communication*, 1967, p. 62 ff.

[125] This metaphor of the stew and this perspective come from, Daniel Goleman, *Emotional Intelligence*, (New York: Bantam Books, 1997), p. 10 ff.; and Daniel Goleman, Richard Boyatzis, Annie McKee, *Primal Leadership*, (Boston: Harvard Business School Press, 2002), p. 5 ff.

[126] Goleman, *Primal Leadership*, 2002, p. 8 ff. For a more complete discussion on the "ripple effect" in leadership see, Wallace Bachman, "Nice Guys Finish First" in Richard Brian Polley, A. Paul Hare,

and Philip Stone (eds.), *The SYMLOG Practitioner: Applications of Small Group Research*, (New York: Praeger, 1988).

[127] An example of a high-chair tyrant is described in Mark Bodnarczuk, *Diving In*, (Boulder, CO: Breckenridge Press, 2009), p. 1 ff.

[128] Powerful informal leaders also have the capability to resonate people on destructive frequencies. Goleman, *Primal Leadership*, 2002, p. 5 ff.

[129] See Howard Gardner, *Leading Minds: An Anatomy of Leadership*, (New York: Basic Books, 1995).

[130] See Argyris, *Action Science*, 1985; and Peter Senge, Art Kleiner, Charlotte Roberts, Richard Ross, and Bryan Smith, *The Fifth Discipline Fieldbook*, (New York: Currency Doubleday, 1994).

[131] See Luft, *Group Processes*, 1984.

[132] See Bossidy and Charan, *Confronting Reality*, 2004.

[133] Jim Collins, *Good to Great*, (New York: Harper Business, 2001).

[134] See Senge, *The Fifth Discipline*, 1990); Senge, *The Fifth Discipline Field Book*, 1994); and Sarita Chawla and John Renesch, (eds.), *Learning Organizations*, (Portland, OR: Productivity Press, 1995).

[135] Argyris, *Overcoming Organizational Defenses*, 1990, p. xiii.

[136] Argyris, *Knowledge for Action*, 1993, p. 15.

[137] For more details see, Argyris, *Knowledge for Action*, 1993, p. 45, and Argyris, *Action Science*, 1985, p. 292 ff.

[138] Argyris, *Knowledge for Action*, p. 20.

[139] Some of the items on this list are modified versions of the defense routines found in Argyris, *Knowledge for Action*, p. 45, and Argyris, *Action Science*, p. 292 ff.

[140] Argyris, *Overcoming Organizational Defenses*, 1990, p. xii ff.

[141] Argyris, *Overcoming Organizational Defenses,* 1990.

[142] Hanna, *Designing Organizations for High Performance*, 1988, p. 38.

[143] For a more complete discussion of causal analysis see Malcolm Craig, *Thinking Visually: Business Applications of 14 Core Diagrams*, (New York: Continuum International Publishing Group, 2000); Kevin Kelleher, *Cause-and-Effect Diagrams*, (New York: Joiner/Oriel Inc., 1995); Bjorn Anderson and Tom Fagerhaug, *Root Cause Analysis*, (Milwaukee, Wisconsin: ASQ Quality Press, 2006); Max Ammerman, *The Root Cause Analysis Handbook*, (New York: Productivity Press, 1998); and James Pershing, (ed.) 3rd edition, *Handbook of Human Performance*, (New York: Pfeiffer, 2006).

[144] See Daniel Denison and William Neale, *Denison Organizational Culture Survey Facilitator Guide*, (Ann Arbor, MI: Denison Consulting, LLC, 2002).

[145] Non-response error also includes non-responses to specific items of a survey, negatively impacting the validity of that survey.

[146] It is important to note that specific survey questions for the BCI Level II are weighted more heavily as a measurement of the six perspectives along the critical path of the Open Systems diagram shown in Figure 1; e.g., Leadership Focus, Resources and Policies, Decisions, Rewards, Just Culture, and Management Philosophy.

[147] There are three levels of analysis that can be used to identify scoring patterns in the BCI data: strategic patterns, tactical patterns, and basic patterns. Strategic Patterns are at the Open Systems level and inter-radar levels, including Key Stakeholders; inter-radar patterns such as HH, LL, HL, and LH that span a given report; and squandered organizational energy and squandered psychological energy. Tactical Patterns are at the radar or graph level, including Strategic View; Execution; Organizational Climate; Four Ways of Working; Emotional Messages; and Organizational Trust Index. Basic Patterns like the ones described here are the scoring patterns of HH, LL, HL, and LH for a specific scale (like Leadership Focus) for the populations and work-groups that participated in the BCI.

[148] It is important to note that the populations in the BCI Level II are weighted differently to reflect the fact that in day-to-day realities of organizational life, managers have a powerful effect (emotional resonation) on those who report to them. Consequently, the responses of managers are weighted in the data shown on this chart based on the number of levels in an organization. As a rule of thumb, top managers are weighted as ten, middle managers are weighted as seven or five, supervisors are weighted as three, and staff members are weighted as one. The influence of managers must be more

heavily weighted because they possess formally delegated authority and are accountable for the work-group's performance. More specifically, the influence of managers is tied to the part of the human brain (amygdala) that produces and senses emotions that functions like an open-loop system; e.g., our emotional connections to other people (like our boss) help to establish the shared moods and emotional responses of entire groups of people. Like an invisible wireless network, work-group members send and receive 93% of their communication through body language and tone of voice. Daniel Goleman argues that employees take their emotional cues from the top – everyone watches the boss. Even when a manager is not highly visible their attitudes affect the moods and emotions of direct reports and this ripples down through the organizational levels like a domino effect creating an emotional climate throughout the organization. Over time, a manager's ability to resonate the emotions and moods of their employees repeatedly creates either destructive or constructive patterns-of-interaction within work-groups or an entire organization.

[149] Peter F. Drucker, "Managing Oneself" in the *Harvard Business Review*, March-April 1999, Volume 77, Number 2, pp. 69-70.

[150] It is often helpful to place these *kairos* events on an organizational timeline as described in the next section.

[151] Carl Jung referred to these as "accidental" symbols because the "pairing" between the physical object or location and the underlying ideas, feelings, attitudes, beliefs, and assumptions were most often the results of experiences that a person happened to have in a given location of space-time. For example, if while on a trip to Denver a man and his wife decide to get divorced, "Denver" will come to symbolize sorrow, relief, or both to the couple depending on their view of the relationship and the event. For a more thorough treatment of Jung's teaching on symbols see, June Singer, *Boundaries of the Soul*, (New York: Anchor Books, 1994); C.G. Jung, *Psyche & Symbol*, edited by Violet S. de Laszlo, (New York: Anchor Books, 1958); and C.G. Jung, *Memories, Dreams, Reflections*, (New York: Vintage Books, 1989).

[152] See Porter, *Competitive Advantage*, 1998; Porter, *Competitive Strategy*, 1980; George S. Day and David J. Reibstein (eds.), *Wharton on Dynamic Competitive Strategy*, (New York: John Wiley & Sons, Inc., 1997); Carl W. Stern and George Stalk Jr. (eds.), *Perspectives on Strategy from the Boston Consulting Group*, (New York: John Wiley & Sons, Inc., 1998); and Kim and Mauborgne, *Blue Ocean Strategy*, 2005.

[153] The Left-Hand Column is described in more detail in, Chris Argyris, *Action Science*, 1985; and Senge, *The Fifth Discipline Fieldbook*, 1994.

[154] Kotter and Heskett, *Corporate Culture and Performance*, 1992, p. 46 ff.; and John Kotter, *A Force for Change: How Leadership Differs from Management*, (New York: Free Press, 1990).

[155] Collins and Porras, *Built to Last*, 1994, p. 46 ff.

[156] See Milton Friedman, *Capitalism and Freedom*, Fortieth Anniversary Edition, (Chicago: University of Chicago Press, 2002); and Milton Friedman and Rose Friedman, *Free to Choose*, (New York: Harcourt, Brace, Jovanovich, 1980).

[157] Collins, *Good to Great*, 2001; Collins and Porras, *Built to Last*, 1994; Peter Drucker, *The Essential Drucker*, 1st edition, (New York: Collins, 2001); Peter Drucker, *Management Challenges for the 21st Century*, 1st edition, (New York: Collins, 1999); Peter Drucker, *Innovation and Entrepreneurship*, (Harper Business, 1985); Jay Galbraith, *Designing Organizations*, (San Francisco: Jossey-Bass, 2002); Al Ries and Jack Trout, *Positioning: The Battle for Your Mind*, (New York: McGraw-Hill, 2001); Harry Beckwith, *Selling the Invisible: A Field Guide to Modern Marketing*, (New York: Warner Books, 1997); Harry Beckwith, *The Invisible Touch: The Four Keys to Modern Marketing*, (New York: Warner Books, 2000); Harry Beckwith, *What Clients Love*, (New York: Warner Books, 2003); Larry Bossidy and Ram Charan, *Execution*, (New York: Crown Business, 2002); Bossidy and Charan, *Confronting Reality*, 2004; Porter, *Competitive Strategy*, 1998; Porter, *Competitive Advantage*, 1998; Deming, *Out of Crisis*,1986; Peter Drucker, "Managing Oneself" in the *Harvard Business Review*, March-April, 1999; Robert Kaplan and David Norton, "The Balanced Scorecard – Measures That Drive Performance" in the *Harvard Business Review*, January-February, 1992; Jim Collins, "Level 5 Leadership: The Triumph of Humility and Fierce Resolve" in the *Harvard Business Review*, January 2001; Harold J. Leavitt, "Why Hierarchies Thrive" in the *Harvard Business Review*, March 2003; Jaques, *Requisite Organization*, 2006; Jaques and

Clement, *Executive Leadership*, 1994; Jaques and Cason, *Human Capability*, 1994; and Elliot Jaques, *The Life and Behavior of Living Organisms: A General Theory*, (Westport, CT: Praeger, 2002).

158 The Chronbach's Alpha reliability coefficients for the six scales that compose the Strategic View radar graph are as follows: Leadership Focus is .85 (N=7 items); Resources and Policies is .80 (N=4 items); Planning and Deployment is .90 (N=5 items); Strata and Talent is .87 (N=6 items); Business Context is .91 (N=5 items); and Business Results is .77 (N=6 items).

159 Hanna, *Designing Organizations for High Performance*, 1988; Sharp and McDermott, *Workflow Modeling*, 2001; Deming, *Out of Crisis*, 1992; Davenport, *Process Innovation*, 1993; Paul Harmon, *Business Process Change*, (New York: Morgan Kaufman Publishers, 2003); Juran, *Quality Control Handbook*, 1979; Alfie Kohn, *Punished by Rewards*, (New York: Houghton Mifflin, 1993); Ram Charan, "Conquering a Culture of Indecision" in the *Harvard Business Review*, April 2001; Harold D. Stolovitch and Erica J. Keeps (eds.), *Handbook of Human Performance Technology*, 2nd edition, (San Francisco: Pfeiffer, 1999); and Jaques and Clement, *Executive Leadership*, 1994.

160 The Chronbach's Alpha reliability coefficients for the six scales that compose the Execution radar graph are as follows: Decisions is .87 (N=6 items); Rewards is .94 (N=5 items); People is .89 (N=5 items); Processes is .85 (N= 5 items); Information is .86 (N=5 items); and Structure is .89 (N=5 items).

161 Edgar Schein, *The Corporate Survival Guide*, (San Francisco: Jossey-Bass, 1999); Schein, *Organizational Culture and Leadership*, 1992; Schein, *Process Consultation Revisited*, 1999; Kotter and Heskett, *Corporate Culture and Performance*, 1992; David Cooperrider, Diana Whitney, and Jacqueline Stavros, *Appreciative Inquiry Handbook*, (San Francisco: Berrett-Koehler Publishers, 2005); Diana Whitney and Amanda Trosten-Bloom, *The Power of Appreciative Inquiry*, (San Francisco: Berrett-Koehler Publishers, 2003); David Cooperrider, Peter F. Sorensen, Diana Whitney, and Therese Yaeger, (eds.), *Appreciative Inquiry*, (Champaign, IL: Stipes Publishing, 2000); Deal and Kennedy, *Corporate Cultures*, 2000; Argyris, *Action Science*, 1985; Argyris, *Knowledge for Action*, 1993; Rapaille, *The Culture Code*, 2006; Wilkins, *Developing Corporate Character*, 1989; Baum, *The Invisible Bureaucracy*, 1987; Bridges, *Managing Transitions*, 1991; Ichak Adizes, *Corporate Lifecycles*, (Paramus, NJ: Prentice Hall, 1988); Miller, *Barbarians to Bureaucrats*, 1989; Rollo May, *The Courage to Create*, (New York: W.W. Norton & Company, 1975); Arthur Koestler, *The Act of Creation*, (New York: Arkana Penguin Books, 1989); Anthony Storr, *The Dynamics of Creation*, (New York: Ballantine Books, 1993); Peter Frost and Sandra Robinson, "The Toxic Handler: Organizational Hero and Casualty" in the *Harvard Business Review*, July-August 1999; Robert J. Herbold, "Inside Microsoft: Balancing Creativity and Discipline" in the *Harvard Business Review*, January 2002; Diane L. Coutu, "The Anxiety of Learning" in the *Harvard Business Review*, March 2002; Teresa M. Amabile, "How to Kill Creativity" in the *Harvard Business Review*, September-October, 1998; Carol Lavin Bernick, "When Your Culture Needs a Makeover" in the *Harvard Business Review*, June 2001; Jaques and Clement, *Executive Leadership*, 1994; and Elliot Jaques, *Creativity and Work*, (Gloucester, MA: Cason Hall & Co., 1998).

162 The Chronbach's Alpha reliability coefficients for the six scales that compose the Organizational Climate radar graph are as follows: Just Culture is .88 (N=5 Items); Management Philosophy is .92 (N=8 Items); Constructive Conflict is .86 (N=5 Items); Tradition is .83 (N= 5 items); Creativity is .87 (N=5 Items); and Openness to Change is .80 (N=5 Items).

163 See Collins and Porras, *Built to Last*, 1994, p. 80 ff.

164 See Collins and Porras, *Built to Last*, 1994, p. 80 ff.

165 For a more detailed discussion of the process of an issue being undiscussible within a culture and organizational defense routines emerging to preserve the status quo see, Argyris, *Overcoming Organizational Defenses*, 1990, p. xiii; Argyris, *Knowledge for Action*, 1993, p. 45 ff.; and Chris Argyris, *Action Science*, 1985, p. 292 ff. For a more complete discussion of the nature of the unconscious in organizations see, Murray Stein and John Hollwitz (eds.), *Psyche at Work*, (Wilmette, IL: Chiron Publications, 1995); Baum, *The Invisible Bureaucracy*, 1987; Edgar H. Schein, *Organizational Psychology*, 3rd edition, (Englewood Cliffs, NJ: Prentice-Hall Press, 1980); Uri Merry and George Brown, *The Neurotic Behavior of Organizations*, (New York: Gardner Press, Inc. 1990); Anne Wilson Schaef and Diane Fassel, *The Addictive Organization: Why We Overlook, Cover Up, Pick Up the Pieces, Please the Boss & Perpetrate Sick Organizations*, (San Francisco: Harper San Francisco, 1990); Michael A. Diamond, *The

Unconscious Life of Organizations: Interpreting Organizational Identity, (Westport, CN: Quorum Books, 1993); Larry Hirschhorn, *The Workplace Within: Psychodynamics of Organizational Life*, (Cambridge, MA: MIT Press, 1990); Manfred F.R. Kets de Vries and Danny Miller, *The Neurotic Organization*, (San Francisco: Jossey-Bass,1984); Arthur D. Coleman, *Up From Scapegoating: Awakening Consciousness in Groups*, (Wilmette, IL: Chiron Publications, 1995); Anton Obholzer and Vega Zagier Roberts (eds.), *The Unconscious at Work*, (New York: Routledge, 1994); and Peter Herriot (ed.), *The Individual and Organization*, European Journal of Work and Organizational Psychology, volume 7, number 3, September 1998.

[166] The Chronbach's Alpha reliability coefficients for the scales that compose the Four Ways of Working graph are as follows: Type 1 Production is .87 (N=8 Items); Type 2 Connection is .88 (N=6 Items); Type 3 Direction is .85 (N=6 Items); and Type 4 Integration is .87 (N=7 Items).

[167] See Gottman, *Why Marriages Succeed or Fail*, 1994.

[168] Because 55% of communication is visual-body language, 38% is tone of voice, and only 7% is word choice, e-mail leaves out 93% of the communication. Regardless of the intentions of the sender, it's difficult for recipients of e-mails not to project their own meaning into the message to fill the 93% communication void. More times than not, this results in destructive conflict. In fact, Dunbar argues that the impersonality of communicating electronically through e-mail makes people less discrete in their interactions with others than face-to-face communication; e.g., they are more likely to be abusive when angry. Dunbar compares this "net rage" to the phenomenon of "road rage" where people in cars escalate to anger much more quickly than they probably would have had they been involved in face-to-face contact with the same person. See Dunbar, *Grooming, Gossip, and the Evolution of Language*, 1997, p. 204 ff.

[169] This section echoes Gottman's more detailed descriptions of Criticism found in Gottman, *Why Marriages Succeed or Fail*, 1994, p. 72 ff.

[170] Some methods for doing this can be found in the "Client-Centered" approach to listening proposed by Carl Rogers in Carl Rogers, *On Becoming a Person*, (Boston: Houghton Mifflin Company, 1961). Another more popularized method can be found in Stephen R. Covey's Habit 5, "Seek first to understand, then to be understood" in Covey, *The 7 Habits of Highly Effective People*, 1991.

[171] This section echoes Gottman's more detailed descriptions of Contempt found in Gottman, *Why Marriages Succeed or Fail*, 1994, p. 79 ff.

[172] For a description of confirming, rejecting, and disconfirming others as people see Watzlawick, *Pragmatics of Human Communication*, 1967, p. 83 ff.

[173] For a description of confirming, rejecting, and disconfirming others as people see Watzlawick, *Pragmatics of Human Communication*, 1967, p. 83 ff.

[174] This section echoes Gottman's more detailed descriptions of Defensiveness found in Gottman, *Why Marriages Succeed or Fail*, 1994, p. 84 ff.

[175] Many of the principles of trust that hold in professional relationships also hold in intimate relationships.

[176] This section echoes Gottman's more detailed descriptions of Stonewalling found in Gottman, *Why Marriages Succeed or Fail*, 1994, p. 93 ff.

[177] For a discussion of the problem of Group Entrapment, see Luft, *Group Processes*, 1984, p. 174 ff, and Watzlawick, *Pragmatics of Human Communication*, 1967, p. 187 ff.

[178] The Chronbach's Alpha reliability coefficients for the four scales that compose the Destructive Emotional Messages radar graph are as follows: Criticism is .90 (N=6 items); Contempt is .96 (N=6 items); Defensiveness is .94 (N=6 items); and Stonewalling is .87 (N=6 items).

[179] See Covey, *The 7 Habits of Highly Effective People*, 1989; Stephen M.R. Covey, *The Speed of Trust: The One Thing That Changes Everything*, (New York: Free Press, 2008); Arky Ciancutti and Thomas Steding, *Built on Trust: Gaining Competitive Advantage in Any Organization*, (Chicago: Contemporary Books, 2001); and Mike Armour, *Leadership and the Power of Trust: Creating a High-Trust, Peak-Performance Organization*, (Dallas, TX: Life Themes Press, 2008).

[180] See Deming, *Out of Crisis*, 1992, pp. 59-62.

[181] See Abraham Maslow, *Maslow on Management*, (New York: John Wiley & Sons, 1998), p. 20.

[182] See Abraham Maslow, *Toward a Psychology of Being*, (New York: John Wiley & Sons, 1999), p. 72.

[183] The Chronbach's Alpha reliability coefficients for the six scales that compose the Organizational Trust Index radar graph are as follows: Truth is .88 (N=3 Items); Integrity is .89 (N=3 Items); Power is .90 (N=3 Items); Competency is .92 (N=3 Items); Values is .85 (N=3 Items); and Recognition is .90 (N=3 Items).

[184] The approach taken here is based on the model described in Miller, *Barbarians to Bureaucrats*, 1989. It also echoes the approach taken in Adizes, *Corporate Lifecycles*, 1988.

[185] Peter Drucker, *Management Challenges for the 21st Century*, 1st edition, (New York: Collins Business, 2001).

[186] Jim Collins, *Good to Great and the Social Sectors: Why Business Thinking Is Not the Answer*, (Boulder, CO: Jim Collins, 2005).

[187] See Collins and Porras, *Built to Last*, 1994, p. 46 ff.

[188] See Kotter and Heskett, *Corporate Culture and Performance*, 1992.

[189] Collins and Porras, *Built to Last*, 1994.

[190] See Schein, *The Corporate Culture Survival Guide*, (1999), p. 33.

[191] For a more complete discussion on hidden costs in an organization's structures, system, and culture see, J.M. Juran (ed.), *Quality Control Handbook*, 3rd edition, (New York: McGraw-Hill Book Company, 1979), p. 5-1 ff.

[192] This is based on the assumption that a senior manager's fully loaded salary is $200,000 per year, a line manager's fully loaded salary is $150,000 per year, a supervisor's fully loaded salary is $100,000, and a staff member's fully loaded salary is $75,000. More specifically, we are assuming eight hours/day and five days/week, with 200 days/year worked = 1,600 hours/year with the following fully-loaded dollar-per-hour rates: a) top managers = $125/hr, b) middle managers = $94/hr, c) supervisors = $75/hr, and d) staff = $47/hr.

[193] This model was originally described in Schein, *The Corporate Culture Survival Guide*, 1999, p. 124 ff.

[194] For more details on learning anxiety and survival anxiety see, Schein, *The Corporate Culture Survival Guide*, 1999), and Schein, *Organizational Culture and Leadership*, 1992.

[195] For situations in a for-profit setting see, Jim Collins, *Good to Great*, (New York: Harper Business, 2001). For situations in a non-profit or government setting see, Collins, *Good to Great and the Social Sectors*, 2005.

[196] The seven step process described below can be formulated into a set of change-levers that can guide an overall change strategy and which "map" to the Breckenridge Change Equation. For example: a) increase revenue to $50 in four years by building a marketing and sales engine with the goal of driving positive change (COI), b) build enterprise-wide structures and systems to increase capacity and capability with the goal of meeting the demand at $50 in revenue (COI), c) disrupt ineffective actions/interactions shown on the Interaction Map (and others) and create intended patterns-of-interaction that get the desired result (POI), d) train and mentor-coach managers and supervisors in the tools, principles with the goal of getting the organization's leadership to "speak with one voice" (ROI), and e) embed change using Say-Do, modeling, a commitment to course correction, and the key embedding mechanisms. Change-levers like these can be used to focus the time and energy of the organization on culture change that addresses key business issues and the organization's strategic direction.

[197] Jim Collins discusses the fact that there is no one defining action or program that creates the kind of quantum change that takes an organization from good-to-great. Instead, deep, sustainable change happens as the outcome of a cumulative process – a "step-by-step, action-by-action, decision-by-decision, turn-by-turn of a flywheel – that adds up to sustained and spectacular results." See Jim Collins, *Good to Great*, (New York: Harper Business, 2001), p. 165.

[198] See Schein, *The Corporate Culture Survival Guide*, 1999, p. 15 ff.; Schein, *Organizational Culture and Leadership*, 1992, p. 16 ff.; Hanna, *Designing Organizations for High Performance*, 1988, p. 42 ff.; Kotter and Heskett, *Corporate Culture and Performance*, 1992, p. 3 ff.; and Collins and Porras, *Built to Last*, 1994, p. 43 ff.

[199] The list below is an adaptation from Wilkins, *Developing Corporate Character*, 1989, p. 123 ff.

[200] See Schein, *The Corporate Culture Survival Guide*, 1999, p. 102.

[201] See Kotter and Heskett, *Corporate Culture and Performance*, 1992, p. 79.

202 Schein, *The Corporate Culture Survival Guide*, 1999, pp. 124-125, and p. 128 ff.

203 See William Bridges, *Transitions*, (Cambridge, MA: Perseus Books, 1980); and William Bridges, *Managing Transitions*, (New York: Addison-Wesley Publishing Company, 1991).

204 Schein, *The Corporate Culture Survival Guide*, 1999, p. 132.

www.ingramcontent.com/pod-product-compliance
Lightning Source LLC
Chambersburg PA
CBHW080532220326

41599CB00032B/6288